Beyond Bias

The PATH to End Gender Inequality at Work

ANDREA S. KRAMER
ALTON B. HARRIS

NICHOLAS BREALEY
PUBLISHING

BOSTON · LONDON

First published in 2023 by Nicholas Brealey Publishing
An imprint of John Murray Press

An Hachette UK company

27 26 25 24 23   1 2 3 4 5 6 7 8 9 10

A CIP catalogue record for this title is available from the British Library.

Library of Congress Control Number: 2022947920

ISBN 978-1-3998-0148-5
US eBook 978-1-3998-0770-8
UK eBook ISBN 978-1-399-80150-8

Printed and bound in the United States of America.

John Murray Press policy is to use papers that are natural, renewable, and
recyclable products and made from wood grown in sustainable forests.
The logging and manufacturing processes are expected to conform to the
environmental regulations of the country of origin.

John Murray Press Ltd
Carmelite House
50 Victoria Embankment
London EC4Y 0DZ
Tel: 020 3122 6000

www.nbuspublishing.com

For Cynthia, again, and the brilliant, fulfilling,
productive life she has ahead of her

CONTENTS

PART IV: PUTTING IT ALL TOGETHER

INTRODUCTION

It's Time to Take a New PATH

There is something seriously wrong with current efforts to end workplace gender inequality. Although virtually all major organizations sponsor some sort of diversity initiative, anti-bias training, or inclusive behavior workshops, over the past 30 years women have made little progress in moving into business, professional, or nonprofit leadership positions.

From the 1950s to the early 1990s, women made substantial—even dramatic—progress entering and advancing in nearly all segments of the American economy.[1] However, this progress slowed dramatically by the mid-1990s.[2] Despite the time, effort, and resources that this country's

*"Remember, you can do **anything**...
but for only 80 cents to every dollar earned by a man."*

www.CartoonStock.com

major organizations have devoted to diversity, equity, and inclusion (DEI) initiatives, women's participation in business, professional, and nonprofit leadership has barely improved. The obvious question is why.

In this, our third book on gender inequality, we answer that question. In *Breaking Through Bias* we provided women with practical, effective, and accessible methods and techniques for advancing in their careers despite the prevalence of gender bias in their workplaces. In *It's Not You, It's the Workplace* we demonstrated that women's frequent workplace conflict with each other is not due to women's inherent hostility toward one another but to the gender-based obstacles they experience in career advancement. In both books we suggested how the bias-driven barriers to career advancement might be eliminated, but their primary objective was to help women cope with their workplaces as they found them—biased, unequal, and structured to keep women from achieving career success comparable to men's.

This book is very different. It is not about how to succeed in unequal workplaces, but about how to bring about workplace equality. This book is about ensuring women and men can experience workplaces that are equally rewarding, engaging, and inclusive. It is about how decision-makers can help ensure that their organizations offer women and men equal access to career advancement opportunities. It is about how leaders can create workplace cultures that enable women and men to thrive, grow, and succeed.

We believe it's time for a new approach to ending workplace gender inequality. This book presents that new approach. We call it "PATH." It is an integrated, comprehensive, and multifaceted program for ending gender inequality in all of its aspects in all types of workplaces.

- **P**rioritize elimination of exclusionary behavior
- **A**dopt discrimination-resistant methods of personnel decision-making
- **T**reat inequality in the home as a workplace problem
- **H**alt unequal performance reviews, career advice, and leadership opportunities

PATH is not another effort to encourage individuals to be less biased, to become more sensitive to women's unique career obstacles, or to behave in a more inclusive manner. Indeed, PATH does not attempt to directly reduce or eliminate individuals' biases.

Rather, PATH provides senior leaders and managers with straight-forward ways in which they can change their organizations' systems, processes, and practices so that women and men have equal and fair opportunities for career advancement and experience equally inclusive, supportive, and safe workplaces.

Our belief—and the assumption underlying PATH—is that career outcomes will only change when changes are made in systems, processes, and practices. PATH shows decision-makers how to make these changes while strengthening productivity, efficiency, creativity, autonomy, and profitability.

PATH's workplace changes are not radical, but sensible, practical, and entirely realistic changes designed to create fair, equal, and equitable workplace outcomes for women and men. We have no interest in tearing down or blowing up established ways of doing things. Rather, PATH seeks to show how, through a series of small wins, leaders can make their workplaces fairer, more equal, and more inclusive for everyone. Moreover, when people within a workplace can see real progress being made at eliminating gender inequality, their sense of purposeful engagement increases. As Teresa Amabile and Steven Kramer wrote in the *Harvard Business Review*, "Of all the things that can boost emotions, motivations, and perceptions during a workday, the single most important is making progress in meaningful work."[3]

Workplace gender inequality is a systemic problem that is caused by the operation of workplace systems, processes, and practices. Most existing DEI initiatives do not, however, focus on the systemic nature of this problem. Rather, they focus instead on trying to reduce gender inequality by increasing people's awareness of their unconscious biases. The assumption is that people will, as a result, behave in less biased ways. But increasing awareness does not necessarily change behavior. After all, given that biases are unconscious it is hard to control their influence on our behavior. As we discuss in Chapter 5, increasing aware-ness of unconscious biases has done little to decrease workplace gender inequality.

To end such inequality and realize the promise of inclusive work-places, we need to incorporate PATH's workplace changes into our current DEI efforts. There are two fundamental causes of workplace gender inequality: structural discrimination and individual discrimi-nation. Structural discrimination is the way that gendered workplaces' day-to-day, taken-for-granted personnel-management practices systemi-cally advantage men and disadvantage women. Individual discrimi-nation is the consistent, predictably biased ways in which individuals behave in the context of gendered workplaces. Because of structural discrimination, the personnel-management practices in gendered work-places operate in systemic ways in unequal career outcomes for women and men. Because of individual discrimination, women's workplace experiences are much less pleasant, engaging, and inclusive than those of men.

PATH changes workplace structures that change individual behav-ior. As Rosabeth Moss Kanter, professor at the Harvard Business School, writes, "To understand (or change) outcomes, we must focus on structures…as well as individual behaviors and perceptions. Structure and behavior are constantly interacting and reinforcing each other."[4] PATH provides organizations with the processes, tools, and techniques to help dismantle structural discrimination. As a result of those changes, employees are exposed to—and begin to internalize—new, fairer, more egalitarian norms, expectations, and values. Adoption of PATH will not transform organizations overnight. It will, however, allow them to make steady, measurable, and meaningful progress toward inclusive, discrimination-free workplaces and truly welcome diversity and dif-ference. PATH presents a carefully structured series of *small wins* that American business, professional, and nonprofit organizations can achieve as they steadily progress toward full gender equality.

What We Don't Cover in This Book

This book is focused on ending gender inequality at work. There are, of course, many other areas of inequality that are matters of serious concern. In limiting our focus, we are not in any way implying that workplace gender inequality is more pressing or more important than any other types of inequalities. We focus on workplace gender inequality because it is a discrete, solvable problem, one that we have studied throughout our professional lives. Nevertheless, we'd like to acknowledge some of the other inequalities about which we are concerned but do not address here.

Intersectionality

We are acutely aware that all individuals who identify as women are not members of a uniform, homogeneous group. Women differ in a wide variety of ways—race, ethnicity, religion, age, education, economic status, physical and mental capacity, parental status, and identification as cisgender, non-binary, and LGBTQ+. In other words, among women there is a great deal of what has come to be called "intersectionality."[5] Because of intersectionality—the intersection of gender with race, ethnicity, age, and so forth—achieving gender equality for one group of women will not necessarily mean it has been achieved for others. For example, it is entirely possible that a discrimination-free workplace could be available to white women and not simultaneously be achieved for Black women. Nevertheless, all people who identify as women *experience workplace gender inequality because they are women*. Therefore, while we understand that individual women experience discrimination differently because of their unique social identities, all women suffer from workplace discrimination because they are women. It is that common experience of gender-based discrimination on which this book is focused.

Non-Gender Workplace Inequality

Entirely separate from any gender inequality, many people experience workplace inequality because of race, ethnicity, religion, age, education, economic status, physical and mental capacity, parental status, and identification as cisgender, non-binary, and LGBTQ+ as well. Indeed, workplace discrimination against Asian, Black, Latinx, and Native American men and women is extremely serious and pervasive. We view this discrimination as one of the most important social challenges that our country currently faces.

By focusing solely on gender inequality in this book we are not discounting or marginalizing the seriousness of these inequalities. We only attempt to tackle and solve this one serious and identifiable workplace inequality, about which we know a great deal more because of our experiences, consulting, and research.

Women's Rights and Workplace Gender Inequality

There are troubling signs that women's rights are under attack: their right to make decisions about their personal medical needs; their right to make career choices without damaging public criticism; and their right to pursue lifestyle options, without being condemned for their choices. Perhaps the most obvious and ominous instance of this attack is the Supreme Court's 2022 decision overturning *Roe v. Wade*.[6] In *Dobbs v. Jackson Women's Health Organization*,[7] the Court held, "The Constitution makes no reference to abortion, and no such right is protected…by any constitutional provision including…the Due Process Clause of the Fourteenth Amendment." In the Court's view, such a right is only entitled to Constitutional protection if it is "implicit in the concept of ordered liberty." Past courts have held that a woman's right to an abortion is protected, because it is entailed in her fundamental "freedom to make intimate and personal choices that are 'central to personal dignity and autonomy.'" According to the current Supreme Court, however, this freedom is *not found in the concept of ordered liberty so it is not protected under the Constitution.* The *Dobbs* decision swept away 50 years of women's constitutionally protected reproductive rights overnight.

The *Dobbs* case has triggered further attacks on women's rights with respect to their reproductive functions. For example, many states have introduced legislation to ban contraceptives, and Missouri has banned public funding of intrauterine devices and emergency contraceptive *Plan B* pills.[8] The University of Idaho issued a memorandum advising faculty and staff that they were prohibited under state law from promoting services for abortion or for the prevention of conception.[9] Six states now explicitly grant pharmacists the right to refuse to refill birth control prescriptions on moral or religious grounds.[10] In New York State, a hospital denied medication to a woman that would "effectively manage her debilitating chronic pain" because she was of child-bearing age and the medication "might cause birth defects" if she were to become pregnant; something she was actively taking steps to prevent.[11] And at the date we are writing, the proposed "Right to Contraception Act" appears doomed in the U.S. Senate because of Republican opposition.[12]

It is not only women's rights to control their reproductive functions that are under attack. As we wrote in the second edition of *Breaking Through Bias,* following the 2016 election of our first openly misogynistic president, there was "an astonishing increase in open, hostile, mean-spirited criticism of successful women."[13] In addition, there has been considerable recent growth in explicit, purposeful anti-female criticism designed to intimidate, silence, and demean women. For example, the presence on social media of "men's rights" groups has exploded with their assertions that white men "are victims who are falling prey to feminism, changing social norms, progressive thought and politics."[14]

These strident secular attacks on women's rights have their religious counterparts in the growing evangelical movement. Although "masculine authority, militarism, and the sexual and spiritual subordination of women" have been consistently espoused by this movement for decades, evangelicals have been far more willing in recent years to publicly preach that such a patriarchal world-view should be observed across all of society.[15]

These are serious assaults on women's rights and women's equal status in society at large. To date, however, the broad societal and organizational commitment to workplace gender equality seems to remain strong. Therefore, despite our deep concern about the assaults on women's rights, our focus in this book is exclusively on ending gender inequality in the workplaces of those organizations whose leaders are truly and consciously committed to DEI.

What is Workplace Gender Inequality?

When women and men have conspicuously unequal workplace power, resources, and status, gender inequality *may be* at work. We say *may be*, because these inequalities may be due to factors other than the discriminatory treatment of women. For example, women and men may choose to pursue different career objectives; they may place greater value upon different activities in their lives; and they may enjoy and find satisfaction in different undertakings, commitments, and roles. Accordingly, in this book and in the PATH framework, when we refer to *workplace gender inequality* we are identifying an inequality in women's and men's *opportunities* to acquire power, resources, and status. Workplace gender inequality exists if women cannot attain what they want in their careers because they face explicit or implicit limitations, conditions, or obstructions that men do not face. Gender inequality also exists if men can attain better career outcomes because of privileges, advantages, or resources that women do not have.

> Workplace gender inequality exists if women cannot attain what they want in their careers because they face explicit or implicit limitations, conditions, or obstructions that men do not face.

Given this definition of workplace gender inequality, its eradication does not require that women and men possess *equal* power, resources, and status, or that there is an *equal* representation of women and men at all leadership levels. Rather, it means that women have an equal opportunity to achieve parity and equal representation. Gender *equality* means women and men have equal advancement and leadership opportunities; receive equally challenging and career-advancing assignments; are given equal support, advice, and mentorship; are equally accepted into networks, social activities, and team projects; and are given equally helpful performance reviews, and equal recognition for equal accomplishments, and equal rewards for equal performance. In other words, workplace gender equality is not indicated by a tally of women's and men's respective positions and advancements, but by the extent to which women and men compete for career success on equal grounds.

Cartoons

A word about our use of cartoons to illustrate some very serious issues. Humor can greatly help individuals cope with difficult, biased, and stressful situations.[16] Humor can help to make intellectually complex concepts emotionally compelling. We hope the cartoons in this book do that. We do not want to make workplace gender inequality seem humorous (it is profoundly not funny), but we do want to help readers see that some of the most egregious manifestations of inequality are strikingly ridiculous. As the saying goes, a picture is worth a thousand words, and it is our hope that the cartoons will convey ideas that might have taken us another thousand words to get across. Workplace gender inequality is not a humorous matter, but we believe humor can draw us into closer emotional contact with that reality.

The Structure of the Book

This book is divided into four parts, with a glossary of important terms. In Part I, "Gender Inequality Today," we review some areas of workplace leadership and advancement where the magnitude of gender inequality is particularly egregious. We have focused on these areas to emphasize the extent and depth of the discrimination suffered by women in their careers—and the pervasive underestimation of the extent and gravity of that discrimination. We proceed to show that many of the common explanations given for the existence of workplace gender inequality— premised as they are on some supposedly innate, non-biological differences between women and men—are simply gender myths. Then, we identify the actual causes of gender inequality and how they result from the gendered nature of our workplaces. In these workplaces, structural discrimination is "baked in" to personnel-management systems, processes, and practices. This reinforces the fundamental biases that underly individual discrimination.

We argue that structural discrimination is a *systemic* problem—a problem caused by the nature and operation of organizations' personnel-management systems. Individual discrimination, in contrast, is a *systematic* problem—a problem of consistent, predictably less favorable treatment of women than men by their coworkers. We end Part I by discussing the obvious and not so obvious costs of ongoing workplace gender inequality for organizations, teams, and employees.

In Part II, "We Haven't Made Much Progress," we consider the supposed simple, quick fixes to gender inequality—mandates, laws, and directives—and why they don't succeed in reducing either structural or individual discrimination. Next, we explain why anti-bias training and programs designed to make women more effective at pursuing career success on equal terms with men—programs designed to "fix the women"—are misguided, doing little to end workplace gender inequality. We end this part with a discussion of the reasons men have not been actively involved in DEI initiatives to date; why men are needed in the efforts to create workplaces that are truly diverse, equitable, and inclusive; and how we can help bring men to the table.

In Part III, "The PATH," we introduce and describe in detail the four actions at the heart of the program, the need for organizations to:

- **P**rioritize elimination of exclusionary behavior
- **A**dopt discrimination-resistant methods of personnel decision-making
- **T**reat inequality in the home as a workplace problem
- **H**alt unequal performance reviews, career advice, and leadership opportunities

Business, professional, and nonprofit organizations can use these principles to develop practical, effective, and readily achievable processes, tools, and techniques to end gender inequality in the workplace.

In Part IV, "Putting It All Together," we explain how organizations can implement PATH as the foundation of their personnel-management practices. To do so requires a strongly led, adequately resourced, and thoughtfully structured effort to overcome employees' resistance to change—both status quo bias and men's defense of their current workplace status. We also set out a well-designed and properly implemented plan that explicitly details how and by whom PATH's workplace changes will be made. The final chapter concerns the promise of PATH. It provides an explicit discussion of the benefits that organizations, teams, and individuals will realize once this bold, innovative, and forward-looking initiative is implemented.

PATH is not another plea for people to be less biased, behave more inclusively, or increase their self-awareness of workplace discrimination. Of course these are all highly laudable objectives. But the ultimate goal of ending workplace gender inequality will not be achieved by appealing to individuals' sense of fair play, encouraging them to be better people, or explaining how their unconscious biases can undermine their conscious beliefs. The past 30 years of well-meaning, well-intentioned DEI training has demonstrated this fact. Attacking the symptoms rather than the causes of gender inequality is simply not enough to get us to gender equality. Such desirable individual behaviors will only come about when we have engineered workplace systems that ensure fair, equal, respectful, and inclusive outcomes for women and men. PATH is about changing that workplace context. It is a no-nonsense, specific, and entirely realistic approach to ending workplace gender inequality.

PART I

GENDER INEQUALITY TODAY

Chapter 1

Extent of Gender Inequality

Today, women make up more than 50 percent of American law school graduates.[1] This is a dramatic improvement from the days when we went to law school. The year that Al graduated from law school, only 1 percent of his class were women. When Andie graduated from law school 11 years later, women made up 30 percent of her class. Over a short period of time, a remarkable transformation has taken place in legal education. This same record of women's participation is repeated in other important areas of higher education. Women now earn more bachelor's degrees, more master's degrees, and more doctorate degrees than men.[2] And, women now comprise 41 percent of students working toward a master's in business administration (MBA).[3]

Here's the problem: the dramatic gains that have been made in approaching true gender equality across American higher education have not been matched by similar workplaces advances once these highly qualified graduates enter their chosen career fields.

When we look at the gender composition of the leadership of all major areas of business, professional, and nonprofit activity, there is a distinct pattern of gender inequality, not gender parity. Take private law firms, for example. Although 47 percent of all associates (early career lawyers) are women at the "Am Law 200," only 22 percent of equity partners at these top American law firms were women in 2019, compared with 16 percent in 2007. Not a meteoric growth curve.[4] This lack of

3

Chart 1

Degrees Conferred by Sex: 2018-2019

Associate's degree	**1,012,202**	
Male	396,254	39%
Female	615,948	61%
Bachelor's degree	**1,911,018**	
Male	803,184	42%
Female	1,107,834	58%
Master's degree	**695,616**	
Male	250,842	36%
Female	444,774	64%
Doctor's degree[1]	**163,677**	
Male	71,337	44%
Female	92,340	56%

[1] Includes Ph.D., Ed.D., and comparable degrees at the doctoral level, as well as such degrees as M.D., D.D.S., and law degrees that were classified as first-professional degrees prior to 2010–12

Data in this table represent the 50 states and the District of Columbia. Data are for postsecondary institutions participating in Title IV federal financial aid programs.

Data courtesy U.S. Department of Education. Institute of Education Sciences, National Center for Education Statistics

gender diversity in the leadership of private law firms is mirrored in most segments of the U.S. economy. But just how serious is this underrepresentation? A lot worse than you may think. Let's first look at corporate America, and then at the professions.

Gender Inequality in Corporate Leadership

In 2015, LeanIn.Org and McKinsey & Company started issuing an annual "Women in the Workplace" report. Every year since then, they have surveyed large U.S. corporations to determine the percentage of women working at various managerial levels. In the 2015 report, LeanIn/

McKinsey looked back to data from 2012 for their first breakdown of the gender demographics of corporate leadership. Table 1 shows a comparison of women's participation in corporate leadership; first in 2012, and then in 2022.

Table 1

Women in the Workplace: 2012 vs. 2022

Year	Entry Level	Manager	Sr. Mgr.	VP	Sr. VP	C-Suite
2012	42%	33%	28%	23%	20%	16%
2022	48%	40%	36%	32%	28%	26%

Data from *Women in the Workplace*, October 2022, McKinsey & Company, www.mckinsey.com. Copyright © 2022 McKinsey & Company. All rights reserved. Reprinted by permission.

Women in the C-Suite

The Table 1 comparisons show that there has been some progress made over the past decade. For example, women's C-suite representation now runs at about 26 percent.[5] This representation percentage is similar in companies in the Russell 3000˚ Index (R3000)[6] and those in the Fortune 100. They're closing in on 30 percent.[7] Thus, if we look only at the percentage of women in the C-suite, the progress has been quite impressive. Nevertheless, in many ways, women's C-suite representation masks the true story of the extent of gender inequality in American corporate leadership. First, as the *Women in the Workplace* comparison shows, women make up 48 percent of entry-level career professionals. By the time they get to the C-suite, however, their proportionate representation has dropped by half. What the *Women in the Workplace 2022* study does not show is that women are *not* being promoted to the important seats of power in boardrooms or to named executive officer (NEO) positions across the United States.

> What the *Women in the Workplace 2022* study does not show is that women are not being promoted to the important seats of power in boardrooms or to named executive officer (NEO) positions across the United States.

The SEC requires publicly held companies to disclose the identities and compensation of their NEOs, defined as the chief executive officer (CEO), chief financial officer (CFO), and the next three highest paid corporate officials.[8] NEO positions are critical for career advancement because they serve as stepping stones to the CEO position and to public board directorships. In short, stepping-stone positions lead to *control*. Only three Fortune 500 companies—Accenture, Insight Enterprises, and Kohl's Corporation—include a rare leadership combination of both a woman CEO *and* a woman CFO.[9]

In 2020, Morningstar, a large investor information company, did an analysis of the proxy disclosures of 2,384 R3000 companies for the fiscal years 2015 through 2019. Morningstar found that in 2019, women held just 12.2 percent of all NEO positions and only 6 percent of CEO positions.[10] While these numbers are up from 2015 (when women were just 9.4 percent and 4.1 percent, respectively), fewer than half of the R3000 companies had *any* women NEOs in 2019, and only 12 percent had more than one woman NEO. In other words, at the great majority of American corporations, *men outnumber women by seven to one* in NEO positions. Among Fortune 100 companies, women hold just 13 percent of these NEO positions—the stepping-stone positions for advancement to CEO and board membership.

Women's seemingly noteworthy advancement into the C-suite is due largely to their promotion to positions without profit and loss (P&L) responsibility. Thus, women hold 38 percent of *staff* as opposed to *line* C-suite positions, such as chief human resources manager (CHRM), general counsel (GC), and chief commercial and marketing officer (CCMO).

These positions are known as *terminal positions*. They are not often considered as stepping stones to more senior leadership roles.[11] The Stanford Closer Look Series "Diversity in the C-Suite" report concludes that women's presence in the C-suites of Fortune 100 companies is skewed toward lower-potential positions. The report notes that women disproportionately serve "in terminal functional roles that are not typically a path to becoming CEO" or "to corporate board service."[12] Among the broader group of R3000 companies, women hold only 10 to 11 percent of the stepping-stone positions and 25 percent of the other C-suite positions.[13]

The management consulting firm, Korn Ferry, has provided a detailed analysis of this inequality in the roles women and men hold in the C-suite. Analyzing the gender demographies of C-suites at the 1,000 largest companies, Korn Ferry found that women make up only 6 percent of CEOs, 12 percent of CFOs, and 18 percent of chief information officers

"A glass ceiling?... Don't be ridiculous. The sign works just fine."

www.CartoonStock.com

(CIOs).[14] Indeed, other studies suggest that only 8 percent of company divisions are led by women with P&L accountability.[15]

The dramatic underrepresentation of women in stepping-stone and P&L positions is, in part, explained by the fact that men receive access to the kind of information and encouragement that is needed to pursue such roles with much greater regularity than do women. In a 2018 study of 3,038 U.S. professionals, only 14 percent of women as opposed to 46 percent of men were encouraged to consider P&L roles, and more than three times as many men had received detailed information on career paths leading to P&L jobs within the two years preceding the survey's data collection.[16]

In addition to men's informational and counseling advantages, women are also held back from obtaining stepping-stone positions because of gender stereotypes. In a 2017 study of more than 2,600 senior executives, women were found to be just as likely as men to possess the kinds of skills and charisma that are predictive of success as a future CEO.[17] Yet, women CEO candidates were 28 percent *less likely* than their male peers to secure these top spots.[18]

Gender Inequality in Managerial Compensation

Another key indicator of the true extent of gender inequality in corporate leadership is managerial compensation. ADP Research Institute (ADPRI) analyzed gender pay records of about 13 million employees across all managerial levels of 30,000 firms in eight economic sectors in 2019.[19] ADPRI divided these managerial positions into a number of levels and found gender pay gaps at every level. Interestingly, these pay gaps increased and decreased as women moved up the corporate ladder, and in ways that do not appear to make any sense.

ADPRI concluded that women appear to hit a "glass wall" at the top managerial levels, where they fell short of parity with men by 23 percentage points.[20]

" While you'll be doing the work of three men, Ms. Hopkins, you'll be getting paid the work of one woman. "

www.CartoonStock.com

Gender Inequality in the Broader Ranks of Management

Women's underrepresentation in corporate leadership is not limited to C-suite positions, or to managers at the NEO level. The *Women in the Workplace 2022* survey shows that women and men are nearly equal in their representation in entry-level positions, but that soon changes. Immediately afterward, men start their leadership ascent rising to 60 percent of managers, 64 percent of senior managers, 68 percent of VPs, 72 percent of SVPs, and 74 percent of C-suite executives.[21]

Of course, as men's representation increases at ever-higher leadership levels, women's representation decreases, in inverse proportion. By the time women reach the C-suite, they hold only 26 percent of these positions and fewer than 16 percent of the NEO positions. The ascent of men and the descent of women in senior leadership roles is reflected in Graph 1.

Graph 1

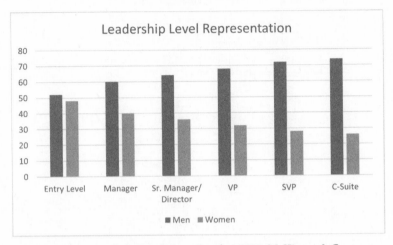

Gender Inequality in Non-Profit and Private Firm Leadership

The substantial gender inequality in corporate leadership is reflected across many other sectors of the American economy. As we have already seen in the legal profession, women and men have been graduating from law schools at about parity since 2017. But women make up only 22 percent of equity partners. Although 58 percent of college students are now women, fewer than a quarter of college and university presidents are women.[22] Women now outnumber men in medical schools,[23] but they make up only 16 percent of deans and 18 percent of departmental chairs at these schools. And, the upper echelons of clinical medical practices are no better for women.[24] In consulting, 39 percent of the professional workforce is women, but women are 17 percent of consulting firm partners.[25] In financial service firms, women account for 22 percent of *all* leadership positions.[26] Among the 100 leading architectural firms, only three are led by women, 10 percent of the top roles (including partner) are held by women, and 16 percent of these firms have no women in any management roles.[27] In the science, technology, engineering, and math (STEM) fields, women make up a paltry 3 percent of CEOs and 19 percent of company board members.[28]

The entertainment industry is awash with discrimination. Of the 100 top-grossing Hollywood films in 2020, women made up only 16 percent of the directors, 12 percent of the writers, 28 percent of the producers, 18 percent of the editors, and a (heartbreakingly measly) 3 percent of the cinematographers.[29] In the same year, women made up only 34 percent of the major characters in top-grossing films[30] (a relatively high number within the industry, perhaps indicative of the long history of women serving as totems in filmmaking). And women only filled 5.2 percent of the CEO positions at major television and movie studios.[31]

Excellent application, would you like to come back when you're a man?

www.CartoonStock.com

Common Reactions to Gender Inequality in Leadership

Many people react to statistics that clearly show the severe underrepresentation of women in business, professional, and nonprofit leadership by claiming that inequality is due to women's personal career and lifestyle choices.[32] If pressed, they will claim that if there is any gender discrimination, it is so small as to be inconsequential.

Horatio Alger and Gender Inequality

Leaders often say that their workplaces operate as meritocracies where discriminatory obstacles do not exist to block women's career ascent.[33] Indeed, senior leaders' strong convictions that career progression is based solely on merit is commonplace, reflecting the pervasive belief that "social rewards and status" in America are due entirely to individual merit and hard work.[34] This perspective on the essential fairness in workplaces is illustrated by the Horatio Alger "rags to riches" stories for young adults and the children's book, *The Little Engine That Could*. The not-too-subtle message that these stories convey is that anyone can get ahead and achieve whatever they want, *if* they have the talent *and* are willing to work hard enough.[35] In fact, the belief that society operates in accordance with meritocracy principles presumes that there is a direct tie between social status and the efforts and abilities of individuals. Such a belief, of course, "legitimizes existing status differences among individuals and groups, and helps to justify the status quo."[36]

Therefore, if there is gender inequality in business, professional, and nonprofit leadership it is because women either don't have men's leadership abilities, or they don't work as hard as men do because of personal lifestyle choices.[37]

> If there is gender inequality in business, professional, and nonprofit leadership it is because women either don't have men's leadership abilities, or they don't work as hard as men do because of personal lifestyle choices.

The Cumulative Effect of Incremental Discrimination

The belief that gender inequality in senior leadership is due to the difference in women's and men's abilities is often bolstered by claims that obstacles to advancement are slight, at best. Unfortunately, even small discriminatory obstacles result in large gender disparities in senior leadership teams.

The incremental effects of small biases are illustrated by a 1996 computer simulation that shows a large, discriminatory impact of slight unequal treatment.[38] In this well-cited simulation, published in *American Psychologist*, Richard Martell and his co-researchers assumed a hypothetical organization had eight hierarchical employment levels, ranging from entry-level to senior management. They further assumed that the hypothetical organization had 500 entry-level employees and 10 employees at the highest senior management level. At the beginning of the computer simulation, women and men were equally represented *at all eight levels*. Everyone in the company received a randomly generated rating (evaluation), with women being scored on a scale of 1 to 100 and men on a scale of 1 to 101. Men's 1 percent advantage meant that men had a clear, if only very small, advantage over women. The simulation then assumed that periodically (say twice a year) there was a 15 percent attrition rate for employees at each of the eight levels. Employees with the highest ratings moving up to the next level, and new employees were added at the entry level. The attrition/promotion simulation process was run enough times so that no employee who had been at the company at the beginning of the simulation was still there at the end. At this point, even though women and men had started out equally represented at all eight hierarchical levels, men's 1 percent advantage over women meant that men advanced to 65 percent of this hypothetical organization's senior leadership positions, with women making up only 35 percent of the positions.[39]

A one percentage point difference between the ways in which women and men are treated in the workplace can have a dramatic effect on their career advancement. Even tiny inequalities in the basis of which women and men are evaluated, for example, allow men to gain substantial advantages over women.

Expanding upon the 1996 simulation model, a 2022 computer simulation model sought to link gender disparity to six empirically identified ways in which gender bias manifests within organizations. Assuming that these factors had a small (typically 2 percent disadvantage) effect on women's careers, men ended up holding, after a series of promotion and turnover simulations, 84 percent of the hypothetical organization's top leadership roles.[40]

A further point can be drawn from these simulation models. It is not the absolute magnitude of any special instance of discriminatory treatment that is important but the cumulative effect of consistent and continuous discriminatory treatment. This is the clear takeaway from this sophisticated computer modeling. If seemingly trivial instances of unequal treatment constitute a systematic pattern, it is easy for them to become systemic organizational problems as well—and in a chronically insidious manner. Subtle and seemingly insignificant discriminatory treatment—while easily ignored—can add up to become very significant over time.

The progression from seemingly insignificant to dramatic inequality is well illustrated by the 2018 resignation of Professor Lenore Blum from her tenured professorship at Carnegie Mellon University (CMU). When she resigned, Blum was the Distinguished Career Professor of Computer Science and had been on the CMU faculty for 20 years. Despite her senior status and many honors, she resigned over what she described as endemic sexism. Blum said, "Subtle biases and microaggressions pile up, few of which on their own rise to the level of 'let's take action' but are insidious nevertheless."[41] Moreover, such biases and microaggressions create a double bind for women. As Blum noted, if women call attention to these slight displays of discrimination, "Attempts to point them out label you a complainer or 'difficult.'"[42] Yet, if women do not point them out, they risk continuing to suffer from cumulative, discriminatory treatment.

Blum, apparently, was not alone in viewing CMU as harboring sexist behavior. In a 2016 CMU survey, when asked if another faculty member had made "an assumption about you based on your birth sex," 62 percent of the women but only 10 percent of the men answered "yes."[43] And

CMU is far from unique. A Pew Research Center survey conducted in 2017 found that women were three times more likely than men to say they experienced repeated, small slights at work because of their gender.[44]

A Pew Research Center survey conducted in 2017 found that women were three times more likely than men to say they experienced repeated, small slights at work because of their gender.

If women and men consistently and predictably experience unequal career outcomes, it is likely that they also experience unequal workplace treatment. These inequalities may be identified in the assignments received; the networks available to them; the training, mentoring, or sponsorship they are provided; the exclusionary behaviors they encounter; the evaluations and the compensation they receive; or the resources available to them. This seems to be borne out by a *Fortune* opinion survey of more than 10,000 businesswomen who called for "an end to systemic discrimination and harmful stereotypes," when asked the simple question, "What needs to change for more women to reach their full potential?"[45]

Discriminatory Impact of the Pandemic

At the time we were writing this book, more than one million people had died from the COVID-19 virus and related health issues; and close to 100 million people have contracted the virus in the United States.[46] More Americans have died in this pandemic than in the Second World War and all subsequent wars in which the United States has been involved, combined. In addition to the human toll, the pandemic has also taken a rough toll on the American economy. Today, many economic dislocations related to the pandemic remain with us.

Discriminatory Impact of the Pandemic in the Home

The pandemic quickly exposed in painful, human terms the extent of the challenges that working women face at home. It is no secret that women and men spend unequal amounts of time on childcare and home-related tasks.[47] When the pandemic forced most schools and day-care facilities to close, far more women than men with young children were forced to choose between taking care of their children and continuing with their jobs. As a consequence, Misty Heggeness, a senior advisor and principal economist at the U.S. Census Bureau, and her coauthors observed, "Working mothers are either willingly leaving jobs or are being forced out in extraordinary numbers."[48]

"Would you have liked any help?"

www.CartoonStock.com

Mothers who were able to continue working full-time—which included most women in management positions—were more negatively affected by school and daycare closures than their male counterparts.

These mothers reduced their work hours four to five times more often than comparably situated fathers.

In a survey of the Stanford University faculty, those faculty members with dependents (50 percent of women compared with only 33 percent of men) spent more than four additional hours each day on caregiving.[49] Accordingly, these women had less time to pursue their professional endeavors, significantly reducing their participation in the kind of critical work needed for career advancement. As Jennifer March Augustine and Kate Prickett remarked in a 2022 article published in *Demography*, mothers increased the amount of time they spent in balancing paid work with caregiving by 346 percent, compared to fathers.[50] Using time-use data from the *American Time Use Survey*, the authors noted that while fathers had marginal increases in their caregiving responsibilities, they were "not in activities that parents tend to rate as more stressful or intensive, such as supervising children's schooling and multitasking at work."[51]

As a result of the pandemic, the gender gap in work hours grew by 20 to 50 percent. This gender gap held true for women with male partners *even when both partners worked full-time*. Mothers with male partners reduced their work hours five times more often than did fathers.[52]

> During the pandemic, "mothers increased the amount of time they spent in balancing paid work with caregiving by 346 percent, compared to fathers."
>
> —Jennifer March Augustine and Kate Prickett

Gender inequality in the home has a severe impact on women's career opportunities. Because of this inequality, women face a clear tension between career advancement and their family and other domestic commitments. As a result, women want or need better flexibility, yet flexibility comes at a price that is often ignored in the frequent calls for "work/life balance."[53] As we will see in Chapter 10, organizations can do a great deal through their personnel policies to lessen the significant discriminatory impact of homelife inequality on women's career advancement.

KEY TAKEAWAYS

- Women's underrepresentation in senior leadership is far more severe than might be assumed if we only consider the *Women in the Workplace 2022* data as shown in Table 1. Behind that data are many dramatic inequalities in women's career advancement. The gender bias that exists in the C-suite is well known. What is less understood are the processes that determine who get promoted into key stepping-stone positions toward senior leadership roles, how, and why.
- Corporations are not the only workplaces characterized by gender inequality in their leadership ranks. Drastic inequalities in the gender representation in organizational leadership are reflected across all spheres of American economic life.
- Computer simulation models show that tiny amounts of incremental discrimination can accumulate over time to result in outsized gender discriminatory impacts.
- The COVID-19 pandemic has highlighted gender inequality at work and at home.
- The many problems with workplace gender inequality are widespread and enduring, and their negative collective impact is not only corrosive, but extremely subtle.

Chapter 2

Causes of Gender Inequality

GENDER INEQUALITY IS PERVASIVE IN American workplaces. As women try to climb leadership ladders, they increasingly encounter gender-based obstacles.[1] Women experience less career support, job satisfaction, and advancement opportunities than do men.[2] They also are more likely to encounter instances of workplace bullying and incivility, microaggressions, and harassment.[3]

Workplace gender inequality is painfully apparent. But what are its causes, and why can't we seem to identify them as readily as we would like? Perhaps the best way to zero in on workplace gender inequality is to first identify those causes that are most frequently given for it, and point out the mistaken assumptions underlying them.

Not surprisingly, people—particularly people at the top of major economic and professional organizations—would like to believe that gender inequality is due to factors outside of their control. Therefore, the paucity of women in business, professional, and nonprofit leadership roles is often attributed to women lacking the ambition, ability, or commitment to succeed. Too many leaders would prefer to simply believe these explanations.

As a result, explanations are commonly given for gender inequality: what we call, "The Five Gender Myths." We will not detail the academic interchanges on each of these myths. Rather, we will simply describe them, and note the profound ways in which they tend to play out.

The Five Gender Myths

Myth 1: Women and Men Are Fundamentally
Different in Nonbiological Ways

Many people believe that because of nature or nurture—heredity or environment—women and men have fundamentally different psychological and emotional characteristics.[4] This belief is reflected in judgments about women's and men's respective fitness for various workplace roles, their ability to take on challenging responsibilities, and their competence as leaders.[5] Although some neurological differences have been identified in female and male brains, there is no evidence that these difference lead to behavioral or competency differences that are relevant to workplace performance.[6]

With respect to roles, responsibilities, and leadership, women's and men's abilities are more similar than they are different.[7] With respect to *abilities and characteristics relevant to workplace performance and career success, there is no meaningful difference between women and men*.[8] As the following graphs illustrate, the difference in women's and men's heights is dramatic, but their difference in critical leadership traits, like self-esteem and confidence, is insignificant.[9]

Importantly, people persist in refusing to acknowledge women's and men's essential similarities. After all, they *see* differences in their daily workplace interactions. They don't *see* that when women and men display different behaviors at work, it is because they are treated differently, not because they are inherently different.

> They don't *see* that when women and men display different behaviors at work, it is because they are treated differently, not because they are inherently different.

Graph 1

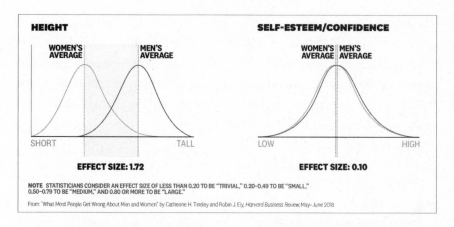

Reprinted with permission from "What Most People Get Wrong About Men and Women" by Catherine H. Tinsley; Robin J. Ely. Harvard Business Review, May 2018. Copyright 2018 by Harvard Business Publishing; all rights reserved.

Myth 2: Women Lack the Ambition to Handle Intense Competition[10]

There is a broadly held narrative that women lack the ambition to drive high performance when intense competition, high-stakes negotiation, and stressful interactions come into the mix. This narrative can describe and considerably shape workplace perceptions.[11] Studies show, however, that women perform as well as men in competitive and stressful situations. Women often share their emotions and are more confident in doing so—but, this should not be mistakenly assumed to mean that women can't take the heat. It is not that women lack the resolve; it is simply that they are more likely to be candid about especially challenging situations at work.[12] When women receive the same training, resources, and opportunities as men, they can perform in all career-relevant situations with the same competence, effectiveness, and confidence.[13]

Myth 3: Women Are Not as Self-Confident as Men[14]

A popular narrative nowadays is that women lack the self-confidence needed to compete on equal terms with men.[15] In 1973, Stephen Goldberg argued that it is natural for women to play a subordinate role to men's higher status because "women are not for psychological reasons as motivated to obtain [it]."[16] More recently, in *Lean In: Women, Work, and the Will to Lead*, Sheryl Sandberg, former COO of Meta Platforms, wrote, "Women hold ourselves back in ways both big and small, by lacking self-confidence, by not raising our hands, and by pulling back when we should be leaning in."[17]

But whether the myth is stated in its old or its new form, the belief that workplace gender inequality is due to women's lack of confidence has things precisely backward. Such inequality is not caused by women's lack of confidence. It is caused—if it exists at all—by the fact that women do not receive equivalent opportunities, resources, and support, resulting in their losing confidence over time.[18]

While women are regularly told that they need to show more confidence in order to progress in their careers, women find themselves trying to walk a "tight rope of exuding just the 'perfect' amount of self-confidence: a psychological challenge men rarely face."[19]

As Darren T. Baker, an assistant professor at UCD Michael Smurfit Graduate Business School in Ireland, and Juliet Bourke, a professor at UNSW Business School in Australia, wrote in their *Harvard Business Review* article "How Confidence Is Weaponized Against Women," the focus on women's supposed lack of self-confidence "deftly distracts leaders from addressing structural barriers to gender equity. We suggest that this risk/reward profile means it is now time to declare a moratorium on the confidence narrative."[20]

> The focus on women's supposed lack of self-confidence "deftly distracts leaders from addressing structural barriers to gender equity."
> —Darren T. Baker and Juliet Bourke

Myth 4: Women Cannot Deal with Risk and Danger[21]

Numerous studies have shown that women are no less interested in entering risky or dangerous situations and no less adept in delivering high performance in them than men. Today, women are establishing an impressive record of achievement in military combat duty.[22] Women are very capable of understanding an organization's enterprise-wide risks and of handling complex related modeling scenarios. Women have proven themselves to be just as capable of identifying, confronting, managing, and mitigating risks as are men. Women's strengths in these areas have important implications for organizational leaders as they seek to manage new market developments, and value retention activities in increasingly competitive markets that require an ability to effectively manage risk and opportunity.[23]

Myth 5: Women Are Caregivers

The last gender myth is that women would rather focus on domestic life than pursue challenging careers. There is little evidence, however, that women in comparison to men would prefer to devote their time to caring for children, spouses, and parents. There is also little evidence that they may welcome the chance to become members of the *sandwich generation*—caring for both the young and the old simultaneously—while attempting to advance at work.[24] Indeed, there is little difference in women's and men's interests pursuing careers and parenthood. Studies show that women and men are equally dedicated to their careers, regardless *of their parental status.*[25]

Moreover, research firmly establishes that women are far more likely to be pushed out of their careers than they are to opt out or step back *for reasons of personal preference,* whether to care for family members or for other reasons.[26]

> Women are far more likely to be pushed out of their careers, than they are to opt out or step back *for reasons of personal preference,* whether to care for family members or for other reasons.

The Five Gender Myths are not only demonstrably false, but they deflect attention away from the root causes of workplace gender inequality. Dwelling on supposed differences can lead people to assume that efforts to end workplace gender inequality are pointless and beyond their control. These attitudes flourish in gendered workplaces and it is because workplaces are gendered that gender inequality exists.[27]

Gendered Workplaces

America's workplaces are gendered because men run, control, and shape their operation:

- *Male-dominated*: authority and power are vested (primarily) in men
- *Male-identified*: masculine norms, values, and expectations define the behavior that is regarded as good and desirable
- *Male-centered*: men's experiences, behaviors, and work patterns constitute what is considered to be "normal"

As Sapna Cheryan and Hazel-Rose Markus confirmed in their *Harvard Business Review* article, "Rooting Out the Masculine Defaults in Your Workplace," most workplaces operate in accordance with what they referred to as "masculine defaults."[28] "Masculine defaults are a form of gender bias in which characterizations and behaviors typically associated with men are rewarded and considered standard practice."[29] The gendered nature of our workplaces results in two powerful forces that drive gender inequality: structural discrimination and individual discrimination. (We look at them in the following section.)

The gendered nature of American workplaces is particularly insidious because, as Cheryan and Markus point out, the problems are harder to pin down when "women are paid less, passed over for promotions, and harassed." In gendered workplaces with masculine defaults, "the doors are often presented as open for both men and women, which makes it *seem* like there's equal opportunity; but the workplace rewards and favors standard stereotypically masculine characteristics and behaviors."[30]

"I'm right there in the room, and no one even acknowledges me."

www.CartoonStock.com

We need to be clear from the outset: the gendered nature of our workplaces is no one's "fault." The fact that most of America's workplaces are male-dominated, identified, and centered is the consequence of a very long history. Workplace structures were formed at a time when only men pursued careers, The businesses, professions, and trades were created as men's preserves; nonprofit organizations as women's volunteer-only efforts. Indeed, until about a hundred years ago, women were effectively excluded from activities where they could earn income or own assets; activities through which it was possible to acquire power, resources, and status.

Of course, great progress has been made in recent years toward the integration of women into American workplaces—but despite this progress, little has been accomplished in changing their basic gendered structures characterized by male defaults. To achieve gender equality now, we need to change these structures. Well-intended and generously resourced DEI initiatives have not resulted in this change, however, because current DEI efforts have not been focused on the root cause of the inequality— the structure of the workplace.

PATH offers a focused, well-conceived, practical to help enable organizations to make needed changes. Therefore, before we dive into the details of PATH in Part III and its implementation in Part IV, we need to take a close look at gendered workplaces and the two discriminatory forces that bolster them—structural discrimination and individual discrimination.

Systemic and Systematic Gender Discrimination

Structural discrimination is a systemic problem that results from the established, consistent, and predictable ways in which an organization's systems, processes, and practices operate to produce unequal outcomes for women and men. The norms, values, and expectations inherent in such structurally biased workplaces operate to foster discrimination at the individual level. Gender inequality is, thus, both a systemic and a systematic problem. Structural discrimination is fueled by the established and accepted ways in which personnel are managed. Individual discrimination is fueled by the fact of structural discrimination. Ending workplace gender inequality depends on changing the systems, workplaces *and* the norms, values, and expectations inherent in such operations.

A gendered workplace's structural discrimination not only leads to unequal outcomes for women and men, but it also creates the internal contexts within which people interact with each other. When workplace structures are discriminatory, the behaviors of individuals in those workplaces will in all likelihood fall in line with the inherent discriminatory norms. Such individual discrimination is what makes women's workplace experiences less pleasant, engaging, rewarding, and safe than those of men.

Structural discrimination is the day-to-day, taken-for-granted operation of personnel-management practices in gendered workplaces. Structural discrimination results in *systemically* unequal career outcomes for women and men. Individual discrimination is the consistent, predictable, gender-discriminatory decisions, behaviors, and attitudes of people in those workplaces that flourish in the context of structural discrimination. Individual discrimination causes women to *systematically* experience unequal workplace treatment. Thus, the dual aspect of workplace gender inequality involves (1) the institutionalized, structural career disadvantages that women experience *because they are women*, and (2) the personal slights, rudeness, exclusion, and harassments women face *because they are women*.

- **Structural discrimination** is the day-to-day, taken-for-granted operation of personnel-management practices in gendered workplace.
- **Individual discrimination** is the consistent, predictable, gender-discriminatory decisions, behaviors, and attitudes of people in those workplaces that flourish in the context of structural discrimination.

As a result of structural discrimination, women and men receive unequal career advancement opportunities; unequal access to resources, support, and encouragement; and unequal chances to develop, practice, and refine their leadership abilities.[31] Because of individual discrimination, individuals (both women and men) tend to systematically regard, treat, and evaluate women less favorably than men; to expose women to incivility, microaggressions, exclusionary behaviors; and to subject them to harassment or outright abuse. Because of individual discrimination, individuals (women and men) tend to evaluate women's performance, accomplishments, and potential as inferior to men's—even when they are objectively the same.

Structural and individual discriminations are consistent features of gendered workplaces. But what sustains these discriminatory forces and the very existence of gendered workplaces? Why are they so resistant to change, and why don't they just fade away? These are the questions to which we now turn our attention.

Stereotypes and Structural Discrimination

Structural discrimination in gendered workplaces are the explicit manifestation of gender stereotypes. Because of gender stereotypes, women are presumed to be "communal," men to be "agentic." This means that women are expected to be and assumed to be caregivers, warm, emotional, and deferential. Men, on the other hand, are expected to be and assumed to be leaders, independent, forceful, and decisive.[32] Underpinning these gender stereotypes are the fundamental assumptions that men are superior to women with respect to the tasks, roles, and responsibilities related to workplace performance, leadership, and commitment.

Cecilia Ridgeway calls these assumptions our "status beliefs" about the relationships of women and men. As she writes in *Framed by Gender: How Gender Inequality Persists in the Modern World*, "It is these status beliefs" that help shape "*gender* as a distinct principle of inequality with its own dynamic potential to change or persist."[33] These status beliefs have no basis in fact. They are sustained and reinforced, however, by the everyday experience of women's and men's unequal workplace roles, responsibilities, and opportunities. Because of persistent status beliefs, men are provided with more resources and power than women.[34] Indeed, because of structural discrimination, women are treated less favorably than men with respect to hiring decisions,[35] performance evaluations,[36] achievement assessments,[37] compensation determinations,[38] leadership development opportunities,[39] and promotion decisions.

PATH is specifically designed to counter the discriminatory effects of gender stereotypes and their embedded status beliefs. Workplace changes under PATH are focused on altering how roles, responsibilities, and opportunities are allocated; how resources and power are acquired; and how status is obtained and reinforced. Through a series of practical, effective, and achievable adjustments to a workplace's personnel management practices, PATH offers a practical, effective, and achievable way to end structural discrimination and thereby eliminates the context that favors individual discrimination.

> Through a series of practical, effective, and achievable adjustments to a workplace's personnel-management practices, PATH offers a practical, effective, and achievable way to end structural discrimination and thereby eliminates the context that favors individual discrimination.

But where do the gender stereotypes that support structural discrimination originate? In his book *Public Opinion*,[40] originally published in 1922, Walter Lippmann makes clear that such gender stereotypes are acquired through participation in our shared cultural experience. As he writes, "In the great blooming, buzzing confusion of the outer world we pick out what our culture has already defined for us, and we tend to perceive that which we have picked out *in the form stereotyped for us by our culture.*"[41] Gender stereotypes are, thus, an instance of what has been called *culture in the mind*.[42] People's inevitable tendency is to incorporate the stereotypical assumptions about women and men into their expectations, belief patterns, and workplace systems.[43]

Gendered workplaces, therefore, reflect culture's gendered nature. It is important to note, however, that PATH does not take on the gendered nature of our entire culture. As we will see in Chapter 5, and Part III, PATH is not an effort to eliminate gender stereotypes from society, the status beliefs embedded in them, or any other aspect of the *culture in the mind*. And PATH's goal is not to de-bias individuals or transform the gendered nature of our shared cultural context. Quite the contrary, PATH seeks to eliminate structural discrimination in our workplaces. It acknowledges the power of stereotypes but prevents them from affecting an organization's workplace decisions, policies, and practices. In other words, PATH is premised on the belief that we can end workplace gender inequality without trying to change the gendered nature of American culture as a whole. Nevertheless, because the workplace is where power, resources, and status in our culture is primarily acquired, by changing the gendered nature of our workplaces, PATH can be expected to have a major impact on the broader culture.

The Four Biases and Individual Discrimination

In gendered workplaces, women's and men's unequal career outcomes are the result of stereotypes and the status beliefs inherent in the structure and operations of those workplaces. These unequal career outcomes are consistent with the beliefs, expectations, and preconceptions people have because of their shared cultural experiences. Unequal career outcomes also result from the expectations and preconceptions people have about other people (and themselves) because of their social identities (which will inevitably be further shaped by intersectionality). In other words, structural discrimination in gendered workplaces produces unequal career outcomes for women and men in ways that are consistent with how individuals, because of culture in the mind, are inclined to believe things ought to turn out anyway. As a result, there are no effective checks in gendered workplaces on individuals' biases, indeed, structural discrimination fosters the biases leading to individual discrimination. PATH's basic strategy is to disrupt structural discrimination, we can do much to prevent individual discrimination from having the outsized influence that it has now.

But what exactly are these biases and what is their workplace influence? For our purposes, we can identify four fundamental biases: *affinity, gender, out-group,* and *status quo.* Together and separately, these biases are at the root of individual discrimination in the workplace. Therefore, we need to understand the nature and operation of these individual biases, and how they can be prevented from having such pernicious effects on women's workplace experiences and on their career progression.

Affinity Bias

Affinity bias is reflected in people's tendency to favor those who are like us. It causes men to prefer to assign work to, socialize with, and provide support for other men. Because of affinity bias, male leaders are far more likely to hire, befriend, and rely on other men than on women.[44] One study found that affinity bias was the overriding factor in 78 percent of all hiring decisions.[45] Indeed, men's affinity bias is so powerful that white men are more likely to accept Black men into their networks than they are to accept women of any race.[46] Given the power of affinity bias, it is not surprising that the straight, white men who lead most of America's major economic organizations tend to surround themselves with other straight, white men.[47] These leaders *naturally* think first of men like them when they seek support or advice, allocate career opportunities, assign jobs, staff projects, and hand out rewards.[48]

People's preferences for people who are like them is part of human nature. Plato observed that "similarity begets friendship," and Aristotle wrote that people love those who are like themselves.[49] This "birds of a feather flock together" tendency is what social scientists call homophily; literally, "love for the same." As a result, affinity bias is a powerful influence in the formation of workplace alliances, personal relationships, and networks of all sorts.[50]

Although affinity bias does not necessarily involve a conscious discriminatory intention, it powerfully drives workplace discrimination experienced by women. For example, McKinsey found that only 20 percent of the members of the executive teams at 1,000 large companies (all led by men) were women, and more than a third of these companies had no women at all on their executive teams.[51] Even among companies whose executive teams had the greatest gender diversity, very few of the women had a sense of equality, acceptance, and belonging—the key components of an inclusive workplace culture. Only 21 percent of the comments from female respondents were positive about feeling included in their workplaces, while 61 percent were negative.[52] McKinsey concluded that these responses make clear "the challenge that even the more diverse companies still face in tackling inclusion.... Hiring diverse talent isn't enough—it's the workplace experience that shapes whether people remain and thrive."[53]

Affinity bias is a powerful force working against women's sense of inclusion. That is why, as we explore in Chapter 8, PATH prioritizes the elimination of workplace exclusionary behaviors—many of which are a form of affinity bias. Affinity bias must be overcome to achieve truly inclusive workplaces.

Gender Bias

Gender bias is the manifestation of the status beliefs embedded in gender stereotypes. It involves valuing the masculine over the feminine; preferring to have men rather than women in high-profile leadership positions; and expecting men to perform more competently, behave more competitively, negotiate more effectively, and display stronger career commitments than women.

Because of gender bias, women and men do not receive equal treatment in regard to:

- the ways in which they are raised[54]
- the educational advice they receive[55]
- the career choices they are encouraged to make[56]
- the company roles into which they are tracked[57]
- the hiring, compensation, and promotion experiences they have[58]
- the ways in which they are expected to behave[59]
- the homelife responsibilities they bear[60]

Unlike affinity bias, which appears to be a fundamental aspect of human nature, gender bias is socially inculcated; it is the result of immersion in society's practices, expectations, and norms.[61]

Gender bias, like gender stereotypes more broadly, is a form of *culture in the mind*—a discriminatory perspective on women's and men's respective characteristics, abilities, and potential. PATH is specifically designed to prevent gender bias from influencing decision-makers' formal personnel-related decisions. As we will see in Chapter 9, PATH does not attempt to de-bias individuals. Rather, it changes the context in which decision-makers act so that their behavior is less likely to be influenced by gender bias.

Out-Group Bias

Out-group bias leads people to disparage those who are different, not in their in-group: people who are other. There is a very thin line between people being favorably inclined toward people who are like them (affinity bias) and feeling uncomfortable with people who are not like them. And there is another very thin line between people feeling uncomfortable with people who are not like them and disparaging or expressing hostility toward them (out-group bias). These lines are more likely to be crossed when, because of gender bias, women (members of an out-group) are systematically subject to devaluation in comparison with men (members of an in-group).

> Out-group bias leads people to disparage those who are different, not in their in-group: people who are other.

Because of outgroup bias, women experience workplace microaggressions and incivilities far more than men.[62] It leads people to exclude women from career-enhancing and socially valuable networks.[63] And it can also result in falsely held beliefs that it is acceptable to assert power over women from crude hazing, to outright sexual harassment and assault. Because of out-group bias, women's pursuit of leadership positions not only can be difficult but also dangerous.

A striking and upsetting illustration of the nature and operation of out-group bias is Jane Elliott's "Blue Eyes, Brown Eyes" study.[64] Elliott divided her all-white third-grade class into two groups: those with brown eyes and those with blue and non-brown eyes. On the first day of the study, Elliott told her students that those with brown eyes were superior, smarter, and more responsible than those with blue eyes. Her entirely fictitious characterizations quickly led to changes in the children's behavior. The brown-eyed students became arrogant, domineering, and overbearing, while the other students became frightened, timid, and uncertain. On the second day of the study, Elliott reversed the characterizations of the groups, and the children quickly reversed their behaviors.

Elliott never told the students how to behave toward students with different eye colors. Nevertheless, hostile, exclusionary behaviors arose spontaneously once the in-group members were convinced of their superiority. In other words, out-group bias does not need any real, meaningful distinctions between members of the in-group and those in the out-group. Quite to the contrary. It happens because of the erroneous associations of qualities and values with insignificant personal characteristics. This is, precisely, the nature of gender stereotypes. It is not the actual differences between men and women that matter. Rather, it is the qualities, characteristics, and capacities that are unjustifiably associated with insignificant and irrelevant differences between women and men. PATH provides specific, practical techniques (as we will see in Chapters 8 and 10) for preventing the exclusionary behaviors caused by out-group bias.

Status Quo Bias

Status quo bias is reflected in people's resistance to change, their preference for the familiar, and their discomfort with the unfamiliar. Because of status quo bias, when given the choice between changing their current situation and leaving things as they are, most people will choose to stick with the familiar—even when the change carries a real chance of being better off.[65] Status quo bias can be thought of as a preference for "the devil you know," rather than "the devil you don't." And, while there is considerable variation among individuals in their aversion to change;

status quo bias causes almost everyone to resist significant workplace changes to one degree or another—including those who would prefer to see a reduction in gender inequality.[66]

"This really is an innovative approach, but I'm afraid we can't consider it. It's never been done before."

www.CartoonStock.com

Nobel Prize–winning psychologist Daniel Kahneman and his long-time collaborator Amos Tversky found that the source of status quo bias is people's greater aversion to loss than their pleasure in gain. In their now classic paper, "Prospect Theory: An Analysis of Decision Under Risk," they concluded: "The aggravation that one experiences in losing a sum of money appears to be greater than the pleasure associated with gaining the same amount."[67] In other words, losses loom larger than gains when compared to, or weighted against, each other. Kahneman has speculated that this asymmetry has an evolutionary origin:[68] "Organisms that treat threats as more urgent than opportunities have a better chance to survive and reproduce."[69]

In their book *Nudge: Improving Decisions about Health, Wealth, and Happiness*, Richard Thaler and Cass Sunstein characterize status quo bias as a "Kind of cognitive nudge, pressing us not to make changes, even when changes are very much in our interest."[70] As a result, status quo bias results in people having a "general tendency to stick with their current situation."[71]

The status quo in gendered workplaces involves the ascendancy of status beliefs as to the inherent workplace supremacy of men over women. Because of the power of status quo, the changes recommended by PATH will inevitably be resisted even if they promise to make things better for everyone. Accordingly, in Chapter 12, we specifically address ways to overcome status quo bias in implementing PATH's recommended workplace changes.

Going Forward

PATH does not attempt to directly eliminate the biases underlying individual discrimination—a misguided exercise in our view. It seeks to end structural discrimination and changes the workplace context that facilitates individual discrimination. PATH, therefore, involves a two-pronged approach to eliminating workplace gender inequality. It attacks structural discrimination by changes to personnel-management systems, processes, and practices. It eliminates the incentive to support individual discrimination. PATH seeks to create an environment where women and men can both flourish.

KEY TAKEAWAYS

- The Five Gender Myths are often cited to excuse or avoid dealing with gender bias in the workplace. But myths are just that: falsely held beliefs. The workplace reality is that:

  – Women and men do not differ in ways relevant to career success.

- Women are not less well-suited for intense competition, high stress, or leadership than men.
- Women are just as confident as men in their careers.
- Women are no less capable than men in dealing with risk and danger.
- Women are no more likely than men to choose homelife over career.

- The Five Gender Myths undermine efforts to end workplace gender inequality. When people focus on supposed differences in women's and men's career-relevant characteristics, capacities, or attitudes, they ignore the real causes of gender inequality and dismiss the value of efforts to disrupt them.
- The real causes of workplace gender inequality are to be found in the nature and operation of gendered workplaces and the behavior of people in those workplaces. Thus, there are two interrelated fundamental causes of gender inequality: structural discrimination and individual discrimination.

  - *Structural discrimination* results from the status beliefs embedded in gender stereotypes. It is the day-to-day, take-for-granted operation of personnel-management systems that systematically advantages men over women.
  - *Individual discrimination* is the consistent, predictably biased way in which individuals behave in the context of gendered workplaces. As a result, women are seen as less committed to their careers and they are assumed to be less-effective leaders.
  - Structural and individual discriminations are baked in to gendered workplaces so that women both systemically (due to structural discrimination) and systematically (due to individual discrimination) experience gender inequality.

- The four fundamental biases that underlie individual discrimination are affinity bias, gender bias, out-group bias, and status quo bias.

- *Affinity bias*: the natural, instinctive inclination people have to associate with people who are like them.
- *Gender bias*: the socially conditioned human inclination to regard men as more capable, competent, and effective leaders than women.
- *Out-group bias*: the negative feeling toward or hostile and exclusionary treatment of out-group members (women) by in-group members (men).
- *Status quo bias*: the preference for, or greater comfort with, the familiar than the unfamiliar. Status quo bias works in tandem with men's defensive reactions when confronted with the prospect of workplace change that would (in their eyes) reduce their power, resources, or status.

Chapter 3

Impacts of Gender Inequality

Workplace gender inequality has a severe negative affect on women, men, and their organizations. It hurts team efficiency, effectiveness, and cohesion; it undermines women's career aspirations, opportunities, and engagement; and it handicaps organizations' effectiveness in realizing their goals.

We have a long history of workplace gender inequality. It is deep-rooted in the structure and operation of our workplaces. And as we will see, the incremental steps PATH has been designed to take has this history in mind.

Ending gender inequality will have enormous payoffs for organizations and their employees. In addition, because the workplace is an important source of individuals' power, resources, and status, ending gender inequality in the workplace will have a beneficial impact on American society as a whole.

Gender Inequality Inhibits Collaboration

When men can move easily into leadership, and women struggle to overcome gender barriers, the efficiency, effectiveness, and productivity of the entire enterprise are damaged. Differences in workplace treatment (structural discrimination) fuel differences in employee treatment of people different from them (individual discrimination). Together, structural and individual discrimination are profoundly harmful to organizations, teams, and individuals.

When gender-diverse collaboration is possible, employees report more positive workplace experiences and organizational outcomes improve.[1] Gallup, for example, found that gender-diverse teams performed better than single-gender teams, in part because they bring "different viewpoints, ideas, and market insights to projects."[2] In a *Harvard Business Review* article, Sylvia Ann Hewlett and her coauthors concluded that "leaders who give diverse voices equal air time are nearly twice as likely as others to unleash value-driving insights, and employees in a 'speak up' culture are 3.5 times as likely to contribute their full innovative potential."[3]

> "Leaders who give diverse voices equal air time are nearly twice as likely as others to unleash value-driving insights."
>
> —Sylvia Ann Hewlett

Companies, teams, and individuals are more productive, more creative, and more effective at problem solving and coping with difficult situations in cultures that encourage diversity and inclusion. Without inclusive mixed-gender collaboration, group think become all too common.[4] Bringing together different ideas and unique perspectives in a collaborative environment generates smarter outcomes.[5] As Laura Tyson, former chair of the Council of Economic Advisers and a distinguished professor at the University of California, Berkeley, puts it, "diversity of teams, diversity of input, diversity of perspective, diversity of education lead to better solutions and more effective solutions."[6] A 2017 report from Bentley University also concludes, "It is clear from a multitude of sources, improving gender representation in the workplace benefits everyone— it is good for our workplace culture, our professional development, our society, our personal lives, and the financial bottom line."[7]

www.CartoonStock.com

Let's consider some additional benefits of mixed-gender teams and inclusive workplaces:

- Men become more reflective, process information more thoroughly, and are more open-minded when there are women on their teams.[8]
- Collaborative, diverse teams lead to smarter, better-informed decision-making processes, while blocking problematic behaviors that foster insularity and close-mindedness.[9]
- Collaborative mixed-gender teams are better at problem-solving than men-only teams.[10] They are especially good at solving complex problems in complex environments.
- Companies with inclusive diverse leadership teams have less in-group/out-group tension and more harmonious working environments for everyone.[11]
- Inclusive senior leadership teams with more than 30 percent women—a *critical mass of women*—are more profitable than those without gender-diverse leadership.[12]

Gender Inequality Inhibits Happiness

There is plentiful empirical evidence that both women and men benefit from increased fairness, equality, and equity in their workplaces. Gender equality makes workplaces more congenial, productive, and efficient. Simply put, people are happier when their workplaces are free of gender inequality. This is apparent from studies that show that people in countries with the greatest degree of gender equality report being significantly happier than people in other countries with less gender equality.[13]

A University of Minnesota study reached the same conclusion. Researchers considered a wide range of inputs to better understand conflicting data and conclusions in earlier research as to the role of gender equality in advancing happiness in industrialized democratic societies. Considering a variety of equality indicators—the Gender Empowerment Measure (GEM), the Gender Development Index (GDI), the Gender Inequality Index (GII), and the Gender Gap Index (GGI). They concluded that people living in societies with the greatest degree of gender equality enjoyed significant improvements in their measure of "life satisfaction."[14]

As we will see in Chapter 6, men often incorrectly assume that workplace gender equality has no personal benefit to them. They are ignoring the likelihood they will enjoy significant improvements in their personal situations' quality of life.

Gender Inequality Inhibits a Sense of Community

Everything simply works better for everyone in environments free of discriminatory structures, processes, and behaviors. When women and men can work collaboratively in environments with inclusive diversity, they develop a sense of community, a sense of being a "We." They share the same core work values, have common goals and objectives, and respect one another's vital differences. Such a sense of "We" extends far beyond single DEI programs or initiatives. When women and men work side by side on equal terms, with a justified sense of equal status, organizations, teams, and individuals all do better.

> When women and men can work collaboratively in environments with inclusive diversity, they develop a sense of community, a sense of being a "We."

Gender Inequality Weakens Performance

When leaders are committed to ensuring a diversity of perspectives, of social identities, and a sense of inclusive community, teams are far more able to unlock their innovative potential than non-diverse teams.[15] Indeed, a "speak-up" culture is a direct result of better organizational innovation.[16] This, in turn, encourages an organization's management to nurture innovation in the development and launch of distinctive products and services and to successfully bring them to market.

As a 2017 Boston Consulting Group (BCG) study found, there is a clear causal relationship between leadership diversity and "innovation revenue."[17]

BCG defined innovation revenue as the share of revenue that a company receives from new products and services in its most recent three-year period. Among the companies included in the study, those with management diversity ratings above the median had, on average, 38 percent greater innovation revenue than those companies below that median. BCG found that this increase in innovation revenue occurred when women filled at least 20 percent of all management positions. Simply having a higher percentage of women employees overall did not increase the company's innovation revenue. BGC concluded that it is gender equality in management that contributes to companies' improved performance, while simply increasing workforce diversity without more does little.[18]

BCG's findings are not unique. Harvard researchers concluded that diversity was a driver of company success, enabling early-mover advantages in taking new offerings to market, and signaling the use of "best practices" in telling investors that the company is well run.[19] When companies are better run, everyone involved with them enjoys the benefits.

Gender Inequality Inhibits Inclusion

Gender diversity is not gender equality. Simply increasing the number of women or other traditionally underrepresented people in an organization's management structure does not automatically lead to a more innovative organization. Robin Ely and David Thomas forcefully made this point in a *Harvard Business Review article*, "Taking an 'add diversity and stir' approach, while business continues as usual, will not spur leaps in your firm's effectiveness or financial performance."[20]

> "Taking an 'add diversity and stir' approach, while business continues as usual, will not spur leaps in your firm's effectiveness or financial performance."
>
> —Robin Ely and Davis Thomas

Diverse participants need to be welcomed, valued, and heard. Indeed, without such inclusivity, a mere *check-the-box approach* to leadership diversity may actually decrease a company's performance by increasing workplace tensions and conflict.[21]

KEY TAKEAWAYS

- **Collaboration**: mixed-gender collaboration improves organizational outcomes, as well as workplace experiences for employees.

- **Navigating Adversity**: diverse and inclusive companies and teams are more productive, creative, and effective at solving problems and in coping with adversity.
- **Productivity**: gender diversity in the context of a fair, equal, and inclusive culture makes for a more productive and efficient workplace.
- **Purpose**: when people collaborate in an inclusive environment, they develop a sense of being a "We." They share core values, develop common goals and objectives, and respect each other's differences.
- **Innovation**: a pleasant, respectful workplace encourages different perspectives, viewpoints, and ideas. It helps unlock innovative potential. People are better able to trust each other, rejecting groupthink and close-minded attitudes.
- **Performance**: diversity alone does not automatically lead to more successful organizations, more productive teams, or more engaged and satisfied employees. To achieve these important benefits, a gender-diverse organization must aim to ensure *bona fide* team inclusion, with all participants feeling welcomed, valued, and heard.

PART II

WE HAVEN'T MADE MUCH PROGRESS

Chapter 4

There Are No Quick Fixes

A N OBVIOUS QUESTION TO ASK is whether there is a simple, direct, and effective way to end gender inequality. Surely, there must be a quick fix for this persistent problem: a straightforward, decisive action to permanently end workplace gender inequality.

"We need to develop a long term strategy to achieve consistent quick fixes."

www.CartoonStock.com

Unfortunately, there are no such quick fixes. The inequalities that result from structural discrimination can only be eliminated through fundamental changes to an organization's systems, processes, and practices. And the gender inequality that results from individual discrimination can only be reduced by changing the workplace context within which individuals make decisions, relate to other people, and evaluate other's performance, accomplishments, and potential.

To see why we need PATH's approach, it is useful to understand why mandates have not been successful and can't prevent discriminatory behavior.

Legal Mandates

Perhaps the quickest and presumably most effective way to address the problem would be to legally mandate companies have some degree of gender diversity in their leadership. As a consequence, a great deal of attention is paid toward efforts that impose legally mandated gender quotas of one sort or another at various levels of company leadership. On their face, such legal mandates seem to offer relatively effortless way to increase women's representation in workplace leadership. After all, most European countries have minimum participation levels for women in senior leadership.[1] And these legal mandates work. For example, corporations based in France, Norway, Sweden, and Italy now include more than 35 percent women on their boards of directors. In France—where corporations are subject to the most rigorous quotas—women make up almost 45 percent of their board members. As we are writing this, the European Union has proposed that most corporations headquartered in its member states must have at least 40 percent women as non-executive directors, or at least 33 percent women among all directors.[2]

Perhaps the best known of these legal mandates in the United States is California law S.B. 826 ("Gender Mandate"). The Gender Mandate, as it was enacted in 2018, required all publicly held companies with principal executive offices in California to have at least one woman director;

two women directors if the company had five director positions; or three women directors if the company had six or more board positions.[3] Modeled on that law, Washington State passed a similar law.[4]

The problem with such legal mandates *in the United States* is that they have shaky legal status. Unlike Europe, the U.S. Constitution, as well as many of the individual states' constitutions in the United States, make government-mandated quotas highly questionable, if not outright illegal. These constitutions have "equal protection" provisions that guarantee that the government will not treat anyone differently from anyone else because of their gender, race, ethnicity, or other fundamental characteristics. As the U.S. Supreme Court declared more than 40 years ago, "the guarantee of equal protection to all persons" does not permit any group of people to be entitled to any governmental protection that is "greater than that accorded to others."[5] It is not at all surprising, therefore, that in May 2022, the Gender Mandate was found to violate the California Constitution's guarantee of equal protection.

> As the U.S. Supreme Court declared more than 40 years ago, "the guarantee of equal protection to all persons" does not permit any group of people to be entitled to any governmental protection that is "greater than that accorded to others."

The court found that any classification by the State of California that affects two or more "similarly situated groups" in an unequal manner is constitutionally suspect. The court found that "men and women are similarly situated for purposes of [the] gender-based quota." To enforce the Gender Mandate, California, therefore, would have needed to go back and demonstrate that it had a "compelling state interest" in adopting the Gender Mandate. The judge found that California did not demonstrate such a compelling state interest, but that the clear purpose of the Gender Mandate was "gender balancing." Indeed, the court did not find any evidence of "any specific, purposeful, intentional and unlawful discrimination." Therefore, California did not have a compelling governmental interest to intervene in company board selection processes. As a result, the judge said that the Gender Mandate violates the equal protection clause of the California Constitution. (The Gender Mandate is also being challenged in federal court, on the ground that it violates the U.S. Constitution's equal protection clause.) While the California secretary of state has announced she intends to appeal the court decision, we agree with most legal scholars that the Gender Mandate is likely to be unconstitutional.[6]

Given United States laws, diversity quotas, including gender mandates, imposed by laws in the United States are likely to be unconstitutional. To overcome these barriers, governments would need to demonstrate that gender inequality is the result of purposeful, intentional discrimination in the decision-making practices of public companies. Without such a "compelling state interest," government-imposed quotas will not be a way out of America's workplace gender inequality. Governmentally imposed diversity quotas cannot provide a quick fix to U.S. workplace gender inequality.

Quasi-Legal Mandates

If government-imposed quotas will not pass muster, what about quotas imposed by non-governmental entities? The answer is not clear but it may be difficult to rely on the viability of quasi-legal mandates. The Nasdaq Stock Market is a self-regulatory organization that is subject to oversight by the Securities and Exchange Commission (SEC). The Nasdaq is authorized to prescribe requirements for those companies that list their securities for trading on its market. In 2018, Nasdaq proposed that all companies subject to its jurisdiction—well over 1,000 companies— should have at least one woman and one member of a disadvantaged group on their boards. Perhaps the thinking behind the Nasdaq proposal was that a board diversity mandate from a self-regulatory organization would not be subject to the same constitutional prohibitions as a government-imposed mandate. Even though Nasdaq's rules must be approved by the SEC, which is a federal government agency, the rules of self-regulatory organizations have generally been held not to be government action.[7] And the equal protection guarantees only apply to governmental actions.

As years passed without the SEC approving Nasdaq's board diversity mandate, it became clear that the SEC was not going to do so—and it did not. While the SEC has not publicly stated the reasons why it did not act, we assume that the delay was, in large part, due to the SEC's belief that Nasdaq's rules should not be used to solve social problems, as opposed to increasing the sorts of information about companies that are useful to investors. As a likely compromise, when Nasdaq's rule change was finally approved (almost four years later), it no longer included a compulsory board diversity mandate. Rather, the final rule simply requires companies to make disclosures about the makeup of their boards, setting out aspirational diversity objectives, and not quotas.

Under the final rule, most Nasdaq-listed companies are expected to have at least two diverse board members, defined as people who self-identify as female or as an "underrepresented minority." A company that cannot comply with this requirement—or simply chooses not to comply—must explain why it is not complying. Nasdaq has no authority to question or evaluate the merits of a company's explanation for noncompliance.

Even though Nasdaq's gender diversity rule could potentially affect more than 1,000 publicly traded companies, it is uncertain as to whether it will have any impact on the board diversity of any of these companies. Indeed, while Nasdaq's listing standards will provide information about the extent and nature of a company's board diversity, this is not very different from board diversity disclosures now required by an increasing number of U.S. states, including Illinois, Maryland, and Pennsylvania.[8]

Given the slow death of Nasdaq's initial board diversity mandate, it appears likely that diversity mandates from quasi-governmental organizations (such as Nasdaq) are no more likely than actual governmental mandates to provide a quick fix to gender inequality. In fact, as we're writing, Nasdaq and the SEC have both been sued over the final watered-down version of Nasdaq's disclosure rule. The plaintiffs allege that the final rule is discriminatory and unconstitutional. Nasdaq and the SEC have both responded that Nasdaq actions are not a prohibited governmental action, and investors are interested in information about board diversity.[9]

Despite the success of such mandates in Europe, we must find alternate solutions to workplace gender inequality in the United States. After all, the U.S. has had strong anti-discrimination laws on the books for more than 60 years and those laws have accomplished little in ending workplace gender inequality.[10]

"UNFORTUNATELY, WE'RE APPROACHING THE EXPIRATION DATES ON MOST OF OUR QUICK-FIX SOLUTIONS."

www.CartoonStock.com

Disclosure Mandates

In the absence of legal or quasi-legal gender diversity mandates, several states, like Nasdaq, now require companies subject to their jurisdiction to disclose the gender composition of their boards of directors. While these disclosure mandates are legally permissible, we don't know what these requirements will do to end gender inequality. The well-known civil rights lawyer Cyrus Mehri suggests that mandatory disclosure requirements hold "great promise" for advancing DEI.[11] He proposes that the federal government should require all public companies to disclose the race and gender of their 200 highest-paid employees.[12] According to Mehri, such disclosure would tell us information about employees in a company's "decision-making pool." He thinks that such disclosures would incentivize companies to improve their diversity practices "to be best in class."[13] Thus, according to Mehri, such disclosure would have "a cascading effect," motivating companies to increase their senior leadership diversity.[14]

Along similar lines—but in a way that does not involve equal protection considerations, because they are not imposed by a government—large investors have successfully pressured companies in which they hold stock in (such as Moody's Investors Services Inc., Nike Inc., Union Pacific Corp., and Walmart Inc.) to publicly release the demographic data that they currently report to the Equal Employment Opportunity Commission.[15] Referred to as EEO-1 data, this information reveals a company's workforce race, ethnicity, and binary gender makeup.[16] Such annual EEO–1 reports are currently required of companies with more than 100 employees and some federal contractors. Although the EEO–1 data is confidential, companies can, of course, choose to voluntarily release their reports.[17]

Mehri makes disclosure of such data sound like it could be the silver bullet that deals a final blow to gender inequality. We are doubtful. The gender composition of the directors and executive leadership teams of most publicly held companies has been on full display for many years with no indication such disclosure has motivated them to increase the representation of women. Likewise, publicly held companies are subject to anti-discrimination and equal opportunity policies, but these policies have not done much to increase the diversity of their senior leadership. We are skeptical, therefore, that disclosure requirements will provide a quick fix to workplace gender inequality. We agree that disclosure has some real benefits and must be continued to show where progress is being made. With that said, however, we don't think that disclosure alone will lead to significant reductions in workplace gender inequality.

Private Mandates

As we are writing, several prominent private efforts are underway to require gender quotas for public company board of directors. A number of large investment firms, investment banks, private equity firms, and others have sought to force the companies that they do business with, or that they invest in, to increase the gender diversity of their leadership ranks. For example, BlackRock, the country's largest money manager, has announced that the companies in which it invests must have at least two women on their boards.[18] Other money managers (such as State Street) have said they will vote against board slates proposed by public companies if the slates do not include women.[19] Goldman Sachs, a prominent investment bank, has said it will no longer take a company public if the company does not have at least one woman on its board.[20]

With respect to diversity in law firms, a number of large corporations, including Hewlett Packard, Macy's, Meta Platforms (formerly Facebook), MetLife, and Novartis have told the law firms representing them that they will take their legal business elsewhere or discount the fees they are charged unless the legal teams working on their matters have significant gender and racial diversity. Meta, for example, requires that half of the lawyers working on its projects are diverse in terms of race, gender, sexual orientation, or disability.[21]

Obviously, it will take more than a few institutional investors, investment banks, and major consumers of legal services to overcome the lack of gender diversity in American workplaces. But such private activism can't hurt.[22]

Although private mandates cannot offer a quick fix, they are raising awareness of workplace gender inequality. Another concern is that at present, most private businesses have their own lack-of-diversity issues. (For example, women are only 30 percent of Meta's C-suite executives,[23] and just about 30 percent of Goldman Sachs's executive leaders.[24])

We applaud these private initiatives and hope they can start to get other businesses to increase the gender diversity of their leadership. Private nudges toward greater gender diversity are very welcome but are hardly a quick fix to the persistent issue of workplace gender inequality.

> Private nudges toward greater gender diversity are very welcome but are hardly a quick fix to the persistent issue of workplace gender inequality.

Self-Imposed Mandates

Some large, prominent companies have imposed mandates for themselves. Under these programs, the companies will financially benefit if they achieve specified diversity objectives, and they will face financial disadvantages if they don't. BlackRock, for example, arranged with its banks that the interest rate it will pay to access its $4.4 billion credit facility will go up or down depending on how well it does on three different standards, one of which is how many women it has in senior leadership roles.[25] The private equity firm The Carlyle Group announced it will link its CEO's compensation to the success the firm has achieved in hiring diverse candidates, fostering an inclusive culture, and diversifying the boards of its portfolio companies.[26] And, a handful of companies, including BASF, Intel Corp., and Johnson & Johnson, have tied their managers' compensation to diversity targets.[27]

Along similar lines, it has been suggested that companies adopt so-called simple rules that will "automatically" achieve gender equality. An example of such a simple rule was set out in an article in the November 2021 edition of the *Harvard Business Review*.[28] In that article, three well-regarded diversity scholars argued that the primary cause of gender inequality in business leadership is simply the difference in women's and men's promotion rates. The authors, therefore, proposed a "simple and straightforward" concept that they call the "gender proportionality principle."[29] It provides that managers should promote employees so that each level in an organization's leadership hierarchy reflects the gender composition of the level immediately below it. For example, if women make up 40 percent of first-level managers but 48 percent of entry-level professional employees (which are the representations found in the *Women in the Workplace 2022 report* we saw in Chapter 1), an organization should set a goal to reach 48 percent women managers in level two in "a reasonable yet challenging timeframe."[30] According to the authors, "Over time, the gender proportionality principle helps organizations grow their gender diversity throughout the entire hierarchy."

Although the gender proportionality principle might have an initial appeal, if vigorously enforced we fear it would suffer from the same fate as all other metric-driven mandates. There is no escaping the fact that the gender proportionality principle is a quota system. As such, it will be seen by American employees—both women and men—as directly at odds with their belief that their workplaces should be meritocracies. It also suffers from the same serious downsides we see with other self-imposed mandates.

Downsides of Mandates

In our opinion, mandates have at least three serious downsides.

- They look like quotas and as such can provoke backlash in the workplace, and managers could resist them as constraints on their discretion and autonomy.[31]

- People who are hired or promoted in compliance with these mandates might be unfairly viewed as "tokens" and their abilities discounted without regard to their actual merits.[32]
- They can distract managers from focusing on their primary job, which is to contribute to their organization's productive, efficient, and profitable operations. As Max Bazerman, a professor at the Harvard Business School, puts it, "The more people are checking off boxes, the less they are focusing on how to make their organization both fair and excellent."[33]

Because of these downsides, we are not fans of mandates of any sort. The structural changes PATH recommends are carefully designed not to provoke backlash. It poses no danger of tokenism or to distract managers from "minding the store."

> The structural changes PATH recommends are carefully designed not to provoke backlash. It poses no danger of tokenism or to distract managers from "minding the store."

There Are No Quick Fixes

Unfortunately, there are no quick fixes to workplace gender inequality because there are no quick fixes to the structural or individual discrimination that drives such inequality. In large part, we have not been making progress at ending gender inequality because we have not allowed ourselves to see how deeply and tenaciously it is embedded in the very fabric of our workplaces.

Unless we address systemic discrimination, we are never going to make real progress in ending workplace gender inequality. Without addressing the fundamental causes of gender inequality and doing the hard work needed to establish PATH as the foundation of a company's personnel-management practices, we will continue to keep running in

"*Aha! Just as I suspected!*"
www.CartoonStock.com

circles and patting ourselves on the back for our bold, unequivocal commitments to gender equality while doing nothing to make such equality a reality.

> It's time to specifically address what is wrong with our current diversity programs and acknowledge why we haven't made any real progress over the past 30 years.

Ending gender inequality requires a comprehensive, multifaceted program. It is by no means beyond an organization's realistic capabilities, but it does require a persistent and focused endeavor. Implementing PATH may be challenging, but it promises real progress in return—not just a feel-good manifesto but strong, progressive, achievable steps toward the ultimate goal of eliminating workplace gender inequality. It's time to specifically address what is wrong with our current diversity programs and acknowledge why we haven't made any real progress over the past 30 years.

KEY TAKEAWAYS

- There is no quick fix for gender inequality. The inequalities from structural discrimination can only be eliminated through fundamental changes to a company's systems, processes, and practices.
- Although some countries have had success imposing diversity mandates, the U.S. Constitution (and most, if not all, state constitutions) does not permit any group of people to receive any protection from the government that is "greater than that accorded to others."[34] This means that we cannot make significant progress at ending gender inequality through government and quasi-legal mandates.
- Beyond constitutional limitations, we need to recognize the limited power of laws in the United States to deal with the fundamental causes of gender inequality. There have been strong anti-discrimination laws on the books in the United States for more than 60 years, but they have done little to end gender inequality in our workplaces.
- Private mandates and self-imposed incentives connected to gender equality are on the rise but come with serious drawbacks, such as being interpreted as quotas, tokenism, or distracting managers from their "minding the store." They can be met with backlash.
- Some respected scholars have suggested "simple rules" that "automatically" achieve gender equality. Our concern is that these metric-driven approaches have the same downsides we see with private mandates and self-imposed incentives. They are also directly at odds with many Americans' belief that their workplaces are—or at least should be—meritocracies. Metric-driven

approaches can lead to employee resentment and can, ultimately, work against achieving an inclusive workplace culture.

- We have not made progress at ending gender inequality because we haven't allowed ourselves to see how deeply and tenaciously it is embedded in our workplaces.
- Unless we address the systemic inequality caused by structural discrimination, we will not make progress toward ending workplace gender inequality.

Chapter 5

Diversity Training Doesn't Work

APPROXIMATELY 98 PERCENT OF AMERICAN companies have some sort of gender DEI programs.[1] Because of this, DEI consulting has become big business. Very big business. Globally, more than $7.5 billion was spent on DEI programming in 2020, and it is anticipated to increase to $17.2 billion by 2027. The United States market for DEI alone is estimated to be $3.7 billion, and it is expected to compound at an annual growth rate of more than 13 percent through that seven-year period.[2] Every year business, professional and nonprofit organization executives work hard to strengthen workplace diversity, with 86 percent of North American financial executives expanding DEI training budgets, according to a survey by OneStream Software.[3]

In addition to this enormous budget spend, the popular press, social media, and a large number of books and articles promote the benefits of DEI and condemn the harms caused by gender-biased workplaces. Yet, despite the time, resources, and attention, very few organizations have made meaningful progress toward increasing the proportion of women in their senior leadership ranks, much less realizing the benefits in doing so.[4] With so much time, attention, and money being paid to this issue, something must be wrong with the common approaches to solve this problem.

We believe there are three fundamental mistakes with the current approaches to gender diversity training:

- Most diversity training is focused on "de-biasing" individuals. This simply doesn't work: people cannot be trained out of their biases with de-biasing training.
- A great deal of effort is devoted to "fixing" women. Women are urged to change their leadership style; increase their confidence; and become more vocal. Such efforts are misguided, demeaning to women, and ineffective in reducing workplace gender inequality.
- Most diversity training is focused on the symptoms of gender inequality but not the fundamental causes of gender inequality (systematically discriminatory workplace systems, processes, and practices).

> Most diversity training is focused on the symptoms of gender inequality but not the fundamental causes of gender inequality (systematically discriminatory workplace systems, processes, and practices).

Let's consider each of these approaches in turn.

1. Individuals Can't Be Trained Out of Bias

Through workshops, videos, role-playing exercises, prescribed reading, and moderated discussions, most DEI programs focus on training individuals. This training (which includes anti-bias and anti-harassment training) is intended to help people become knowledgeable about the nature and extent of bias; to become aware of their own (generally unconscious) biases; and to aid them in ensuring that their biases do not influence their behaviors. The assumption underlying such training is that increasing knowledge and awareness of bias will reduce the presence

*"Are you sure it doesn't contravene
the Sex Discrimination Act, Harry?"*

Punch Cartoon Library / TopFoto

of bias in the workplace and reduce the discriminatory barriers women face in pursuing their careers.

Much of the impetus behind individualized de-bias training stems directly from *Title VII of the Civil Rights Act of 1964*, which forbids employment discrimination because of sex.[5]

There are benefits to increasing knowledge and information about how biases result in different workplace experiences for women and men. Making people aware of their own biases, however, has proven to be largely ineffective in changing their attitudes and behavior. Let's examine why this is the case.

Research Regarding Anti-Bias Training

A 2009 comprehensive review by Harvard and Yale academics of 985 studies of programs designed to reduce biased behavior by increasing awareness of one's own bias found little or no evidence that they were effective.[6] These programs were wide-ranging in their approaches, including:

- workplace diversity initiatives
- anti-bias education
- multicultural education
- dialogue groups
- cooperation training
- moral and values education
- intergroup contact
- education in reconciliation techniques
- media interventions
- intercultural and sensitivity training
- cognitive training
- miscellaneous other techniques and interventions

The researchers did not find evidence that any of these approaches reduced the biased behavior of the people who had participated in the training. In fact, the researchers concluded that the studies "[do] not reveal whether, when, or why [anti-bias] interventions reduce prejudice in the world."[7]

More recently, a 40-year analysis of 260 studies on discreet anti-bias training programs similarly concluded that while many programs increased participants' cognitive knowledge about bias and its effects, none was particularly effective in changing attitudes or behaviors.[8]

Another study that looked at 17 promising anti-bias training programs found that only eight of them reduced unconscious (implicit) biases. Even when the programs did reduce unconscious bias, the reduction vanished after 24 hours.[9] Worse still, none of these programs resulted in any measurable changes in the participants' explicit biases or actual behaviors.[10]

Together, these exhaustive research studies demonstrate that anti-bias training has little or no effect in reducing discriminatory decisions affecting women's career advancement. It might be argued, however, that it is not that anti-bias training in and of itself is ineffective, rather that the training must be done in specific ways to be effective. Let's examine this idea.

Finally, a 2018 study of unconscious bias training (UBT) by the Equality and Human Rights Commission of the United Kingdom could find no evidence to indicate that UBT is effective for behavior change.[11]

Compulsory versus Voluntary Programs

Putting aside for the moment the question of whether anti-bias training of any sort can reduce biased behavior, there is the issue of whether it is better to make such training compulsory or voluntary. The argument for compulsory training is obvious: unless you make the training, compulsory, you may not reach those people who need it the most. On the other hand, people who are required to attend compulsory training resent the training and are likely to ignore its positive message or worse. Let's look at the pros and cons of both approaches.

Compulsory Programs

Compulsory training ensures that all supervisors are aware of the extent, nature, and discriminatory consequences of unconscious bias. After all, supervisors, particularly middle managers, are the group whose personnel decisions, if biased, are likely to have the most severe adverse consequences for women's careers. Male supervisors are likely to be the most reluctant group to voluntarily participate in anti-bias training. We know that compulsory training provokes anger and hostility.[12]

One study, for example, found that participants reported greater animosity to diverse group members *after* such training than before the training.[13]

Voluntary Programs

We have found that voluntary training is far more likely than compulsory training to be accepted, making it more effective for those people who participate.[14] Its drawback, however, is that the employees least likely to participate are likely to be those with the lowest levels of awareness about their own biases and the most in need of training.[15] Management that chooses to provide voluntary programs might encourage participation through incentives, continuing education credits, networking event, access, and senior leadership sessions. (It is worth noting that Google's *Unconscious Bias @ Work*,[16] Facebook's *Unconscious Bias Training*,[17] and Microsoft's *Self-Paced Online Unconscious Bias Training*[18]—three thoughtfully designed diversity training programs—are all voluntary.)

Supervisor Participation

Supervisors—in particular middle managers—are positioned to make biased career advancement decisions that can have direct, adverse consequences for more junior women's progress.

Six of One, Half Dozen of the Other

In the end, though, it may not make much difference if anti-bias training is compulsory or voluntary, or who attends. There is no conclusive evidence that either type of program reduces biased behavior, diminishes discriminatory outcomes, or increases the promotion of women in leadership. As Frank Dobbin, of Harvard University, and Alexandra Kalev, of Tel Aviv University, point out, whether anti-bias training is voluntary or compulsory, such "training alone [does] not change attitudes or behavior, or not by much and not for long."[19]

> Whether anti-bias training is voluntary or compulsory, such "training alone [does] not change attitudes or behavior, or not by much and not for long."
>
> —Frank Dobbin and Alexandra Kalev

The ineffectiveness of traditional anti-bias training was confirmed by Edward H. Chang and his research colleagues in a large field experiment involving employees of a global company. The experiment consisted of a voluntary training program that sought to determine if a stand-alone online diversity program could affect employees' attitudes and behavior toward women at work.[20] The format and length of the program (limited to one hour) was typical of the types of diversity training frequently offered by most major American corporations. The program was designed in accordance with what are considered to be best practices to accomplish the following:

- raise awareness about the pervasiveness of stereotypes and bias
- provide scientific evidence of the discriminatory effect of stereotyping on important workplace behaviors
- destigmatize and expose participants to their own stereotyping
- provide evidence-based strategies for overcoming stereotyping
- allow employees to practice evidence-based strategies to combat stereotyping by responding to different workplace scenarios

More than 2,000 people took part in this program. Participants were randomly given one of three types of training: gender bias training, general bias training, and psychological safety and active listening training that did not mention stereotypes. Neither gender-bias nor general-bias training had any measurable effect on participants' behavior—except for a small effect on the behavior of women participants from the United States, hardly the primary group diversity trainers seek to influence. The researchers concluded, "The lack of change in the behaviors of dominant group members indicates additional remedies [beyond such diversity training] are needed to improve the overall workplace experiences of women and racial minorities."[21]

Diversity Training That Might Work

There has been quite a bit of pushback against the conclusions that all diversity training programs fail to change behavior. For example, researchers writing in the *Harvard Business Review* argue that two types of diversity training show some promise in changing behavior.

Perspective Taking

The first type of diversity training that could offer benefits involves participants engaging in perspective taking—mentally walking in someone else's shoes. The researchers had students write a few sentences about the challenges they imagined members of a marginalized group might experience. They were then tested with respect to their "pro-diversity attitudes and behavioral intentions toward those marginalized groups."[22] The researchers reported that participants said that their attitudes and "behavioral intentions" improved, after this exercise, and these positive effects persisted when the participants were retested eight months later. No information was provided, however, about the extent of the students' real-world behavioral changes, or whether the report of their "behavioral intention" resulted in actual changes in their behavior.

Specific, Measurable, and Challenging Goal-Setting

The second type of diversity training that the researchers claim holds promise is called "SMC goal-setting." It involves asking participants to set specific, measurable, and challenging (but attainable) personal goals to increase workplace diversity. (The Google training course *Unconscious Bias @ Work* does this.[23]) The experiment again involved undergraduate students, and the researchers reported that goal-setting with respect to promoting diversity led to more positive diversity attitudes nine months after the training. They gave no evidence, however, as to how much the participants' diversity attitudes increased or whether the goal-setting had positively influenced their actual behavior.

Although perspective taking and SMC goal-setting seem to produce some positive effects, these experiments require further validation to see if the techniques can increase positive workplace outcomes for women or reduce workplace gender inequality. While organizations should certainly consider including these types of techniques in their overall diversity efforts, the fact remains that diversity training programs need to be combined with other initiatives to increase workplace gender diversity equity, and inclusion.

Defensiveness Avoidance

It has also been claimed that diversity training specifically designed to avoid defensiveness on the part of white men can work to decrease biased behavior. In one study, the training material was presented in the context of actual day-to-day workplace activities, and it provided participants with action-oriented bias mitigation strategies. Researchers found that eight months after participating in this type of training, employees at a global technology company reported engaging in these strategies to mitigate the bias that had been highlighted in the training.[24] However the researchers were appropriately understated in their conclusion, "Unconscious bias training can be a useful component of [other] diversity and inclusion efforts."[25]

The Inescapable Conclusion

Based on the available research and our personal experiences, stand-alone diversity training, whether compulsory or voluntary, does little to change attitudes, beliefs, or behaviors, even over an extended period of time. It helps educate employees about gender inequality, women's workplace advancement obstacles, and an organization's broader diversity goals. Indeed, there is no evidence that diversity training—on its own—will reduce workplace gender inequality or strengthen women's representation in senior leadership.

Indeed, there is no evidence that diversity training—on its own—will reduce workplace gender inequality or strengthen women's representation in senior leadership.

This is not surprising. Providing people with the information they need to make good (unbiased) decisions doesn't do much to stop them from making bad (biased) decisions. As public health expert Victor Strecher, of the University of Michigan, puts it, "We've known for over 50 years that providing information alone to people does not change their behavior."[26] Many people still smoke, despite knowing the risks of tobacco use.[27] Children exposed to drug education programs aren't any less likely to try illicit drugs.[28] Providing people with information about workplace sexual harassment doesn't reduce its prevalence.[29] Increasing people's awareness of the role of unconscious bias in fueling workplace gender inequality and stereotypes and biases does not reduce their biased behavior. In the simplest of terms, people can't be trained out of their biases.

That said, diversity training programs designed to increase participants' knowledge about bias and its harmful effects on women's careers can be a highly beneficial part of a comprehensive and multifaceted program. It is useful for people to share a common language so they can talk about bias and the need for diversity and inclusion. As we discuss in Chapter 7, PATH expressly depends on such training. Indeed, many existing programs can usefully be adapted to and integrated with PATH.

2. Programs to "Fix the Women" Are Misguided and Ineffective

Many leaders remain unaware of major challenges in their current organizations. "They underestimate the obstacles confronting an employee of a diverse group, perceiving a workplace with far less bias than actually exists."[30]

> Many leaders "underestimate the obstacles confronting an employee of a diverse group, perceiving a workplace with far less bias than actually exists."
>
> —Matt Krentz

This lack of awareness is all too apparent from a survey of faculty, staff, and alumni at Stanford University's Byers Center for Biodesign.[31] The survey found that 80 percent of men believe their workplace "empowers women to reach their full potential," while only 36 percent of women agree. In addition, 84 percent of men believe their organization's promotional criteria for women and men are the same, but only 35 percent of women agree. Moreover, men overwhelmingly attribute gender disparities within the leadership ranks to individual choices made by women and men. As noted in Chapter 2, it is a commonplace myth that women prefer to balance the needs of homelife and career. Women, by contrast, believe that they are held back by stereotypes and exclusion from important communication networks and influence because of systemic gender discrimination.

Because of such blind spots, senior leaders can fail to see, much less comprehend, the gender-based obstacles to women's career advancement.[32] Because of the widely held belief that workplaces operate as meritocracies,[33] senior leaders can believe that if women are not advancing in their careers as far and as fast as men, it is because women are doing something wrong. The assumptions are that women are not confident enough; their behaviors are not forceful enough; and their career commitments are not strong enough. In other words, these leaders can believe that women can succeed in their careers to the same extent as men if they have the will and display the commitment, attitudes, and behaviors for such success.[34] Such beliefs have led to the proliferation of programs designed to "fix the women, primarily by" making them more confident and capable of self-promotion.[35] The common underlying premise is that women don't get ahead because they lack confidence. This lack of confidence "is presented as being entirely an individual and personal matter, unconnected to structural inequalities or cultural forces."[36] A misguided belief.

www.CartoonStock.com

This "fix the women" approach to dealing with gender inequality in leadership is reflected in the advice offered in the large number of books written by women who have been successful in their careers. A look at these books reveals that the authors present a remarkably similar set of recommendations. To achieve career success women need three things: (1) confidence, (2) control, and (3) courage.[37]

Confidence

With respect to confidence, Sheryl Sandberg (formerly of Meta Platforms) displays the common theme of these authors when she writes, "Women are hindered by barriers that exist within ourselves. We hold ourselves back in ways both big and small, by lacking self-confidence, by not raising our hands."[38] While Sandberg and other women authors acknowledge that some gendered barriers exist, they emphasize that, for the most part, if women just become more confident, they will be able to overcome them. As Michelle Mone, co-founder of Ultimo Lingerie, writes, "If you've got those ingredients [that is, passion, determination, and a 'can-do' attitude], nothing will stop you."[39]

Control

Another common theme is that women can achieve career success if they can just remain in control at all times in their personal lives and in their work lives. Indeed, women can "have it all," successfully combining a high-powered career and a satisfying homelife, as long as they exercise tight control over both spheres. These authors thus present success as a matter of personal choice and responsibility: If women make the right choices, success can be theirs; if not, failure is their own fault.

Courage

On the topic of courage, Arianna Huffington, founder and CEO of Thrive Global and founder of *The Huffington Post*, is typical when she writes, "[Our female] fears of sticking our necks out because of how we'll be perceived often causes us to sabotage our careers.... If you want to succeed big, there is no substitute for simply sticking your neck out."[40]

These advice books and company programs designed to fix women obviously don't consider the structural discrimination that women face in their workplaces or the individual discrimination they face every day at work. Indeed, the implicit assumption of the entire "fix the women so they can succeed" thinking seems to be that structural and individual discrimination are inevitable, that they probably cannot be changed, and they are essentially irrelevant. Rather, women can succeed if they would take more risks and demand seats at the leadership table. The implication is that gender inequality is their fault[41] and therefore women can end it all by themselves. It is hard to think of a more wrongheaded or perverse view of the state and cause of workplace gender inequality.[42]

3. Ignoring Structural Discrimination

Because of the focus on anti-bias training and programs to fix women, leaders have shown little interest in addressing the structural forces driving workplace gender inequality.[43] The pervasive assumption of diversity training is that gender inequality will end if people will just become more aware of their biases, and women will just try harder.[44]

> The pervasive assumption of diversity training is that gender inequality would end if people will just become aware of their biases, and women will just try harder.

But organizations have been pursuing this approach for at least the last 30 years, and they have achieved little in bringing about real change in their leadership. The failure to confront the structural discrimination in their workplaces and the workplace cultures that allow individual discrimination are the primary reasons we have made little progress to end gender inequality.

Increasing individuals' awareness of their unconscious biases and teaching women to be more confident will not reduce—much less end—gender inequality. Without a program that directly attacks both structural and individual discrimination, company management is just playing around the edges of workplace gender inequality.

> Without a program that directly attacks both structural and individual discrimination, company management is just playing around the edges of workplace gender inequality.

Most business, professional, and nonprofit organizations currently do diversity training of one sort or another,[45] and many have programs specifically designed to help women become more confident and self-assertive.[46] Yet, few of these organizations have programs to end exclusionary behavior in the workplace (as we address in Chapter 8) or to change the workplace's personnel systems, processes, and practices (as we address in Chapter 9). These sorts of structural changes are the only real hope we have of confronting structural discrimination so we can achieve fair, equal, and equitable career outcomes for women and men. "Although raising awareness is a clear and necessary prerequisite to fostering self-regulated unbiased behavior, awareness alone does not change culture."[47] PATH is about changing structures and cultures.

KEY TAKEAWAYS

- With so much attention and money being spent on DEI programs and with so little progress being made, something must be wrong with what we are doing to improve gender diversity, equity, and inclusion, or else it is an expensive public relations exercise.
- "De-biasing" individuals simply can't be achieved in any broad and meaningful sense. A few techniques may offer promise but need further study. Related training doesn't reduce biased behavior, diminish discriminatory outcomes, or increase the promotion of women into leadership positions.
- Diversity training focuses on the symptoms (individual discrimination) but not the causes of workplace gender inequality (structural discrimination). This distinction helps inform PATH's fundamental approach.
- A great deal of effort is devoted to "Fixing the Women." The belief that women's attitudes, behaviors, and personal choices are the fundamental reasons they are not advancing in their careers as far and as fast as men is based on a fundamentally misguided view placing the blame squarely at women's feet.

- Far too little attention is being paid to structural discrimination, that is, the group of systemic factors that perpetuate gender inequality.
- We need to directly confront both structural and individual discrimination if we are to move forward, reduce negative impacts, and strengthen positive operational outcomes and rewards across the entire workplace.

Chapter 6

Men Aren't Involved

AS WE SAW IN CHAPTER 5, fix the women programs and anti-bias training sessions[1] that target individual employees have not helped to achieve gender equality at work.[2] Current DEI efforts are not making significant progress at ending workplace gender inequality because they are not addressing the systemic nature of the problem: the structural discrimination inherent in an organization's management systems, processes, and practices. But there is a second and simpler reason: men are not involved in efforts to end workplace gender inequality. As Michael Flood, an Australian sociology professor, correctly observes, "There is little doubt gender injustice will only end when men join with women to put an end to it."[3]

> "There is little doubt gender injustice will only end when men join with women to put an end to it."
>
> —Michael Flood

Men lead most major businesses and professional organizations; men control the majority of our country's organizational resources; and men wield far more power—social, economic, and political—than do women. Without men's active support to end workplace gender inequality, half of the potential participants in this effort—the more powerful and better-resourced half—remain on the sidelines.

Men's lack of involvement is readily apparent. When we speak to company diversity committees, hold workshops on gender diversity and inclusion, or consult on DEI initiatives, the people we deal with are women, almost exclusively. Moreover, women write most of the books and articles addressing gender equality. Women make up the great majority of people who express concern about the need to end gender inequality, engage in concrete efforts to bring this about, and thoughtfully critique the current workplace status of women and men. As a result, and quite understandably, ending workplace gender inequality is too often seen as a woman's issue.

Where are the men? Why aren't they active participants in the efforts to build truly fair, equal, and inclusive workplaces?

In this chapter we look at the reasons that men aren't involved, and how we can get them enthusiastically involved. Of course, apart from being uninvolved, some men can also forcefully oppose efforts to achieve gender equality. We focus on such opposition and how to help overcome it in Chapter 12. For now, though, let's look at why men of good will, men who generally express strong support for workplace gender equality, are not actively engaged in the effort to bring it about.

Why Are Men AWOL?

A great many men express strong support for workplace gender equality. A national survey from Equimundo: Center for Masculinities and Social Justice[4] found that 67 percent of men believe that women face "major barriers" in their professions that men don't face, and 60 percent of men support having more women leaders in their workplaces.[5] A recent Pew Research Center survey found that 49 percent of Americans believe that women and men should have equal rights; 28.5 percent believe society has different expectations of women and men; and 27 percent believe there are not enough women in positions of leadership and power.[6]

A survey by the Center for Talent Innovation (CTI) found that 42 percent of "majority men" (defined as white, straight, cisgender men) are "true believers," that is, they believe that gender diversity and inclusion are "very important," and that women and men do not have equal access to career opportunities.[7]

Surveys such as these make it clear that many men favor more gender-diverse workplaces. Unfortunately, few of them actively participate in programs, initiatives, or public efforts to bring about increased gender equality. These men are "absent without leave" (AWOL). Based on our many years spent fighting for gender equality, we believe there are five reasons that men of good will—the true believers—are on the sidelines, not on the front lines, of these efforts:

1. Men don't think that gender equality is their fight and, as a result, they don't believe they have the psychological standing to join it.
2. Men fear backlash from women and other men if they become active advocates for gender equality.
3. Men worry that if they get involved, they will say or do the wrong thing and be thought of as unenlightened, ignorant, or worse.
4. Men are unsure about how, where, and when they should join the battle for gender equality.
5. Men feel they are too busy to get involved in an effort that doesn't seem to have any personal payoff for them.

Leaders must address all of these core concerns. Let's consider each of them, and discuss how each one can be overcome to ensure that men of good will can be brought into the efforts to achieve gender equality.

1. It's Not My Fight

Men can be reluctant to actively advocate for workplace gender equality because they don't see it as their fight. When the objective of gender equality is characterized as *increasing women's power, resources, and status*, men don't see that as their issue. They lack the psychological standing to join the fight.[8] In the simplest terms, people are said to lack psychological standing to participate in an activity, or effort if they believe they are not legitimately affected by the outcome; they have no stake one way or the other; or their participation would be gratuitous, unwarranted, or without justification. Accordingly, workplace gender equality is seen by many men as a woman's issue, a woman's objective, and a woman's fight in which they have no stake, one way or the other.

When men feel they lack psychological standing, they hang back and stay on the sidelines. Although they can be supportive, they don't believe they have a role to play. When men do attempt to play a role in gender diversity efforts, they often see themselves—and can be seen by women—as outsiders. Thus, male respondents in the 2019 "White Men's Leadership Study" identified the primary reason they were reluctant to participate in DEI initiatives was their "sense of exclusion" from the effort.[9] Indeed, 70 percent of respondents noted they were not certain that they would be welcomed by women if they attempted to participate.[10]

Andie: Recently Al and I walked into the meeting room for a workshop we were conducting on building gender inclusivity in the medical profession. A number of participants were already seated and as we walked in some looked confused. One woman said to Al, "You're in the wrong session. This one is about gender diversity." Her remark gave us the opportunity to make the point that gender diversity is a goal everyone—women *and* men—need to be working toward.

There is a vicious circle here. Men—true believers—who feel a lack of psychological standing to roll up their sleeves don't participate. As a result, gender equality efforts are overwhelmingly dominated by women, and men come to be seen as outsiders, unconnected to the objective of the efforts. As outsiders, men can sense that they lack psychological standing to join the fight; and, as this belief increases, they continue to remain on the outside.

This vicious circle results in an apparent disconnect between belief and action, and it is common to see men express a strong belief in gender equality, yet do nothing to bring it about. Even men who are vocal about the need to end gender inequality can still refuse to join diversity committees, attend events on gender diversity or events sponsored by women's groups, or advocate for specific policies or practices that would strengthen gender diversity in the workplace. Despite the strengths of their beliefs in the importance of ending gender inequality, men consistently stay away from actively assisting the related efforts.[11] They "believe it is just not their place to act, so they don't."[12]

There are two ways to persuade men that ending workplace gender inequality is their fight. The first is to get them to believe—as Al does (see box)—that men do perform benevolent acts without a self-interested motive so they should also act to correct injustice or improve the conditions of working women.

Most men will make commitments in which they have no personal stake—coaching kids other than their own, volunteering at the local soup kitchen, or sheltering recent refugees. Therefore, they simply need to believe that making life a little better for working women is just as valuable and important a social issue as those to which they already devote their time and effort.

The second way to get men involved is to reframe the goal. When gender equality is not about advancing women but about assuring equitable outcomes for everyone, it immediately becomes an issue in which men have a stake.

In other words, by reframing the objective of ending gender inequality as the establishment of equal and inclusive workplaces—not women's this or women's that—men can see they have legitimacy in advocating to end gender inequality. Another way to persuade men they have standing in the fight for workplace equality is to show them—along the lines we discussed in Chapter 3—that companies work better, teams are more productive, and both women and men are happier in workplaces that offer equal opportunity and fair treatment for everyone.[13]

Al: I have never understood the hands-off attitude expressed by so many men. I have certainly heard it expressed and have watched men shy away from involvement. In life, we often do things for people we care about or are concerned about even if we have no personal stake in the outcome. We might work to provide accommodations for the unhoused, provide school supplies for underprivileged children, or volunteer to assist at an old folks' home. If the justification for these things is simply that you "feel good," then you should join the fight for gender equality if it "makes you feel good." But I don't think we do these things simply because they make us feel good. There is something deeper and more valuable than a sense of pleasure. They are things that should be done, that are important, and that will make someone else feel better. Indeed, there are many reasons I devote so much of my time and effort to ending gender inequality, but primarily I do it because it will make women's lives better. And this makes workplaces better for everyone.

2. Fear of Backlash

Men are often hesitant to participate in diversity efforts for fear that they will encounter backlash. Adam Grant, an organizational psychologist and professor at the Wharton School, writing in the *Atlantic*, observes, "When a cause seems inconsistent with our self-interest, we fear that we'll incur a backlash [if we advocate for it], so we hold back. What business do men have speaking up for women? [As a result] many men who would like to see more women leaders are afraid to speak up about it."[14]

The fear of backlash is different from feeling a lack of psychological standing. The lack of psychological standing is an internally driven sense of illegitimacy—a feeling that "it's not my place" to advocate for women. Fear of backlash, however, is a concern about the possibility of facing external disapproval or the loss of status. This backlash can come from both men and women.

"Damn it, Hopkins, didn't you get yesterday's memo?"

www.CartoonStock.com

Backlash from Men

Men often disapprove or criticize men who advocate for women's advancement because of their belief that such advocacy is inconsistent with traditional male values—promotion of "masculinity," maintenance of male solidarity, and disparagement of the feminine. Backlash from women typically comes from the suspicion that men's real motivation is something other than the achievement of gender equality. Regardless of its origin, the fear of backlash unquestionably prevents a substantial number of men from actively joining the fight to end gender inequality.

> Regardless of its origin, the fear of backlash unquestionably pre-
> vents a substantial number of men from actively joining the fight to
> end gender inequality.

Backlash from Women

What about backlash from women? Men advocating on behalf of women's
advancement can face backlash from women for entirely different reasons than the ones they face from men. A story told by Professor Adam
Grant illustrates the sorts of reasons for backlash from women. He said, "I
facilitated a conversation for a group about gender and leadership. A man
raised his hand to share his support for bringing more women into leadership positions. I expected enthusiastic reactions from his female peers, but
instead, his comment was greeted with skepticism. One woman directly
questioned his intentions: What was his ulterior motive? Was he trying to
ingratiate himself with women to improve his dating prospects?"[15]

There are a variety of reasons why many women are skeptical of
men's sincerity when they publicly advocate for women's advancement.
Often women's reaction can be something like, "What right does he have
to speak for us?" Lily Zheng, writing in the *Harvard Business Review*,
comments that many men tell her, "'It seems like I'm not wanted in the
room when D&I conversations happen.' Others say, 'It feels like I'm part
of the problem.'"[16] Thus, the skepticism and hostility men can experience
from women often reflects women's belief that ending gender inequality
is a woman's issue in which men have no legitimate stake.

Dealing with Backlash

There are effective ways of dealing with backlash.[17] When the backlash
comes from other men, those men with a high awareness of gender bias
are far more willing to enter the fray, ignoring backlash, and openly
advocating for women.[18] Thus, the best way to get men into the gender
equality fight is through knowledge. The more knowledge men have
about the concrete, adverse consequences of gender inequality, the more

likely they are to advocate for its elimination. There are a variety of ways in which organizations can increase men's understanding of the negative consequences to women's careers from gender inequality:

- Sponsor discussions between women and their male colleagues.
- Host moderated men-only conversations about male privilege.
- Present talks by women about their personal experiences with gender bias.
- Present talks by men about what they have done to increase workplace fairness, opportunity, and equity.
- Promote cross-gender mentoring relationships.

One way or another, when men truly appreciate the extent and nature of the negative consequences of gender inequality, they can become far more willing to advocate for gender equality regardless of possible backlash.

By reframing efforts to assure fairness, opportunity, and equity for everyone, men's active involvement should not appear to be suspicious or out of place.

> By reframing efforts to assure fairness, opportunity, and equity for everyone, men's active involvement should not appear to be suspicious or out of place.

By adjusting the perspective, men's involvement is seen as appropriate and understandable. The nuance, however, is to shift the objective from women's advancement to workplace fairness *without* making women feel as though they are being depreciated, or their issues ignored.

An effective way to do this is for organizations to provide "safe spaces" where women can candidly share personal experiences, obtain important advice about coping with their workplace cultures, and seek assistance to develop positive self-images. "Safe spaces" can be very effective in providing women with the opportunity to bond with other women—a critical need in gendered workplaces that will help women cultivate the vital networks that can assist their mutual support, advancement, and future promotion.[19]

3. Concern about Saying "the Wrong Thing"

The American Bar Association (ABA) 2021 report from its Commission on Women in the Profession concluded that a key reason that men don't collaborate with women to end gender inequality is their fear of "saying the wrong thing."[20] This is different from a concern about backlash. Backlash involves being ostracized, criticized, or treated with suspicion. Worrying about saying the wrong thing, however, is a concern that men will appear stupid, unenlightened, or out of touch. As one man commented in the ABA survey, many men "think that if they are not the epitome of the 'sensitive guy' that they will be unfavorably perceived."[21]

www.CartoonStock.com

To become active participants in efforts to end gender inequality, men need to feel comfortable in honestly expressing their opinions, perspectives, and concerns. This means that women need to be prepared to invite men into gender initiatives without being too quick to criticize attitudes that are not as "advanced" as they would like.[22] Men need to be able to openly express their perspectives, beliefs, and experiences without being viewed as cavemen.

At the same time, men must be prepared to thoughtfully listen to what women have to say, to honestly engage with women, and to be willing to change their thinking as women's concerns come into clearer focus. In other words, women and men must be willing to engage in non-defensive, blame-free dialogues. Such conversations can be tricky because one side or the other can easily be misunderstood. But if women and men are patient and willing to give one another the benefit of the doubt, such conversations are possible and unquestionably essential to the collaboration needed to end workplace gender inequality.

4. Not Knowing How, Where, and When to Advocate for Gender Equality

Closely related to men's concerns that they might "say the wrong thing" is their feeling that they don't "know how" to fight to end workplace gender inequality.

More than half of men who responded to the ABA survey reported that not knowing how to support women was a significant reason that they did not participate in gender equality initiatives.[23]

Al: While I realize that many men are uncertain about *how* to advocate for women, I find much of this uncertainty puzzling. After all, what kind of knowledge is needed? Publicly expressing support is often all that is needed and there is no special knowledge required to do that. It's time to give it a try.

Al's view is supported by a recent study that found that when men voice their commitment to gender equality, they decrease women's expectation of "workplace hostility and isolation and increase their anticipated respect, support, and perception that gender equality is seen as 'normative' at this organization."[24]

"I gotta say, this normalization is really starting to
grow on me."

Mark Anderson

Beyond simply expressing support for gender equality, knowing what more to do can be puzzling, particularly given the ineffectiveness of most existing diversity initiatives. While the goal may be clear—actively promoting gender equality for women and underrepresented groups in the workplace—precisely how this can be done is far from clear. This conundrum exists for women and men, and it is one of the reasons we developed PATH so there would be no ambiguity or uncertainty as to how to proceed forward in attacking gender inequality.

5. Men Feel They Are "Too Busy" to Get Involved

We often hear men, particularly senior executives, partners, and managers, say that they have too many other things on their plates to get involved in gender equality initiatives. After all, these men claim they need to run their companies; assure their teams are engaged and productive; and make sure that their people are developing skills, attitudes, and experiences needed to increasingly improve their performance. Although there is some truth in such an attitude, more often than not, this reaction stems from a sense of not wanting to be bothered with an effort that appears unconnected to their principal responsibilities and which holds no personal benefits for them.

As we have already seen, however, it is important to reframe the goal of ending gender inequality to make it clear that men have a definitive stake in ending gender inequality so it no longer seems tangential to their core responsibilities but essential to effectively accomplishing them. In other words, when men see that ending workplace gender inequality will make their companies more productive, their teams more effective, the people they supervise more engaged, and their own jobs more enjoyable, they will suddenly find the time to fight for it.

> Men must be persuaded that they have a definitive stake in ending gender inequality so it no longer seems tangential to their core responsibilities but essential to effectively accomplishing them.

Three Principles to Keep in Mind

Whatever the reasons for men's reluctance to get involved in efforts to end gender inequality, three overriding considerations need to be kept front and center in efforts to enlist men's support.

1. Make Gender Equality Relevant

According to Deloitte, a global network of professional services and consulting member firms, "Diversity of thinking is a wellspring of creativity, enhancing innovation by about 20 percent. It also enables groups to spot risk, reducing these by up to 30 percent. And it smooths the implementation of decisions by creating buy-in and trust."[25] Indeed one research study found that gender-diverse teams made more effective decisions 73 percent of the time—compared with just 55 percent of the time for all-male teams.[26]

The key to getting men of good will to become involved in PATH is to persuade them that this is their fight, too. This is men's fight because *it is about them being more successful at their jobs.* When men—and women—are surrounded by people who are like them, it is usually very easy to develop consensus about procedures, policies, products, and services. But as Jennifer Mueller and her colleagues write in the *Harvard Business Review,* "Consensus-based problem-solving groups are often where innovative ideas go to die. [Homogeneous] groups are highly prone to groupthink—quick agreement around status quo solutions with little discussion or deliberation."[27] When men see this and realize that they need gender-diverse teams to avoid groupthink, they should be easily persuaded to join the fight for ending gender inequality. They should want to create workplaces and teams where gender diversity will flourish, bringing diversity of perspective, ideas, and experience. It also leads people to "*believe* that differences of perspectives might exist among them and that belief makes people change their behavior."[28]

2. Men Need Role Models

Regardless of the benefits of diverse and inclusive workplaces and teams, men may be reluctant to participate in initiatives to end gender inequality unless they see other men are participating in those efforts.[29] Organizations can do this when their senior male executives and influential managers are seen as highly visible in these initiatives. When there are influential male role models, it becomes clear to everyone that active support of diversity initiatives is not only appropriate but is highly valued.

Men will stop being reluctant to join the gender equality fight when they see other men—men they respect and trust—already in the fight.

In this way, men come to see participation as the thing to do, not just an activity with obvious benefits for their companies and their teams. It becomes an expected, common, and well-regarded activity.

3. Building a Community

When women and men collaborate, they develop a sense of community, a sense of being a "We." They become people who share core values, have common objectives, and respect one another's differences. If men can develop a sense of "We" with the women with whom they work, it is a very small step for them to see themselves working with them to bring about an end to workplace gender inequality. In other words, if men are accustomed to working with women, they can easily be persuaded to join with women to make workplace conditions fairer.

There is no reason for men of good will to be on the sidelines of the fight for gender equality. It is their fight too. And with the right encouragement, information, and role models, they will become not just active participants but enthusiastic ones.

Liza Donnelly

KEY TAKEAWAYS

- Gender inequality remains a systemic workplace problem. Men need to be fully engaged, be honest about its existence, and work alongside women to disrupt and end it. It is critical that both women and men are seen as being at the forefront of the fight.
- To date, many men have been absent without leave in efforts to end gender inequality for five key reasons.

1. Men don't think that gender equality is their fight. Enlist men by reframing the objective of the fight. Assure them that it is not about the advancement of women but about building equal and inclusive workplaces for everyone.
2. Men fear backlash if they actively advocate for gender equality. Assure men their involvement is appropriate and necessary. Counter backlash with knowledge. The more knowledge men have about the adverse consequences of gender inequality, the more likely they are to advocate for its elimination. Backlash can come from women as well. We recommend broadening the focus to fairness and equality for *everyone* in the workplace.
3. Men worry they will say or do the wrong thing if they get involved. Host assisted non-defensive, blame-free discussions for all constituencies to help men realize they are welcome. These conversations are never easy, and misunderstanding can quickly arise if people are not willing to give one another the benefit of the doubt; however, such conversations are possible and unquestionably essential. Non-defensive, blame-free discussions are needed to start this process.
4. Men are unsure about how, where, and when to join the fight. Knowing the problem is one issue; figuring out solutions is another. Men are wary of involvement so they need some direction, encouragement and engagement. In short, they need leadership. Indeed, this is precisely why we have written this book:

to lay out how you can effectively end gender inequality in your organization.

5. Men are too busy to spend time on an effort with no perceived personal payoff. Persuade men that ending gender inequality is an essential element of their core workplace responsibilities. Most men can be persuaded when they see that ending workplace gender inequality will make their organizations more productive; their teams more effective; the people they supervise more engaged; and their own careers more rewarding.

- Keep three overriding principles in mind:

  1. Make gender equality relevant.
  2. Identify, empower, and make visible male role models.
  3. Build a community of women and men working together.

PART III

THE PATH

Chapter 7

The PATH

U P TO THIS POINT WE have looked at the extent of workplace gender inequality; its root causes; and its profoundly detrimental impact on the ability of organizations, teams, and individuals to flourish. We have also examined why current efforts to end workplace gender inequality have been only marginally successful; why there are no quick fixes for such inequality; and why men are reluctant to be involved in DEI efforts.

With this background, it is apparent that there is a vicious circle of the structural discrimination inherent in gendered workplaces and the individual discrimination reflected in the behavior of individuals in those workplaces. Structural discrimination leads to unequal workplace outcomes for women and men. The gender stereotypes and status beliefs that drive these unequal outcomes foster individual discrimination. People in these workplaces incorporate expectations of unequal gender outcomes into their own attitudes, judgments, and behaviors. This conduct, in turn, strengthens the persistence of structural discrimination. As a result, there is a process of mutual reinforcement of structural and individual discrimination, a highly pernicious process that most organizations' DEI initiatives have been unable to counter. As Sheen S. Levine, David Stark, and Michèle Lamont write in the *Harvard Business Review*, "In recent years, researchers have documented surprisingly feeble outcomes associated with diversity-training sessions, initiatives to reduce prejudice, and implicit-bias training."[1] It is apparent, therefore, that if organizations simply continue to do DEI as they have been doing it, America's workplaces will continue to be plagued by pervasive, pernicious, and persistent gender inequality.

"We put up new curtains, we repainted the hallways, and we even replaced the lights in the restrooms.

"So why are we still having retention problems?"

Copyright Grantland Enterprises; www.grantland.net

A new, different, and comprehensive approach to DEI is needed. An approach that directly challenges structural discrimination and by doing so offers the realistic prospect of ending individual discrimination. PATH is such an approach. It is a practical, accessible, and effective way for organizations to change the discriminatory outcomes of their personnel-management practices. By doing so, the workplace context that shapes attitudes and expectations changes; and, in turn, behaviors of the participants also change. By attacking structural discrimination, PATH also attacks individual discrimination. In the absence of structural discrimination, the context within which individual discrimination is fostered is changed so that women's and men's workplace experiences become more rewarding, pleasant, and safe.

PATH is an acronym of the first letter of each of the four principal components of the program:

- **P**rioritize elimination of exclusionary behavior
- **A**dopt discrimination-resistant methods of personnel decision-making
- **T**reat inequality in the home as a workplace problem
- **H**alt unequal performance reviews, career advice, and leadership opportunities

The PATH Approach

Gender inequality exists in our workplaces because those workplaces are "gendered": they are male-dominated, male-identified, and male-centered. As a result, they operate to consistently and predictably favor men over women, to evaluate men less critically than women, and to value men's contributions and accomplishments more highly than women's. Gendered workplaces operate in this way because they are structured based on gender stereotypes and the status beliefs embedded in them. Everyday personnel-management practices—the ordinary, taken-for-granted ways in which people are hired, evaluated, given opportunities and responsibilities, and promoted—reflect these stereotypes and status beliefs. A workplace's norms, values, and expectations are internalized by the participants in those workplaces, leading to individual discrimination. As Bob Pease writes in *Undoing Privilege: Unearned Advantage in a Divided World*, individual discrimination is "a result of the attitudes and practices of ordinary people who are not aware of how their [unconscious] assumption of [male] superiority impacts the lives of others."[2]

PATH involves a series of changes to workplace personnel systems, processes, and policies that are designed to undermine the foundation of structural discrimination.

**"I'm willing to try you out, but
you'll have to give up the whole cat thing."**

PATH does not seek to directly de-bias workplace participants. Rather, organizations are provided with the processes, techniques, and tools to change the ways in which personnel decisions, policies, and practices are implemented. PATH is designed to end the expected, routine pattern of unequal workplace outcomes for women and men. Once men's assumed superiority is no longer "baked in" to workplace operations, individuals' unconscious assumptions of such superiority are also undermined.

The changes that PATH recommends are not self-executing. Implementation depends on organizations undertaking a well-led, properly resourced, and fully empowered change initiative to bring about these changes.

In the chapters that follow, we explain the nature of PATH's four components, the essential approaches underlying each of them, why PATH represents a new and effective approach for ending workplace gender inequality, and how organizations can implement its recommended changes.

The Components of PATH

To recap briefly, PATH recommends four sets of actions that organizations need to take to bring about an end to workplace gender inequality:

1. **P**rioritize elimination of exclusionary behavior
2. **A**dopt discrimination-resistant methods of personnel decision-making
3. **T**reat inequality in the home as a workplace problem
4. **H**alt unequal performance reviews, career advice, and leadership opportunities

Although each of these components can be structured as a stand-alone initiative, they are closely interrelated. When implemented as a comprehensive, integrated initiative, PATH provides organizations with the processes, tools, and techniques they need to effectively disrupt both structural and individual discrimination, foster the values inherent in diversity, and achieve an inclusive workplace environment in which employees can enjoy a sense of engagement, satisfaction, and ambition.

PRIORITIZE Elimination of Exclusionary Behavior

Assuring that women and men have equally positive workplace experiences—experiences that are equally challenging, rewarding, and conducive to career growth—depends on organizations creating workplace cultures that explicitly condemn exclusionary behaviors and empower individuals to interrupt such behaviors whenever they witness them. Such exclusionary behaviors include incivility, microaggressions, disregard and dismissal, subtle (and not so subtle) assertions of superiority, demeaning conduct, bullying, harassment, and intimidation. When a workplace is free of such behaviors, employees feel able to speak up and make their views known and are comfortable in challenging consensus thinking.

Such a workplace is psychologically and physically safe; it is welcoming to and supportive of all participants without regard to their social identities, personal characteristics, or life experiences.

Unless employees feel respected, valued, and free to honestly contribute to the advancement of their workplace objectives, gender inequality will still exist no matter what other changes organizations make to their personnel-management practices. Until women and men are assured of equally positive workplace experiences, women will never be able to achieve the same degree of career engagement, satisfaction, and motivation as men.

ADOPT Discrimination-Resistant Methods of Personnel Decision-Making

PATH is not an affirmative action initiative for women. Rather, its changes ensure that all personnel decisions are unaffected by structural or individual discrimination. It provides managers with a variety of decision-making techniques that are resilient to the influence of stereotypes, status beliefs, and individual biases. The guiding principle of this aspect of PATH is that the subjective preconceptions, expectations, and preferences of individual decision-makers need to be eliminated from formal personnel decisions so that these decisions can be made in fair, objective, and transparent ways.

TREAT Inequality in the Home as a Workplace Problem

Inequality in the home can have a discriminatory impact on women's career opportunities in their workplaces. When women are expected to perform the lion's share of home responsibilities—childcare, eldercare, and routine domestic responsibilities—they are unable to engage in workplace activities to the same extent as men (or other women who do not have such significant responsibilities). While organizations cannot directly ameliorate homelife inequality, they can do a great deal to lessen its discriminatory impact in their workplaces. In this regard, PATH recommends specific steps that organizations should take to ensure, to the extent possible, that women's often unequal responsibilities as homemakers and caregivers do not limit their career advancement opportunities. These steps include adopting policies that provide flexible workplace times and locations, adequate parental leaves, financial assistance with caregiving, and well-designed and effective career reentry programs.

HALT Unequal Performance Reviews, Career Advice, and Leadership Opportunities

Organizations are likely to have unrecognized discriminatory practices with respect to how they conduct performance reviews, provide career advice, and offer and support opportunities for leadership development. These practices are often sources of acute workplace gender inequality. PATH sets out structural changes that organizations should make to ensure women and men receive (1) equally candid, constructive, and action-oriented performance reviews; (2) equally ambitious, supportive, and future-oriented career advice; and (3) equally frequent and valuable opportunities to exercise their leadership abilities and receive coaching, support, and recognition when they do.

Getting Started

Before implementing the changes PATH recommends, organizations need to prepare employees for what is to come and why. We have been somewhat dismissive of the value of most diversity training programs simply because of their heavy emphasis on teaching people to behave in less biased ways. But the training programs that should precede implementation of the PATH changes are of a quite different nature. Such training should be focused on increasing employees' knowledge of the extent of workplace gender inequality, its structural and individual causes, its adverse consequences for organizational and team performance, and the damage it does to professional relationships.

Importance of Information

Providing employees with critical information prior to launching PATH is essential to its success. There are three essential concepts that should be incorporated in early training and educational outreach: (1) the understanding that gender inequality is pervasive and needs to be pro-actively countered in the workplace; (2) that gender inequality does not result from any essential differences in women's and men's workplace qualifications; and (3) that the elimination of gender inequality depends on changes to the organization's personnel systems, processes, and practices. Let's look at these in more detail.

1. *Gender inequality is a reality in the workplace.* Organizations can help educate their employees on these realities in a variety of ways.[3] The most straightforward and effective way would be for large organizations to release their EEO-1 data.[4] The Equal Employment Opportunity Commission (EEOC) requires private employers with 100 or more employees and federal contractors with 50 or more employees to annually file an EEO-1 report, providing a breakdown of worker gender, race, and ethnicity in 10 job categories. Releasing EEO-1 data may be viewed by some organizations as too detailed and possibly misleading for employees. But whether or not organizations choose to release their EEO-1 data, in one way or another they need to impress upon their employees the reality that gender inequality exists in their workplace and that they are committed to eliminating it.

2. *Women and men are not fundamentally different with respect to their workplace abilities.* People often believe that women's and men's unequal career outcomes are caused by inherent differences in their abilities, characteristics, or personal preferences. As we saw in Chapter 2, many men (and some women) believe in one or more of The Five Gender Myths—myths concerning the existence of fundamental, nonphysiological differences between women and men. Therefore, organizations need to make every

effort to change this mindset, convince employees of women's and men's fundamental similarities with respect to career capabilities, and that gender inequality exists because of structural and individual discrimination.

3. *Ending gender inequality requires changes in workplace systems, processes, and practices.* It is important that employees understand the profound effects of unconscious bias in their own behaviors. But it is equally important that they understand that workplace gender inequality is systemic and caused by inadequate and inappropriate gender-equal controls in workplace systems, processes, and practices. Consequently, in accordance with the PATH approach, organizations need to inform employees about the changes that will be made in the ways in which personnel management is carried out in the workplace, changes that are designed to make their workplaces fairer and more equal. and their experiences in those workplaces more positive, rewarding, and inclusive.

Efforts to inform employees of the three essential concepts should be ongoing and incorporated into workplace cultures, but once organizations believe the initial messaging outreach has been accepted by a substantial number of employees, it is time to announce the adoption of PATH and provide a summary outline of its four principal components. This will involve an overview of the material we present in the next four chapters. The objective of such an announcement is not to immerse employees in the details of the PATH program but to simply give them a heads up as to what is to come.

KEY TAKEAWAYS

- **Prioritize elimination of exclusionary behavior**: employees feel safe to speak up, make their views known, and dissent from consensus views.

- **Adopt discrimination-resistant methods of personnel decision-making:** hiring and advancement decisions are made and constructed on a fair and objective basis, unaffected by structural or individual discrimination.
- **Treat inequality in the home as a workplace problem**: policies support flexible scheduling and locations of work, adequate parental leave, financial assistance with family care, and well-designed and effective career reentry programs.
- **Halt unequal performance reviews, career advice, and leadership opportunities**: the assessments of workplace performance, career advice, and leadership development programs do not favor men.

Chapter 8

Prioritize Elimination of Exclusionary Behaviors

IN GENDERED WORKPLACES, WOMEN ARE far more likely than men to face exclusionary behaviors.[1] As a result, the first priority of PATH is to assist decision-makers in implementing processes to ensure that their workplace cultures strongly condemn exclusionary behaviors and strongly encourage people to step in and stop such behaviors when they see them. Before discussing how organizations can eliminate exclusionary behaviors from their workplaces, let's look closely at how exclusionary behavior is manifested. Exclusionary behaviors make a person feel unwelcome, not valued as a full participant, not recognized as an important contributor, or not regarded as of equal status or standing. Exclusionary behaviors express themselves in many ways, including:

- incivility, rudeness, and microaggressions
- dismissiveness, condescension, and disrespect
- gaslighting
- humiliation, embarrassment, and ridicule
- disregard, disdain, and dismissal
- exclusion, limitation, and restriction
- idea theft
- bullying, intimidation, and harassment

When women are subject to these behaviors, they become less productive, less creative, less collaborative, and less satisfied. They also become more susceptible to burnout. If women experience workplace exclusionary behaviors, it will not matter that changes are made to personnel decisions, practices, and policies that aim to treat women and men on par with one another, gender inequality will persist.

"That's an excellent suggestion, Miss Triggs. Perhaps one of the men here would like to make it."

Punch Cartoon Library / TopFoto

How Exclusionary Behavior Is Manifested

Women experience exclusionary behavior in a wide variety of ways:

- gratuitous incivility, such as being ignored, talked over, or disregarded
- criticism or insensitive comments about their appearance, clothes, mannerisms, parental status, or homelife choices
- public depreciation of their status or value
- exclusion from career-advancing associations, networks, work-related social activities, and collaborative projects

- gaslighting behaviors and comments made to make them question the legitimacy of their reactions to exclusionary treatment
- not being provided with opportunities equal to men's to develop leadership skills
- having their ideas stolen
- not being recognized for their accomplishments
- being exposed to unwelcome locker room talk, off-color jokes, lewd comments, and crude personal observations
- experiencing stalking, leering, touching, and propositioning
- being bullied, intimidated, or sexually harassed

Because of such exclusionary behavior, women can find their workplaces unpleasant, distasteful, unsatisfying, even frightening. They can experience greater frustration, discouragement, and stress than do men,[2] and they feel less psychologically and physically safe than their male colleagues.[3]

"Cindy is it? Be a love and make us a cup of coffee and some sandwiches would you?"

www.CartoonStock.com

Unfortunately, managers often believe that exclusionary behavior in the workplace originates with a few bad actors, or the thoughtless behavior on the part of otherwise "good guys."[4] Therefore, they typically seek to eliminate such exclusionary behavior through anti-bias and anti-harassment training.[5] We can gain a perspective on just how ineffective such training is at ending exclusionary behavior by looking closely at anti-harassment training.

Anti-Harassment Training

Since the 1970s, many American companies have required their employees to participate in anti-harassment training. In large part, companies have done so to mitigate legal exposure to claims of workplace sexual discrimination.[6] Such training provides organizations with substantial legal protections, even without showing that their training actually reduces workplace harassment.[7] As a result, more than 75 percent of all American companies now provide anti-harassment training.[8]

Despite the proliferation of such anti-harassment training, the EEOC Select Task Force found that much of this training "has not worked as a prevention tool."[9] In fact, workplace sexual harassment remains "widespread" and "persistent," and there is "no evidence" that anti-harassment training has "affected the frequency of sexual harassment experienced by the women in the workplace." Indeed, when women were asked if they had experienced one or more specific types of sexually related exclusionary behavior, approximately 60 percent of the women answered in the affirmative.

In a thoughtful article in the *Atlantic*, Pulitzer Prize winner Caitlin Flanagan argues that the only way companies can eliminate sexual harassment from their workplaces is by creating "a climate and culture that starts at the very top of the company and establishes that harassment is not tolerated and will be punished severely."[10]

Professor Adam Grant observes that the problem of sexual harassment isn't merely one of "bad apples" but of "bad barrels," that is, bad workplace cultures.[11]

" Unfortunately my boss would rather that I show femur
instead of backbone."
www.CartoonStock.com

Toxic Workplace Cultures

Toxic workplaces allow for conditions where sexual harassment can fester. Toxic workplaces take a heavy toll on employees. They suffer from "stress, anxiety, depression, and burnout," and they are 35 to 55 percent "more likely to be diagnosed with a serious physical disease."[12] Toxic workplace cultures also hurt organizational performance: employers that offer medical benefits have increased healthcare costs and employees are "more likely to disengage from their work, bad-mouth their employer on employee review sites like Glassdoor or Indeed, or look for another job."[13] The harms of toxic workplaces were acknowledged in a 2022 report from Dr. Vivek Murthy, the U.S. Surgeon General.[14] Murthy explicitly linked employee mental and physical health to "job factors such as low wages, discrimination, harassment, overwork, and long commutes."[15] To address these issues, the Surgeon General pointed to embedding values in a company's culture, noting that this "will require organizations to rethink how they protect from harm, foster a sense of connection among workers, show them that they matter, make space for their lives outside work, and support their long-term professional growth....A healthy workforce is the foundation for thriving organizations and a healthy community."[16]

A destructive, toxic workplace culture is chillingly exemplified by America's television newsrooms just a few years ago. For example, after Matt Lauer, former host of the *Today* show, was fired by NBC News in 2017, it was revealed that the behind-the-scenes environment at the network resembled a "boys' club," where men would routinely play a crude game in which they would identify the women they would prefer to marry, kill, or have sex with. Inappropriate sexual jokes and rude comments about women were routine.[17]

At CBS, Charlie Rose was fired for making unwelcome sexual advances to current and former employees of *CBS This Morning* (now, *CBS Mornings*). PBS also cancelled his talk show, *Charlie Rose*. Co-workers described a "hostile work environment with no human resource department and Rose essentially running his own fief."[18] At CBS, network CEO Les Moonves and Jeff Fager, executive producer of *60 Minutes,* were both fired because of sexual misconduct. Outside investigators found a pattern of "harassment and violation," noting that the claims against Moonves "were a reflection of the culture at CBS."[19]

Fox News was no better. Former on-air commentator Bill O'Reilly was fired after multiple allegations of sexual harassment and the disclosure of out-of-court settlements of approximately $45 million.[20] That did not prevent O'Reilly from leaving Fox News with a $20 million severance payment.[21] And when former chairman and CEO of Fox News Roger Ailes was forced out, after more than 10 women accused him publicly of sexual harassment, Ailes left with a severance payment of $40 million.[22] *New York Magazine* reported that Fox News was guilty of "grotesque abuses of power," and Ailes's pattern of repeated sexual harassment exposed "a culture of misogyny, corruption and surveillance, smear campaigns, and hush money, with implications reaching far wider than one disturbed man at the top."[23]

While revelations of misconduct at network and cable TV news shows have filled the headlines, these are not the only organizations with toxic workplace cultures. Other companies in entertainment, technology, consulting, and finance have all been exposed as hotbeds of sexual harassment. Workplaces become toxic for women when dominated by men who cultivate cults of personality, and who see themselves as above the rules of civility and the laws against sexual harassment.

Exclusionary Behavior Is All of a Piece

Sexual harassment is not a unique type of offensive behavior that is unrelated to other types of exclusionary behavior. Quite the contrary, it is at one end of a spectrum with incivility and microaggressions are at the other end.

Sexual assault is a crime that should be treated as such. Therefore, sexual assault is categorically different from the exclusionary behaviors that we are concerned about in this book.

What links all manifestations of exclusionary behaviors is that they are all expressions—to one degree or another—of hostility toward, disparagement of, and a sense of superiority over women.[24] Exclusionary behavior, whether conscious or not in its intent, achieves the following:

- puts down women
- shows disapproval of their presence or conduct
- silences their efforts to express themselves
- keeps them "in their place" and out of "men's places"
- demonstrates men's power over them

As we wrote in an article for the *Harvard Business Review* in 2018, all exclusionary behavior is of a piece. The same attitudes, expectations, and sense of entitlement that underlie sexual harassment also underlie incivility and all other forms of exclusionary behavior. As we observed, "Sexual harassment is far more likely in organizations that experience offenses on the 'less severe' end of the spectrum than those that don't."[25]

PATH therefore seeks to effectively prevent workplace sexual harassment by comprehensively addressing all forms of exclusionary behavior. It shows leaders how they can ensure that their culture-defining workplace norms, values, and expectations strongly condemn and eliminate such behaviors, supporting employees' efforts to interrupt those behaviors wherever they do occur.

Workplace Culture

A workplace's culture is the context within which employees pursue their careers; perform job-related activities; and interact with colleagues, managers, and subordinates. Workplace culture is reflected in the standards against which an organization's employees' behaviors are judged acceptable or unacceptable and their attitudes toward (and treatment of) others are regarded as appropriate or inappropriate.

There is a reciprocal relationship between the nature of an organization's workplace culture and the behavior of its employees.

> There is a reciprocal relationship between the nature of an organization's workplace culture and the behavior of its employees.

Studies show that employee attitudes, values, and behaviors tend to reflect the dominant characteristics of their workplace cultures.[26] Employees receive explicit and implicit messages signaling those attitudes and behaviors that will be rewarded and punished, encouraged and disapproved, and valued and disparaged. They observe the conduct

of workplace leaders, see how they treat women, and witness the seriousness with which inequality is regarded.

The only effective way to eliminate workplace exclusionary behavior
is, as Caitlin Flanagan urges, to create "a climate and culture that starts
at the top" of an organization, establishing that exclusionary behavior
"is not tolerated and will be punished severely."[27] But how can organizations create a workplace "climate and culture" that condemns exclusionary behavior?

Workplace Inclusion

A workplace is inclusive when people of all social identities, backgrounds,
and perspectives feel comfortable and safe when interacting in one-on-one
or team settings. In such a workplace, employees have no fear that they will
be subjected to personal criticism, purposeful embarrassment, gaslighting,
denial of resources, or loss of status. That is, they will not face exclusionary
behavior when they choose to actively and fully participate in workplace
activities.

> A workplace is inclusive when employees of all social identities,
> backgrounds, and perspectives feel comfortable and safe when
> interacting in one-on-one or team settings.

Most commentators focus on achieving inclusive workplaces by
changing the attitudes, behaviors, beliefs, and expectations of employees,
encouraging those employees to welcome, value, and respect people of all
social identities, personal perspectives, and life experiences.

While we agree that workplace participants need to behave in inclusive ways, we are skeptical, however, that simply asking people to be more
inclusive is likely to succeed. PATH helps to create inclusive workplace
culture by eliminating exclusionary behaviors that can threaten *physical*

and psychological safety and well-being. As Amy Edmondson, a professor at the Harvard Business School, writes, when people feel psychologically safe, their workplaces are inclusive and they are "comfortable being themselves."[28] People feel psychologically safe when:

1. They know they will not be punished, humiliated, isolated, restricted, limited, or made to feel unwelcome, unvalued, or disrespected *because of who they are.*
2. They are confident that sharing their questions, ideas, concerns, perspectives, and breadth of experiences will not meet with derision, disregard, disdain, or idea theft *because they come from them.*
3. They are certain that the people they work with will not encounter exclusionary behavior *because of who they are, or because contributions come from them.*

Thus, workplace participants feel psychologically safe when they can openly express their ideas, freely present different perspectives, and disagree with dominant or consensus views without fear of provoking exclusionary behavior. When employees feel psychologically safe, teams are better able to adapt to new situations, resolve challenging issues, solve perplexing problems, and innovate in the face of adversity.[29] In addition, when team members feel psychologically safe, they are more likely to respectfully disagree, admit error, and ask for help from one another.[30] Accordingly, psychological safety is a critical driver in determining whether a workplace has a high degree of employee engagement, collaborative decision-making, healthy team dynamics, and effective organizational performance.[31]

Psychological safety is also the key to unlocking the potential of workplace diversity and inclusion. Well-managed diverse teams outperform homogeneous ones.[32] When psychological safety is not prioritized, however, diverse teams can experience misunderstandings, team members can fail to pick up other members' intentions, and achieving consensus can become far more difficult. In contrast, when members of diverse teams have a high sense of psychological safety, they work together and outperform homogeneous ones.[33] In other words, psychological safety is necessary if organizations are to truly benefit from efforts to increase gender diversity.

Andie: Al and I were planning a workshop on building an inclusive workplace with the women's affinity group at a major global engineering firm. We suggested that the most effective way to have a serious discussion about building a collaborative and inclusive workplace was to invite the men to participate in the workshop. Initially, the women on the planning committee objected, saying they did not want the men to participate. They were afraid that the men would take over the meeting and silence the women. Eventually, the planning committee came around, and they were pleased to find that working together to solve problems provided an awareness and built important connections.

Creating an Inclusive Workplace Culture

Although senior leaders have known for some time the value their organizations would derive from an inclusive workplace culture, only minimal progress has been made to date.[34] While few American workplaces have cultures that are truly toxic, many of them are defined by unacceptable exclusionary behavior. In a 2019 article in the *Harvard Business Review*, University of Colorado associate professor Stefanie Johnson, along with her research colleagues, found that while blatant *sexual harassment* declined between 2016 and 2018, *gender harassment* (that is, workplace incivility and other forms of exclusionary behavior that did not rise to the level of sexual harassment) increased.[35] Indeed, the percentage of women reporting gender harassment grew from 76 percent (in 2016) to 92 percent in 2018. Given this increase, the researchers said that "while blatant sexual harassment—experiences that drive many women out of their careers—might be declining, workplaces may be seeing a 'backlash effect,' or increase in hostility toward women." This is a strong driver of gender inequality. "Constant exposure to gender harassment can be just as damaging to women as the most egregious forms of sexual harassment."[36]

> "While blatant sexual harassment declined between 2016 and 2018, gender harassment (that is, workplace incivility and other forms of exclusionary behavior that did not rise to the level of sexual harassment) increased."

The pervasiveness of gender harassment was confirmed at the end of the same period by a 2019 Gallup survey that found that only 48 percent of American women believe that women are treated with respect and dignity, a shocking 14-point decline from 2017. Indeed, the United States received the lowest rating with respect to women's sense of being treated with dignity and respect among 21 countries surveyed by Gallop.[37] The United States also had the largest gap (22 percentage points) between the views of women and men about how women are treated. In the United States, 70 percent of men—but only 48 percent of women—think that women are treated with dignity and respect. In addition, 73 percent of American women report experiencing persistent exclusionary behavior.

> 73 percent of American Women report experiencing persistent exclusionary behavior.

We believe that the lack of progress in eliminating persistent exclusionary behavior is attributable to an unwarranted reliance on training designed to encourage employees to change their behaviors and attitudes. These programs merely address the symptoms of gender inequality and fail to confront the underlying causes of exclusionary treatment. PATH does not seek to change individuals' "hearts and minds" (a questionable exercise in our view). Instead, it focuses on the establishment of processes that render unacceptable these inappropriate behaviors. As a result, employees will be dissuaded from engaging in exclusionary behaviors, and processes will be implemented to interrupt inappropriate behaviors and prevent them from recurring.

A Workplace Behavioral Charter

The first step organizations need to take is create an inclusive workplace culture is to formulate a mutual agreement that all workplace participants will be subject to a mutual agreement in the form of a pact specifying unacceptable behaviors (PATH Charter). This agreement might be thought of as a code of unacceptable conduct, or what has been called "a team charter to establish norms and practices for communication etiquette."[38]

To be effective, the PATH Charter must be "owned" by all workplace participants; reflect their views of the types of behavior that need to be prohibited to feel psychologically safe; and involve clear commitments to support the prohibitions. Developing such a charter can be approached in a variety of ways across different geographical and functional territories.

- Senior management might prepare the first draft to submit to a broad, representative committee of executives, managers, and rank and file career professionals.
- The organization might bring in a consultant to work with management to produce the first draft.
- A working group that includes a diverse representation of participants could prepare the first draft.
- An organization-wide survey could be distributed on an anonymous basis.
- An open-ended suggestion portal can be established.

Whatever the process, everyone who is, ultimately, subject to the PATH Charter needs an opportunity to provide input and to have the ability to object, offer suggestions, and express approval or disapproval.

There are significant benefits when employees know that they have participated in defining the rules to which they will be expected to adhere. Moreover, employees need to explicitly agree that they will not engage in prohibited behavior and commit to interrupt prohibited behavior when they see it. Decision-makers should not shortchange the process of developing the PATH Charter. The more thoughtful and participatory this process is, the more effective it will be in preventing exclusionary behaviors.

> Within the PATH Charter, employees should collectively agree that they will not engage in prohibited behavior and commit to interrupt prohibited behavior when they see it.

The PATH Charter should be as specific as possible in identifying the types of conduct that make workplace participants feel unwelcome, disregarded, or demeaned. For example, a Charter might prohibit behaviors that:

- objectify women to potentially view them as less than fully human
- show disrespect for women through such things as interrupting and talking over them
- depreciate the value of women by assuming they are not as valuable as men
- downplay women's contributions by not giving them the comparable credit as men for their accomplishments
- exclude access to opportunities or resources by offering plum assignments to men and not including women in client and networking opportunities
- assert power over women
- intimidate women
- frighten women
- endanger women

Consider a simple, straightforward example of how a change in a workplace context can change the behavior of the people who work in it. Until recently, the Supreme Court allowed the justices to question lawyers during oral arguments on a free-for-all basis. Female justices were more frequently interrupted by their male colleagues than their male colleagues interrupted each other. According to Justice Sonia Sotomayor, these interruptions had a "great impact on the dynamic" of the Supreme Court.[39] Studies exposing this dynamic led Chief Justice John Roberts to become, in Justice Sotomayor's words, "much more sensitive to the issue." As a result, the Supreme Court established a new process for questioning: supplementing the free-for-all format with a period at the end of each lawyer's presentation when each justice—in order of seniority—has the chance to ask questions without interruption.[40] The Supreme Court's change to how justices can ask questions has led to a shift in the justices' individual behavior. This is precisely the type of change that organizations need to make in their process, practice, and policies. Such a change that prevents the women from being systematically disadvantaged has resulted in different individual behaviors. In Part III, we turn to how PATH's four elements work together to change both structural discrimination and individual discrimination.

In specifying unacceptable behaviors, the PATH Charter should carefully distinguish between *exclusionary behaviors* and *vigorous debate, disagreement, and dissent*. After all, debate, disagreement, and dissent are precisely the types of behavior that an inclusive workplace should seek to foster. While these types of behavior might cause discomfort and conflict, they are not exclusionary, but necessary. Debate, disagreement, and dissent do not disparage, demean, or belittle anyone. Thus, the PATH Charter's purpose is to prohibit exclusionary conduct, not to shield anyone from ideas, opinions, or points of view with which they might deeply disagree, even if they find them to be wrongheaded or deplorable. As long as this agreement or conflict occurs in an atmosphere of civility and respect, the fact that participants may feel uncomfortable does not signify exclusionary behavior. This distinction needs to be clearly articulated in the PATH Charter so that all workplace participants are able to adapt to it and to identify the difference between vigorous disagreement and exclusionary behavior.

In specifying unacceptable behaviors, the PATH Charter should carefully distinguish between *exclusionary behaviors* and *vigorous debate, disagreement, and dissent*. After all, debate, disagreement, and dissent are precisely the types of behavior that an inclusive workplace should seek to foster.

With adoption of the PATH Charter, an organization's management and its entire workforce will have taken a major step toward the elimination of workplace exclusionary behavior. When the norms, standards, and expectations of workplaces are made explicit, most participants will do their best to abide by them. There will still be situations, however, in which exclusionary behavior still occurs. Therefore, there must be a *process* by which such behavior is interrupted to prevent it from happening again.

Intervention and Interruption

When exclusionary behavior occurs, what should be done? Who should be responsible for intervening or interrupting it? As a starting point, the PATH Charter should explicitly state that maintaining an inclusive workplace is everyone's responsibility, and therefore all employees should be prepared to step in to challenge exclusionary behavior *to the extent they are comfortable doing so*. Unquestionably, there will be many situations in which particular employees will not feel comfortable interrupting or challenging exclusionary behavior. It is unrealistic to expect junior women to challenge the exclusionary behavior of powerful men. Likewise, employees may feel that challenging exclusionary behavior from managers poses a serious risk to their careers. And no one is likely to feel comfortable challenging exclusionary behavior on the part of senior leaders.

In addition, people who witness such behavior—bystanders— might be reluctant to interrupt exclusionary behavior for any number of professional or non-career-related reasons.[41] They might dislike confrontation; don't want to "stick their necks out"; believe someone else should deal with the behavior; not want to be bothered; fail to recognize the behavior as exclusionary or only recognize it as exclusionary after they reflect on the incident; or simply do not know what to do when they see it happen.

Therefore, organizational leaders face two distinct problems in ensuring that exclusionary behavior is effectively challenged, and that repetition is prevented. Leaders need to motivate employees to challenge exclusionary behavior even when they would prefer not to do so and, at the same time, they must protect individuals who fear career backlash if they do intervene. PATH deals with these problems in different ways. Let's consider first how best to overcome employees' general reluctance, and then discuss dealing with the risk of career backlash.

Overcoming Bystanders' Reluctance to Intervene

Employees are often reluctant to challenge exclusionary behavior simply because they don't want to have an unpleasant confrontation with another person. Organizational leaders can seek to overcome this reluctance in a variety of ways.

- Leaders can emphasize that effective team performance depends on the efficient acquisition, exchange, and examination of information. Such effective team performance is hindered by exclusionary behavior.[42] When employees come to see exclusionary behavior as a fundamental threat to their ability to carry out their essential functions, they are far more likely to interrupt that behavior when they observe it.
- When the value of workplace diversity is clearly understood, employees will be far more likely to step in to interrupt behavior that diminishes the value of that diversity.
- Thoughtless remarks, incivilities, and off-color jokes can often be effectively interrupted by the use of humor ("Are we really back

in the *Mad Men* era of the 1960s?"); changing the focus ("I think that comment has distracted us from our proper objective"); or by questioning the behavior ("I must not have heard you properly, could you repeat that?").

- Sometimes direct confrontation may be necessary to effectively interrupt exclusionary behavior. Very often, however, less confrontational, assertive, or accusatory techniques can be effective and much easier for reluctant employees to use. ("I don't think I understand what you meant. Can you say it again?").

- Employees need to be trained about the best ways to intervene. Some interventions are best done privately if public intervention is likely to have negative repercussions.

- Seeing others—both managers and colleagues—interrupt exclusionary behavior is often a powerful incentive for otherwise reluctant bystanders to also do the same.[43] When challenging exclusionary behavior is recognized as normal and expected conduct, employees are more willing to emulate such interventions. It is critical, in this regard, that managers and senior leaders actually challenge exclusionary behavior. They must conspicuously model behavior that disrupts exclusionary behavior.

Andie: One all too common example of exclusionary behavior is when a woman (let's call her Beth) makes a valid, interesting, or strategic point at a meeting yet the conversation continues as if she had not said a word. If her point is later restated by a man (let's call him Bill), he is likely to be praised for his insight and ingenuity. It is at this point that the meeting leader or another person should intervene to be sure the woman gets credit for her contribution. The intervenor can say something like, "Thanks, Bill, for restating Beth's point. I thought it was a good one too. Now, Beth, do you have anything more you would like to add?"

If employees are reluctant to directly challenge exclusionary behavior, they might be more likely to report that behavior to management. Therefore, decision-makers need to make it clear that reporting exclusionary behavior is a valuable contribution in strengthening, sustaining, and preserving an inclusive workplace culture. To encourage such reporting, many organizations provide confidential hotlines. Sometimes reaching out to the targeted individual to express support or solidarity can help support the ultimate elimination of exclusionary behavior.

A Team of Dedicated Interveners

The second problem organizations face in assuring that exclusionary behaviors are effectively challenged is the fear of career backlash on the part of employees who experience or witness this behavior. In such situations, if bystanders are willing to report it but not interrupt it—someone else must intervene with the offending party to make sure the behavior is not repeated. Organizations need to designate a group of senior executives who are specifically empowered to respond to reports of exclusionary behavior.[44]

> Organizations need to designate a group of senior executives who are specifically empowered to respond to reports of exclusionary behavior.

The first step is that there needs to be an established and easy-to-use mechanism for anyone—target or bystander—to report exclusionary behavior. This need not be a formal or bureaucratic process. The ability to report an incident to any manager or senior executive (in person or in writing) should be sufficient. Promptly, upon receipt of such a report, a member of the intervention team needs to act. This can be done in a variety of ways. After adoption of the PATH Charter, all that might be required is to make the offender aware of the negative impact of this behavior, that it is unacceptable under the PATH Charter, and the consequences if the behavior occurs again. In most cases, the intervener can focus on reform and "rehabilitation," not on "humiliation, shaming, or angry altercations."[45]

There may be situations, however, in which employees, particularly long-serving male managers, display a consistent pattern of purposeful exclusionary behavior. For example, it is not uncommon for such managers to shortchange women when it comes to assigning career-enhancing projects, leadership responsibilities, or including them in work-related social activities. If these employers cannot be "rehabilitated," we concur with Dr. Jamie Gloor and her colleagues when they write in the *Harvard Business Review* that such employees need to be promptly "moved, demoted, or even removed due to their lack of progress."[46]

PATH purposefully treats intervention as an informal process. In dealing with reported instances of exclusionary behavior that do not rise to the level of bullying, intimidation, or harassment, a determination of

"Miss Gaines, send in someone who reminds me of myself as a lad."

www.CartoonStock.com

"guilt" is not typically the objective. There may be serious infractions that require special treatment but, by and large, the intervention process is simply designed to prevent people from continuing to display unacceptable behavior.

> If these employers cannot be "rehabilitated," we concur with Dr. Jamie Gloor and her colleagues when they write in the *Harvard Business Review* that such employees need to be promptly "moved, demoted, or even removed due to their lack of progress."

Ambiguous Behavior

Whether behavior is, in fact, exclusionary is not always clear. For example, not all types of sexual interest constitute sexual harassment. As Kim Elsesser points out in her book *Sex in the Office: Women, Men, and the Sex Partition That's Dividing the Workplace,* it can be difficult to know when sexual interest is objectionable. As she writes, "Because sexual attraction may often play a role in day-to-day social exchange between employees, the distinction between invited, uninvited-but-welcome, offensive-but-tolerated, and flatly rejected sexual advances may well be difficult to discern."[47] However, behavior that *appears* to a bystander to be unwelcome should be treated as unacceptable. It may not always be possible to distinguish flirting from leering, testing the waters from unwanted attention, and genuine affection from an assertion of power. Nevertheless, interruption or intervention is appropriate whenever workplace decorum is disrupted, there appears to be a loss of psychological or physical safety, or there is a negative effect on team cohesiveness and collaboration. If there is any uncertainty, managers should always step in. Better that unwelcome behavior is stopped than to be concerned that a budding office romance might be identified.

Serious Exclusionary Behavior

Bullying, intentional humiliation, and sexual harassment can be far too serious to be dealt with on an *ad hoc* basis. Sexual assault is a crime and needs to be treated as such. Although we will limit our following discussion to sexual harassment, the recommendations we make are equally applicable to other forms of serious exclusionary behavior.

When sexual harassment is reported, organizations need a compassionate, effective, and timely process to help deal with it. Unfortunately, many organizations' existing processes are ineffective. They are overly bureaucratic, expose the accuser to embarrassment, and create a serious risk of retaliation.[48] The formalities and personal exposure of most processes for dealing with sexual harassment allegations can deter most women from using them. Not surprisingly, therefore, only about 10 percent of women who have been sexually harassed make a formal complaint.[49]

PATH represents a significant departure from such highly formalized reporting processes. As a starting point, PATH recommends against a zero-tolerance policy with respect to sexual harassment because it offers organizations and targets too little flexibility. In contrast, PATH suggests a range of methodologies and possible outcomes be made available to the person who may have been harassed. The guiding principle turns on the wishes of that person. She should be able to report the behavior informally to any manager or executive with whom she feels comfortable discussing the situation or by calling a confidential hotline. She should be free to indicate her desired method of how to proceed and the preferred outcome. For example, many women who have experienced sexual harassment simply want the harassment to stop. Therefore, in some situations, managers may be able to go directly to the offending person and say: "Cut it out." In many situations, this is all it takes to prevent future incidents. Even if the alleged offender pushes back against the allegation, the manager may still be able to resolve the matter to the reporting party's satisfaction by establishing ground rules for any future professional or personal contact. Perhaps the manager can structure workplace locations or responsibilities so that the parties come in contact with each other less frequently, if at all. It is important to note, however, that any such arrangement must not operate to the career disadvantage of the target.

A woman reporting sexual harassment might request that no action be taken unless other people complain or the behavior occurs again. Another possibility is that the target could request that the manager simply monitor the situation, observe the offending party's behavior, and seek to determine if other people are having similar problems with the offending party.

Thus, under PATH, an organization's complaint/resolution process should put the reporting party in full control with respect to whom to report the harassment, what will then happen, and the outcome that the reporting party prefers. If the reporting party doesn't want the alleged offender to know about the report, that's okay—the manager should be able to consult with the target on a confidential basis and help her think through the options.

Not all managers will be sufficiently knowledgeable and capable of effectively dealing with reports of sexual harassment. Therefore, organizations must have well-trained senior executives to whom managers can turn to handle any reports of harassment. These senior executives should be both knowledgeable about and confident in dealing with sexual harassment. Knowledge can be especially important in situations where a person is already traumatized because of current or prior abuse outside of the workplace.

Therefore, these senior executives should not be bound by formal rules of evidence, have no obligation to make any disclosure of the offense (unless the offense rises to the level of criminal activity), or be required to bring about a face-to-face confrontation.[50] Should a person who is alleged to have engaged in sexual harassment dispute the allegation, the matter can often still be resolved without a formal proceeding.

Of course, a reporting person should be able to request a formal investigation and proceed openly against an alleged offender. When this happens, management must take the lead, not leaving the target to carry the burden of the proceeding. Management must treat allegations of sexual harassment as serious breaches of the victim's psychological or physical safety. It is crucial, therefore, that an investigation be conducted with sensitivity to the reporting person's privacy, psychological vulnerability, and freedom from undue notoriety. Further, management must be vigilant in ensuring that no person reporting sexual harassment behavior is subjected to retaliation of any sort.

If the perpetrator has engaged in egregious sorts of behavior, he or she should not be allowed to remain in the workplace. If a perpetrator's behavior does not rise to this level, less serious kinds of internal discipline might be appropriate, such as a leave of absence or a demotion. Punishment is a matter of judgment, but leaders must keep foremost in mind that their ultimate objective is to put an end to all exclusionary behavior without adverse consequences to the reporting person.

KEY TAKEAWAYS

- The first step in PATH is to *prioritize* elimination of exclusionary behavior.
- The primary focus at the beginning of the PATH Program is to ensure that workplace culture condemns exclusionary behaviors and that a company's employees are prepared and motivated to interrupt such behaviors when they see them.
- Women encounter exclusionary behavior in their workplaces far more often than do men.
- Exclusionary behavior is a reflection of individual discrimination (particularly out-group bias) and is a major reason why women often find their workplace experiences more unpleasant, distasteful, and unsatisfying than do men.
- Organizations tend to view the problem of exclusionary behavior as an issue caused by the thoughtless or biased behavior on the part of a limited number of people. They try to deal with it through education and training. This does not work.

- The most effective way to end workplace harassment and diminish exclusionary behaviors against women is to address the causes, not the symptoms, and by building inclusive workplace cultures.
- A workplace culture is inclusive where employees of all social identities, backgrounds, and perspectives feel comfortable to candidly interact with one another without fear of personal criticism, purposeful embarrassment, denial of resources, or loss of status.
- To create an inclusive workplace culture, organizations need to adopt an explicit policy against exclusionary behavior; motivate employees to interrupt exclusionary behavior; and specify an effective process for reporting and punishing this conduct when it occurs.
- We recognize that, in many situations, exclusionary behavior will be tricky to address. To deal with such situations, organizations should designate senior people with well-recognized and extensive authority to whom people can report exclusionary behavior. The people with this authority should view their objective as preventing such behavior while dealing with perpetrators without humiliation, shaming, or angry altercations.
- Sexual and physical assaults are criminal and should be reported to appropriate authorities.
- Organizations can only end exclusionary behaviors when everyone in the organization shares the goal and is equipped with techniques to interrupt and challenge such behaviors so that workplaces are inclusive and more comfortable for everyone.

Chapter 9

Adopt Discrimination-Resistant Methods of Personnel Decision-Making

WORKPLACE GENDER INEQUALITY IS MOST evident in the results of formal personnel decision-making. Compared to equally well-qualified women, men are more readily hired, paid more for the same work, and promoted to leadership roles in greater numbers. In this chapter, we turn to the methods that organizations need to adopt to ensure their personnel decision-making is resistant to the influences of gender stereotypes, status beliefs, and individual biases.

As we saw in Chapter 2, gendered workplaces operate in a manner consistent with gender stereotypes and their associated status beliefs. As a result, personnel decision-making reflects a predictable and consistent pattern of structural discrimination favoring men over women with respect to compensation, leadership development, membership on high-status teams, and career-advancing assignments.

When personnel decisions are made by individuals in a context of structural discrimination, there are no effective checks on their individual biases. There is thus in gendered workplaces a mutually reinforcing relationship between structural discrimination and individual discrimination.[1]

www.CartoonStock.com

The key to ensuring personnel decisions are fair is for organizations to require that personnel decisions are made in ways that resist discrimination.[2] This means that decision-making methods must consistently operate without consideration of gender-specific characteristics, qualities, and behaviors that are irrelevant in the nature of the position under consideration.

The Route to Discrimination-Resistant Decision-Making

PATH identifies seven approaches that organizations can use to ensure that decision-making is fair, objective, and defensible.

1. "Screen" the social identities of the candidates.
2. Ensure decision-makers adhere to specified objective evaluation criteria.

3. Nudge decision-makers to use "slow thinking" in making personnel decisions.
4. Remove gender-relevant discretion, when possible.
5. Separate personnel evaluations from personnel decisions.
6. Appoint diverse teams of decision-makers.
7. Monitor and assess decision-making patterns.

Let's look at each of these approaches and examine the most effective ways to implement them.

1. "Screen" Social Identity

Perhaps the simplest change that organizations can make with regard to personnel decision-making is to "screen" the decision-makers from information that they should not be considering. This can be accomplished by removing all indications of and references to the candidates'

"I see by your résumé that you're a woman."

www.CartoonStock.com

social identities—their gender, race, ethnicity, parental status, age, education, socioeconomic position, sexual orientation, religion, and so on.

The best-known example of such a screening process is the practice of many of America's major symphony orchestras conducting auditions from behind screens (sometimes referred to as "blind auditions"). This simple change substantially increased the gender diversity of these orchestras. In the 1963 season, for example, the Chicago Symphony Orchestra had only three women among its 101 musicians, while the New York Philharmonic had none.[3] Today, after widespread adoption of this screening practice, the participation of women in major symphony orchestras stands at about 36 percent.[4]

Despite some skepticism as to whether screened auditions were responsible for increasing women's participation in symphony orchestras,[5] the technique appears highly effective in assuring that discriminatory factors do not influence hiring decisions. One study found that, depending on the industry, women were 25 to 46 percent more likely to be hired when their gender was not known.[6] Another study found that when résumés included applicants' social identities, only about 20 percent of non-white, non-male, and non-able-bodied applicants made it to the first-round interview. When the application materials were stripped of all information about the applicants' social identities, however, 60 percent of these applicants made it to a first-round interview.[7]

In certain contexts, simple screening is not sufficient to overcome gender bias. One study conducted by researchers at the National Bureau of Economic Research (NBER) considered extensive written proposals for research grants. These researchers found that men's proposals were far more likely to be accepted than women's, even though the proposals had been screened to eliminate explicit references to gender. The researchers found that the unequal gender results were due to the ways in which women and men write their proposals. Women "use fewer of the words favored by reviewers" and more words that the reviewers associated with lower scores. Women had a tendency to choose more "narrow" topic-specific words and fewer "broad" words. Reviewers picked up on these linguistic differences, favoring men's applications over those submitted by women. Interestingly, once the researchers controlled "for the impact of word choice, the gender-based score disparity [was] no longer significant."[8]

This NBER finding is consistent with our discussion in *Breaking Through Bias* on recommendation letters for men often being more influential than those for women because of language differences used in praising the applicant's characteristics. Women are more often described with communal traits ("helpful, kind, sympathetic, nurturing, tactful, agreeable, warm, and willing to help others"), while men are described with agentic traits ("assertive, ambitious, confident, daring, forceful, outspoken, independent, and intellectual").[9] Inevitably, based simply on their recommendation letters men were viewed as more qualified than the women.[10]

Although it is important to recognize that clues to gender can be picked up in extensive written proposals and recommendation letters or when these materials are screened for explicit indications of social identity, screening is highly effective in reducing gender-biased personnel decision-making[11] and in increasing the fairness of those decisions.[12]

> Screening is highly effective in reducing gender-biased personnel decision-making and in increasing the fairness of those decisions.

Screening with Software

Software products are now available for rapidly screening decision-makers from candidates' social identities. Products such as Applied,[13] GapJumpers,[14] and Unitive[15] (to name only a few) help organizations eliminate demographic characteristics from the materials referenced at various stages of personnel decision-making. To date, these solutions have been applied primarily during recruiting, but they hold the promise of being of wider value.[16] A caveat is appropriate, however, about these technologies. Organizations must be sure that any software they employ in connection with their personnel decision-making does not have discriminatory biases already built into them, and that the software is not likely to develop such biases through repeated use.[17]

Shockingly, the Berkeley-Haas Center for Equity, Gender, and Leadership found that 44 percent of the artificial intelligence (AI) programs that organizations were relying on to make personnel decisions had gender-biased considerations embedded in them.[18] Therefore, organizations must monitor the results produced by these technologies just as carefully as they monitor the results of their legacy personnel decision-making frameworks.

"Don wrote our hiring algorithm."

www.CartoonStock.com

Screening Personnel Decisions Beyond Hiring

Although the initial stages of the hiring process are the most obvious place where screening candidates' social identities can reduce discriminatory influences, the technique has value in many other areas as well. For example, when organizations make compensation and promotion decisions solely on the basis of written materials, there is no downside in stripping demographic information from the written materials. Colleges and professional schools have been doing this for a long time—for instance, by identifying test-takers' examinations by number, not name. Indeed, decision-makers should be able to identify a great many situations in which screening social identity is possible without any loss of quality or effectiveness. Even when a final decision cannot (and should not) be made anonymously, it may still be valuable to screen decision-makers from knowing candidates' identities during the preliminary steps in the process. The important point is that when anonymity will not adversely affect the quality or effectiveness of decision-making, it should become routine practice.

2. Specify Objective Evaluation Criteria

When personnel decisions are made on the basis of clear, specific, and objective criteria, those decisions are largely protected from discriminatory influences. Personnel decisions made on the basis of vague, ambiguous, or subjective criteria allow gender stereotypes, status beliefs, and individual biases to influence the decisions.

> Personnel decisions made on the basis of vague, ambiguous, or subjective criteria allow gender stereotypes, status beliefs, and individual biases to influence the decisions.

Professor Shelley Correll and her fellow researchers observe that when evaluation criteria are not specific, or do not require evidence of actual behavior or accomplishments, evaluators are forced to engage in "a sense-making process in which widely shared gender beliefs subtly frame their observations, interpretations, and valuation of employee behavior."[19] In other words, when evaluators can assess employees' performance without the need to present evidence-grounded observations, they are likely to view the same performance differently, depending on whether it involved a woman or a man.

The extent to which the nature of decision-making criteria can affect personnel decision-making is well illustrated by a 2017 study of 30,000 management-track employees at a large retail chain. The women in this group of employees consistently received higher ratings than did the men concerning specific aspects of their job *performance* (objective criteria). The women, however, consistently received lower ratings when rated on their *potential* (subjective criteria). Almost half of the gender promotion gap at this company was found to be due to women receiving lower ratings for potential, despite having received higher ratings for performance.[20]

> The women consistently received higher ratings than the men concerning specific aspects of their job *performance* (objective criteria). The women, however, consistently received lower ratings when rated on their *potential* (subjective criteria. Almost half of the gender promotion gap at this company was found to be due to women receiving lower ratings for potential, despite having received higher ratings for performance.
> —2017 study of 30,000 management-track employees

As important as it is for organizations to strive to ensure personnel decision-making criteria are specific, objective, and require evidentiary support, they also should make every effort that these criteria do not trigger gender stereotypes and status beliefs. For example, a 2020 field study of the evaluations of employees at a Fortune 500 company[21] asked evaluators to assess employees in terms of "helpfulness" and "willingness to take charge." Women were consistently rated more helpful, but that had no influence on their compensation or likelihood of promotion. This was because *helpfulness* is a feminine stereotyped characteristic that is not associated with leadership.

Being seen as helpful, therefore, did nothing to advance the women's careers. On the other hand, when evaluators were asked how likely it was that employees would behave in a "take charge" manner, women and men received equal ratings. But because *taking charge* is a masculine stereotyped characteristic, women's rating in this regard had no impact on their compensation and promotion. We call this the *Goldilocks Dilemma*.[22] Being judged as *helpful* did nothing to advance women's careers because it is not a leadership characteristic, but being judged as willing to *take charge* also did nothing to advance women's careers because it is a characteristic that women are *not supposed to display*. Therefore, when they did, they were viewed as unpleasant, unlikable, and unlikely to be effective leaders.

Formulation of Objective Criteria

The criteria used to make personnel decisions will vary across organizations and among types of decisions. There are, however, four relatively straightforward principles that all organizations should use in formulating the criteria used in their personnel decisions.

1. Criteria should involve objectively determinable characteristics, skills, and accomplishments. When this is the case, concrete examples of conduct consistent with the criteria can be required. For example, to better analyze an individual's people management skills, objective criteria might include:

   - Sets clear expectations for work teams
   - Provides an inclusive environment

- Offers opportunities for employees to grow and develop their careers
- Gives clear, specific, and timely performance feedback
- Recruits, mentors, and retains talented diverse employees
- Effectively delegates projects
- Rewards superior performance[23]

2. Criteria should not call for open-ended commentary on a candidate's personal characteristics or the evaluator's personal preferences. The criteria should be tied to objective items of performance. Criteria should not allow for evaluators to be able to rely on stereotypes and biases to evaluate candidates ("he's a go-getter," "she's aggressive"; "he's busy," "she has trouble with deadlines").

3. Criteria should set out objective ways to assess characteristics that might otherwise be seen as subjective. For example, rather than asking evaluators to rate a candidate's *fit*, they might instead ask about the candidates' support for a sense of community. The criteria for this characteristic might include

- Fosters a positive working and learning environment by ensuring accountability for fairness, cooperation, civility, and professionalism among team members
- Practices and integrates these basic principles of accountability in all interactions.[24]

Likewise, rather than asking about a candidate's *potential*, an evaluator might ask about a candidate's ability to create and rally support for an objective or vision:

- Takes a long-term view of business prospects and objectives
- Builds a shared vision with others
- Ensures that the shared vision is well communicated and understood at all levels of the organization
- Acts as a catalyst for organizational change
- Influences others to translate ideas into action[25]

"What makes you think you'll
fit in here?"

www.CartoonStock.com

4. Criteria upon which personnel decisions are reached should not
involve the use of words that have strong gender associations.
When looking to fill a manager position, for example, it would
be a mistake for an organization to specify that the ideal candidate should be *independent, decisive, logical,* and *forceful.* These
words immediately predispose decision-makers to favor male
candidates. Just as organizations should ensure that job postings are not phrased in gender-stereotyped ways,[26] they should
also formulate the criteria for personnel decisions so they do not
carry obvious stereotypical implications.

Numerical Ratings

To ensure that all candidates are evaluated further on an apples to apples
basis, they should each be given a numerical score for each of the relevant
criterion. Each criterion, in turn, should be given a specified weight in the
final decision. In a technology company, for example, computer coding skill

*"Yes, I use a weighted appraisal
system. Why?"*

Copyright Grantland Enterprises; www.grantland.net

is likely to be more heavily weighted than research skills. In a law firm, the weighting is likely to be the reverse.

When each candidate has been given a numerical rating for each criterion and final scores are determined based on the weights of the criteria, it should be relatively easy for decision-makers to assess the candidates on an apples to apples basis. Of course, there is still the need for the use of subjective discretion in making the final decision—candidates' relative strengths and weaknesses, talents and deficiencies, and experiences, all need to be balanced. In addition, different decision-makers might reach different conclusions after that assessment process. With this stated, when numerical ratings are applied to specified criteria, the final decision is far less likely to be influenced by discriminatory factors than it would have been otherwise.

Skepticism about the Value of Objective
Criteria and Numerical Ratings

Of course, if decision-makers choose to "game the system," they can undermine the value of objective criteria. For example, decision-makers could simply rate favored male candidates more highly on specified criteria than equally qualified female candidates; or, *vice versa*. Because of this possibility, in their book *Getting to Diversity: What Works and What Doesn't*,[27] Frank Dobbin and Alexandra Kalev express serious doubts that objective criteria and numerical ratings lead to fairer personnel decisions. They argue that if organizations were able to use only quantifiable, objective criteria, such as, "the number of laptops assembled or couches sold," they would, indeed, be able to make fairer personnel decisions. But because it is hard to eliminate the possibility of any subjective discretion, decision-makers almost always have "a chance to tip the scale, opening the door to discrimination." Decision-makers also can "build a file" indicating poor performance on the part of disfavored employees while ignoring similar failings of favored employees. Finally, Dobbin and Kalev argue that the existence of supposedly objective criteria often prompts organizational leaders to dismiss allegations of gender inequality because they believe that their objective standards make such inequality impossible. For all of these reasons, Dobbin and Kalev conclude that specifying objective performance evaluation systems do not improve gender diversity.[28]

Dobbin and Kalev undoubtedly raise legitimate concerns. We believe, however, that they are too quick to dismiss the value of objective criteria and numerical ratings. While there is a movement away from numerical ratings in the context of personnel performance reviews,[29] objective criteria and numerical ratings remain an important way to reduce discriminatory outcomes in connection with personnel decisions. Therefore, as part of PATH, we recommend that organizational leaders take three steps to assure that decision-makers cannot "game the system" by merely appearing to adhere to objective decision-making criteria:

- **Inclusivity**: By assuring their workplaces are free of exclusionary behavior, decision-makers have positive incentives *not* to favor one group of people over another.
- **Multiplicity**: When people are being considered for hire or promotion, their candidacy should be reviewed by three or more

decision-makers. By taking such steps, the likelihood that the decision-makers will not deal straight with objective criteria is substantially reduced.

- **Review**: When personnel decisions are reviewed by someone who is not involved in the initial process and who is specifically charged with monitoring career-affecting decisions, initial decision-makers have a strong incentive to actively "play by the rules."

With respect to this last step, as Dobbin and Kalev point out, the appointment of a full-time diversity manager—someone charged with such a review responsibility—significantly increases the number of management jobs held by women.[30]

3. Slow Thinking

Nudging decision-makers to make personnel decisions using what Nobel Prize–winning psychologist Daniel Kahneman calls "slow thinking"[31] is a highly effective way to insulate those decisions from discriminatory influences. As Kahneman points out, people think in two quite different ways: they *think fast* and they *think slow*.

- *Fast thinking* is automatic and effortless, and it occurs without conscious awareness.
- *Slow thinking* is careful, deliberative, and grounded in facts.

Fast thinking is based on experience, preconceptions, instincts, and feelings. We think fast most of the time, allowing ourselves to be guided by our instincts, inclinations, preferences, and beliefs. We are generally confident that our fast thinking will result in appropriate and correct conclusions. Indeed, if we didn't think fast most of the time, we wouldn't be able to get our work done, attend to our daily obligations, or perform well at a whole host of necessary activities.

- *Fast thinking* is automatic and effortless, and occurs without conscious awareness.
- *Slow thinking* is careful, deliberative, and grounded in facts.

The problem with fast thinking, however, is that it is likely to cause us to make systematic errors about the people we like and dislike, of whom we approve and disapprove, with whom we have a sense of comfort and discomfort, and whose traits are familiar and unfamiliar. Indeed, thinking fast when making personnel decisions results in those decisions being highly susceptible to the influence of gender stereotypes, status beliefs, and the four fundamental biases.[32] It doesn't matter that decision-makers sincerely believe they are the least biased, most merit-oriented people in the world. If they think fast when making personnel decisions, those decisions are likely to be influenced by bias. Without any conscious awareness, decision-makers are likely to assign responsibilities to men rather than comparably qualified

"BASED ON YOUR RESUME YOU'RE NOT REALLY
QUALIFIED FOR THE JOB...BUT THERE'S JUST
SOMETHING ABOUT YOU I LIKE!"

www.CartoonStock.com

women; evaluate men's performance more positively than women's objectively similar performance; and prefer to have men rather than women in their work-related networks and social activities. *Fast thinking is the enemy of fair, objective, and fact-based personnel decision-making.*

Under PATH, we recommend that organizations use a variety of techniques to *interrupt* decision-makers' inclination to think fast when making personnel decisions. This can be done by structuring the decision-making context so that decision-makers are nudged toward slow thinking. As Kahneman points out, the voice of our reflective self is "much fainter than the loud clear voice of an erroneous intuition."[33] Therefore, the decision-making context for personnel decisions should be designed to amplify that faint voice of reason. Let's look at three such contexts.

> ...the decision-making context for personnel decisions should be designed to amplify that faint voice of reason.

Collaborative Decision-Making

When two or more people must collaborate to reach a conclusion about a personnel matter, they typically feel obligated to explain to one another the reasons they want to make their decisions the way they do. There is, thus, a back-and-forth dialogue in evaluating alternative outcomes, based on consideration of alternative assumptions, observations, and anticipated outcomes.

People engaged in collaborative decision-making are, in a sense, being held to account. Naturally, they want to be seen as having *good reasons* for why they want to decide a matter in the way they do. Therefore, a reflective, interactive decision-making process is the very essence of slow thinking. It nudges decision-makers to think about their preferred outcome, to carefully formulate their rationale for it, and to contemplate alternative positions. As a result, collaborative personnel decision-making is not likely to be influenced by gender stereotypes, status beliefs, or individual biases.

Comparative Decision-Making

Organizations can encourage slow thinking by requiring that certain types of personnel decisions be made on a comparative basis. When it is, decision-makers must balance the evaluations that multiple candidates have received on the specified criteria—*and* then explain in writing why they have selected the particular candidate they have. It is often hard work to decide among candidates who are all well qualified but in different ways; and, then, to justify the final decision. Such comparative decision-making depends on slow thinking—weighing candidates' different strengths against one another, evaluating the importance of different characteristics in relation to the positions to be filled, and balancing the candidates' positive and negative qualities.

Third-Party Review

Regardless of the process by which personnel decisions are made, if decision-makers know their reasons for making a decision will be reviewed by a third party, they are likely to work hard to come up with good reasons to justify making the decision they do. Third-party review of personnel decisions is, therefore, a powerful incentive for decision-makers to use slow thinking in making personnel decisions.

4. Remove Discretion When Advantageous

A fourth way of reducing the possibility of discriminatory factors influencing career-critical personnel decisions is to eliminate discretion, when this can be done without adversely affecting organizational effectiveness, efficiency, or productivity. Anthony Greenwald, the developer of the well-known Implicit Association Test (IAT), points out that when people make subjective judgments about other people, their judgments are "likely to result in unintended disparities" but to the extent discretion can be eliminated, these "judgments are much less likely to produce disparities."[34]

Examples of how organizations might eliminate discretion include stipulating that all teams must have, say, at least 30 percent women, or that all promotion opportunities must be prominently posted for some time period before they are filled or to require that all employees at specified stages of their careers be assigned to specified types of projects and evaluated in terms of their performance on those projects and responsibilities.

Andie: At my former law firm several years ago, we found that women and diverse lawyers were not getting the same hands-on training as the men. As a result, when it came time for setting compensation or making promotion decisions, men were moving ahead of everyone else. To address this problem, we had our practice groups and departments prepare a checklist of the sorts of projects that were suitable for first-year attorneys, second-year attorneys, and so on for each of their following years of law practice. Each practice group committed to provide these career stepping-stone projects to all of the attorneys in their groups during the designated periods. An attorney could no longer be denied necessary training or the chance to work on projects commensurate with the number of years they had been out of law school. This solved the problem of mid-level associate attorneys—particularly women—from being found to lack the experiences they needed to advance in their careers. Of course, attorneys were still candidly evaluated on how they handled those experiences, but we were able to ensure that they got access to appropriate projects for their tenure.

Reducing discretion can be tricky, however, because it reduces the scope of decision-makers' authority, their ability to decide for themselves how to attain the goals they are assigned to achieve.[35] If decision-makers are resentful of changes to the parameters of their authority, there can be a backlash.

Therefore, organizations need to strike a balance between limiting decision-makers' discretion and preserving their autonomy. For example, our hypothetical requirement that *teams must include 30 percent women* takes away decision-maker discretion with respect to the gender composition of their teams, but it *does not change* their ability to select the individuals who would serve on their teams. Similarly, a policy that limits managers' ability to assign specific types of projects to whomever they choose *would not limit* their discretion with respect to the specific projects going to specific women employees. The important point here is that limitations on discretion must be balanced alongside the need to preserve decision-makers sense of autonomy.

The Rooney Rule

An increasingly popular way to limit discretion is to specify the demographic characteristics of a pool of candidates before a particular personnel decision is made about those candidates. This approach is generally regarded as an application of the so-called "Rooney Rule," adopted by the National Football League (NFL) in 2003[36] and amended in 2020. Named after Dan Rooney, the former owner of the Pittsburgh Steelers, it provides that professional football teams must consider at least two external minority candidates when filling the head coaching job, and at least one external minority candidate for coordinator and senior operational or general manager positions.[37] The Rooney Rule does not require NFL teams to hire minority candidates; it just obligates them to consider such candidates before making their decisions.

Unfortunately, despite what appears to have been the best of intentions, the Rooney Rule has done nothing to significantly diversify NFL coaching staffs. In 2003, the year the NFL adopted the Rooney Rule, there were three Black head coaches; 20 years later at the start of the 2022 to 2023 season, there were still three Black head coaches.[38]

Eliminating discretion in the composition of a candidate pool will do nothing to end discriminatory decision-making if ultimate discretion remains unfettered—which is precisely the case of the NFL, where leadership is free to pick whomever they want to coach their teams. An increasing number of public companies have followed the NFL and adopted variations of the Rooney Rule; unfortunately, with no more positive effect than has been achieved in the NFL.[39]

It's clear, therefore, that reducing discretion simply by requiring that some limited number of "diverse candidates" be included in relevant candidate pools is not going to lead to less discriminatory personnel decisions. Therefore, organizations are urged to create a gender-diverse candidate rule based around the principles of the Rooney Rule; but they should also add two important adjuncts:

1. A process should be put in place to assure that the manner in which the ultimate personnel decision is made is unlikely to be subject to the influence of discriminatory factors. This might be third-party review or mandatory collaborative decision-making. But whatever technique is used, *it must function as an effective restraint on decision-makers' subjective discretion.*

2. The number of women in any candidate pool must be significant. According to Alina Polonskaia, global head of Korn Ferry's DEI practice, a candidate pool must consist of at least 30 percent women to make a meaningful impact on reducing gender inequality.[40] This percentage is supported by an important research study that found that in a candidate pool of four, if there is only one woman, she stands no statistical chance of being hired, but if there are at least two women in the pool, the chance that a woman will be selected increases by 70 percent.[41]

> A candidate pool must consist of at least 30 percent women to make a meaningful impact on reducing gender inequality.

Taken together, the Rooney Rule—plus limitations on the subjective discretion of decision-makers and having a critical mass of women in candidate pool is an effective way of assuring personnel decisions are made in fair, objective, and evidence-based ways.

5. Separate Personnel Evaluations from Personnel Decisions

Organizations can also reduce the influence of gender stereotypes, status beliefs, and individual biases by separating the personnel evaluation process from the personnel decision-making process. At Google, for example, interviewing is done by diverse teams of employees drawn from around the company; and, then, these teams submit detailed written reports of their evaluations of the candidate's qualifications to Google's hiring committee. It is the hiring committee that then makes final hiring decisions. In this way, the subjective preferences, first impressions, and unconscious biases of the interviewers cannot influence ultimate personnel decisions.[42]

Separating the evaluation process from decision-making is a highly effective technique to reduce the influence of discriminatory factors on personnel decisions. The technique can be used with respect to a wide variety of personnel matters beyond hiring. For example, when compensation and promotion decisions are made on the basis of written materials, the decision-making process is likely to be free of discriminatory factors *if* the written evaluations the decision-makers have to work with are thoughtful, objective, and limited to relevant and specified criteria. This is likely to be the case when evaluators know that their decisions will be scrutinized by another person or group making the final decision, *and* the evaluation materials are stripped of demographic information.

We recognize that some organizational leaders might strongly resist separating personnel evaluations from the decision-making process. Objections might include concerns that there are difficult-to-capture-in-writing qualities that can only be addressed if personnel decisions are made by the reviewers who had opportunities to directly interact with the candidates. If organizations choose not to separate evaluations from decision-making, it becomes all the more important that they use the other techniques—screening, slow thinking, adherence to explicit job criteria, and reducing discretion—to prevent discrimination from influencing career-affecting personnel decisions.

6. Appoint Diverse Teams of Decision-Makers

As we have seen, organizations with diverse and inclusive leadership teams are more innovative, better able to reach solutions to complex problems, and are more effective in dealing with unanticipated situations than are homogeneous leadership teams.[43] Likewise, decision-makers are more likely to make fairer and more objective personnel decisions when the teams or groups that make them are diverse. Diverse and inclusive teams are more likely to reach decisions that are free of the influence of gender stereotypes, status beliefs, and individual discrimination. They are also less likely to fall victim to groupthink.[44] Therefore, senior leaders should make every effort to ensure that the teams charged with making personnel decisions include comparable numbers of women and men.

7. Independently Monitor and Assess Decision-Making Patterns

Regardless of the techniques or processes that organizations choose to adopt in ensuring the fairness, objectivity, and evidence-based nature of their personnel decision-making, they need to monitor the results of this decision-making.[45]

> Regardless of the techniques or processes that organizations choose to adopt in ensuring the fairness, objectivity, and evidence-based nature of their personnel decision-making, they need to monitor the results of this decision-making.

Therefore, with respect to all career-critical personnel decisions, organizations need to accurately track:

- the characteristics of the candidates considered,
- the ratings that these candidates received, and
- the characteristics of those selected or highly rewarded.

Organizations can then decide how candidates in different social identity groups fare in the evaluation and selection processes. This information is important because it allows senior leaders to know whether their personnel decision-making is functioning as it should. Under PATH, organizations are not expected to use this information to "manage" personnel decisions—rewarding managers who meet specified gender goals while penalizing managers who don't. Managers should be focused on their fundamental jobs—driving company performance; recruiting; developing and retaining superior talent; boosting the performance of individuals and teams; and collaborating effectively with colleagues. Requiring managers to achieve specified numerical diversity goals would only distract them from this focus.

Nevertheless, organizations should closely monitor the outcomes of their decision-makers' personnel decisions so that they are able to assess any discriminatory patterns within such decisions.

For example, recent research found that 30 to 50 percent of the promotion differential in the data studied was caused by white men being advanced based on their assumed potential, but that everyone else had to prove themselves over and over.[46] By monitoring decision-makers' personnel decisions, senior leaders should be able to spot this sort of pattern and specifically target efforts to eliminate the resulting discrimination.

> ...recent research found that 30 to 50 percent of the promotion differential in the data studied was caused by white men being advanced based on their assumed potential, but that everyone else had to prove themselves over and over.

PATH and Discrimination-Resistant Decision-Making

Personnel decision-making is the most obvious source of women's and men's unequal career outcomes. The discrimination women face in hiring, advancement opportunities, compensation, and promotion are apparent and well established.[47] The seven approaches we have recommended as part of PATH are all effective, practical, and easily administered. Some are more likely to fit at particular organizations than at others. Organizations are not expected to adopt all of these techniques for all personnel decisions, but every organization should make some of them or a combination of them where appropriate. Ending workplace gender inequality depends on organizations making personnel decisions in ways that significantly reduce the possibility that discriminatory factors will affect those decisions. As we have said before, this does not require organization's leaders to radically change the ways in which they operate. It does, however, require decision-making processes to be modified so that historic staffing patterns, established ways of assigning responsibilities, and discretionary control over advancement cannot significantly influence career-affecting personnel decisions.

KEY TAKEAWAYS

- The second step in PATH is to *adopt* methods of making personnel decisions that are fair and free of bias.
- Many powerful factors contribute to workplace gender inequality, but one of the most apparent sources is found in how personnel decisions are made: hiring, assignment of projects and responsibilities, timing and frequency of promotions, and compensation.
- If decision-makers continue to go with their guts when deciding matters of career-affecting significance for their direct reports, we will never eliminate workplace gender inequality.

- We recommend seven ways for companies to confront personnel decisions that perpetuate gender inequality:

  1. Screen the social identities of the individuals who are being reviewed within a personnel decision-making process.
  2. Specify the criteria on which decision-makers are required to make personnel decisions.
  3. Nudge decision-makers to make personnel decisions using "slow thinking."
  4. Remove managers' discretion from those aspects of personnel decisions where this can be done without diminishing the effective, productive, or innovative operation of the workplace.
  5. Separate the evaluation of personnel from the decisions to be made about their advancement.
  6. Ensure that groups making personnel decisions are composed of diverse individuals.
  7. Monitor the patterns that appear within and among evaluators' personnel decisions for the potential of gender bias.

- Carefully measure organization-wide progress toward gender-equal personnel decision-making by accurately tracking the social identities of the individual being considered when personnel decisions are made, as well as the favorable and unfavorable outcomes of those decisions.
- It is valuable to have inclusive and diverse teams charged with personnel decisions because diverse workplaces work better when driving innovation, resisting groupthink, and reaching better solutions to complex problems.

Chapter 10

Treat Inequality in the Home as a Workplace Problem

DEI EFFORTS TEND TO FOCUS exclusively on workplace practices and behaviors that inhibit diversity and inclusiveness in the workplace. As a result, organizations typically ignore the discriminatory impact that inequalities in the home can have on women's workplace experiences and career outcomes.[1] This is a serious oversight, because inequality in homelife responsibilities of women and men who are in domestic partnerships are a major contribution to gender inequality in the workplace.

Homelife inequality takes two different and quite distinct forms. The first, is the priority that many working couples in heterosexual domestic partnerships give to the man's career; and the second, is the greater burden imposed on the woman for childcare, elder care, and other family responsibilities. These two forms of domestic inequality are distinct and have different discriminatory impacts on women's workplace experiences and career advancement opportunities.

Organizations can define and enforce their personnel policies to help ameliorate the impact of homelife gender inequality on workplace discrimination. While the impact of the unequal allocation of domestic responsibilities can be quite effectively addressed, the precedence generally given to the man's career in heterosexual domestic partnerships is very hard for organizations to address. Let's begin by understanding why this is the case.

The Precedence of Men's Careers

Most high-paying, high-status leadership positions demand long and unpredictable hours, extensive travel, and 24/7 availability. Indeed, as people move up the business, professional, and nonprofit leadership ladders, their jobs come to impose more and more demands on them; until, as Indra Nooyi, former CEO of PepsiCo put it, "There is no flexibility at the very top."[2]

But this lack of flexibility not only exists at the top. For example, Goldman Sachs investment bankers average a 95-hour work week—and get five hours of sleep a night. These bankers are seeking to cap their commitments to 80 hours a week.[3] Harvard professor Claudia Goldin calls these highly demanding positions "greedy jobs."[4] Because of the lack of flexibility in greedy jobs, it is a practical impossibility for anyone in a domestic partnership—woman or man—to hold a greedy job unless someone else takes care of the children, performs the great majority of the home-related tasks, and assumes a significantly greater responsibility for all of the other everyday exigencies of homelife. The need of a person

> Because of the lack of flexibility in greedy jobs, it is a practical impossibility for anyone in a domestic partnership—woman or man—to hold a greedy job unless someone else takes care of the children, performs the great majority of the home-related tasks, and assumes a significantly greater responsibility for all of the other everyday exigencies of homelife.

in a greedy job to have someone else to "take care of the kids" is highlighted in a comment of Ursula Burns, the former CEO of Xerox. In an interview with CNBC in 2022, Burns stated that she would not have been able to be CEO if she had not "outsourced" the caring for her children and believed that she needed to go to all of their sporting events.[5]

When someone has or wants a greedy job, there are profound implications for their domestic partnership. Unless a couple is wealthy enough to outsource almost all of their childcare, elder care, and domestic responsibilities, only one of the partners can typically hold or strive for a greedy job. The other partner must assume the lion's share—and then some—of these responsibilities. In other words, if one partner in a domestic relationship holds (or wants) a greedy job, the other

"Of course I put my kids first! Look
at how much I pay the nanny!!"

www.CartoonStock.com

partner usually cannot also hold (or want) a greedy job. Short of hiring other people to perform these services, one partner must step back and give priority to the career of the partner who has (or wants) the greedy job.

Because of gender stereotypes and status beliefs, it is far more likely that the woman will step back while her male partner steps forward. Not surprisingly, therefore, 70 percent of the men who hold the greediest jobs—those who are in the top 1 percent of earners[6] and those in senior business, professional, and nonprofit leadership roles[7]—have stay-at-home domestic partners.

The priority commonly given to the man's career is clearly illustrated in a survey of 25,000 graduates of the Harvard Business School (HBS).[8] In the survey, female and male HBS graduates were equally emphatic in emphasizing the importance of their careers, with a substantial majority

"It's come to my attention, Wycliff, that you're actually planning a life outside the office."

www.CartoonStock.com

of all graduates saying that "opportunities for career growth and development" were important to them. In keeping with their belief in the importance of their careers at the time they graduated, most of the women anticipated that their careers would be just as important and highly valued as those of their domestic partners. As their careers progressed, however, many of their expectations were dashed. Indeed, 40 percent of female HBS graduates reported that their careers were treated as less important and of a lower priority than that of their male partners. Among these couples, the male partners were far more likely to be candidates for greedy jobs than were the women.

But what about those high-potential couples who are committed to career equality, shared childcare responsibilities, and equality in home-related duties? Realistically, both partners will pay a career price. Without one partner taking on the great majority of home-related responsibilities, both partners must reconcile themselves to the lower probability of becoming a partner at a law or consulting firm, landing a big corporate promotion, or entering the C-Suite. As Goldin puts it, "couple equality costs more" as careers get greedier.[9] As a result, in the absence of substantial outsourcing, the rational economic choice for two high-potential individuals is for one partner (typically the woman) to give up on the pursuit of a higher paying, high-status job while the other partner (typically the man) pursues such a job. This allocation between couples often means that men in heterosexual domestic partnerships are much freer than their partners to pursue and hold greedy jobs. And, of course, this is precisely what we see with men holding about 85 percent of senior leadership positions.

This is not a homelife inequality that organizations can do much to counter. To the extent that gender inequality in senior leadership is due to the sheer fact that fewer women than men pursue greedy jobs, organizations can do nothing to change this situation. As long as senior leadership positions are greedy—and men's careers are given precedence by their domestic partners—the playing field for advancement into this rarified realm of high-paying, high-status, and highly inflexible careers remains severely tilted against women.

"Hello. This is Workoholics Anonymous. This is a recorded message. We're in a meeting right now but if you would like to call us again later..."
Punch Cartoon Library / TopFoto

Unequal Domestic Responsibilities

Unlike the inequality couples often give to the priorities of their respective careers, the second form of homelife inequality—unequal responsibilities for child care, elder care, and other home commitments—is something that organizational policies can address. Under PATH, organizations are urged to put in place policies that treat unequal domestic responsibilities as important discriminatory factors that can have dire consequences for the advancement of women in the workplace, the blatant inequalities between mothers and fathers with respect to caring for children. A 2021 poll by the University of Chicago and the Associated Press found that 68 percent of mothers (but only 18 percent of fathers) believe they perform all or most of the homelife tasks.[10] The American Family Survey found that women believe they do two-thirds of all childcare and housework, but men believe that they evenly split homelife responsibilities with their domestic partner.[11] And, the Pew Research Center found that mothers spend more than twice as much time on childcare as do fathers.[12]

This inequality between women and men extends beyond childcare and household responsibilities. It also extends to caregiving for elderly and disabled family members. In 2020, there were 53.5 million unpaid caregivers in the United States. Sixty-one percent of the unpaid caregivers are women, and 61 percent of those caregivers hold jobs.[13] As the average age of Americans continues to increase; so, too, will the collective burden of family caregivers. The number of Americans caring for the elderly and disabled increased by 9.5 million from 2015 to 2020. Unpaid family caregiving—especially for elderly loved ones—is a demographic trend that will continue to grow as the U.S. population ages. Gina Raimondo, U.S. Secretary of Commerce, said that the issues associated with an aging population are "Going to hit the U.S. economy like a 'ton of bricks'."[14] According to Population Reference Bureau's Population Bulletin, "Aging in the United States," there were 52 million Americans who were 65 or older in 2018, and this population group is projected to rise to 95 million by 2060. Our society's reliance on women as unpaid family caregivers for the elderly and the disabled puts even more pressure on working women who already handle the bulk of domestic responsibilities.

Women must increasingly balance their careers with homelife responsibilities that are increasingly expanding to include caring for the elderly. The challenges associated with caregiving for chronically sick and infirm family members can quickly become immense, intense, time consuming, and immediate. As such, caring for elderly and disabled family members has become a DEI issue that organizational leaders must consider and address with sensitivity, thoughtfulness, and integrity.

The pressures of caring for both children and elders is forcing many women to choose between their careers and their domestic responsibilities. During the ravages of the COVID-19 pandemic, working women needed to meet their job responsibilities, educate their children at home, assist elderly relatives and friends, and meet their ongoing domestic responsibilities. With expanded domestic inequality, it appears that many women have left organizations to set up their own businesses so they can create the flexibility they need. According to a study by human resources cloud software company Gusto, in 2021 women established a staggering 49 percent of new businesses in the United States, up from 28 percent in 2019.[15]

"Looking after your parents while you work and take care of your own family is a real bargain --

"Twice the guilt for the same length day."

Copyright Grantland Enterprises; www.grantland.net

To continue to attract, promote, and retain exceptionally capable women at all levels within their organizations, leaders need to understand the challenges that working women face when they often have the primary responsibility to care for both the young and the old. PATH's approach to home inequalities considers these issues as well.

According to a study by human resources cloud software company Gusto, in 2021 women established a staggering 49 percent of new businesses in the United States, up from 28 percent in 2019.

Career Impact of Home Inequality

Women (in general) perform many more home-related activities that do men. This gender inequality has two discriminatory impacts on women's careers. First, it leaves women with less time than men—whether the men are in domestic partnerships or not—to spend on work-related activities. Second, women need to take more time off from their careers than men to handle their larger domestic responsibilities. Women's lesser time at work and more time away from it, are, as Goldin points out, the "principal causes" of the gender gaps in earnings and career advancement.[16]

The fact that women in domestic partnerships with men have fewer hours to devote to their jobs than do comparably situated men has obvious adverse consequences for women's careers. Women cannot take on as many responsibilities; participate in as many work-related social activities; engage in as many networking activities; take advantage of as much mentoring, coaching, and training; or interact as frequently with their supervisors. Moreover, this lack of time to pursue career advancement causes twice as many women as men to work part-time. Among those people who do work part-time, nearly nine times as many women than men make this choice due to family needs.[17]

The *Women in the Workplace 2022* report has some shocking information about the imbalance between women's and men's household responsibilities as they work their way up in their careers. It is no surprise that "women at all levels are far more likely than men to be responsible for most or all of their family's housework and caregiving." But, things get more out of whack when we look at the imbalance between women and men in leadership roles. "Among entry-level employees, women are about twice as likely as men to be doing all of this work; among employees in leadership, the gap nearly doubles."[18] Senior women do 52 percent of housework and childcare but senior men do 13 percent of it.[19]

For women who need to interrupt their careers with time off to deal with domestic responsibilities, the discriminatory impact of absence from the workplace may not be quite so obvious. Yet, employees who interrupt their careers—as mothers do far more often than fathers[20]—pay a steep penalty when they try to return to their careers.[21] For example, one study found that 13 years after earning an MBA, women who have never had a child were almost at career-earning parity with their male counterparts, but those women with a child had fallen significantly behind the men.[22] Another study in the *Harvard Business Review* found that women who take time off after the birth of a child beyond the amount of time provided by their organization's maternity leave policies (if any leave is provided) "can expect to pay a price for their commitment to motherhood when they return to work."[23]

Women who have taken leaves of absence who seek to return to their careers, face a "downward career trajectory," according to Jia Wang, a professor at Texas A&M University.[24] Wang's observation is confirmed by a survey of highly qualified women conducted by Sylvia Ann Hewlett, and Carolyn Buck Luce. They found that when women take time off from their careers in business, they suffer "draconian" financial penalties on their return. After only 14 months away, women's "earning power drops an average of 28 percent."[25] The longer women are out of the workforce, the more severe the penalty they face. Thus, if women are out of the workforce for less than a year, they lose around 11 percent of their earning power; but, if their absence extends to more than three years, that loss in earning power *plummets to 37 percent.*

Personnel Policies to Ameliorate the Workplace Consequence of Unequal Home Responsibilities

Organizations need to adopt personnel policies in four areas to counter the discriminatory workplace impact of women's heavier homelife responsibilities. (It should go without saying that whatever personnel policies are adopted for women should also be available to men.) These policies should include flexible hours and locations of work; assistance with childcare; generous maternity leaves; and easily accessible, effective, and discrimination-free reentry programs. With more control over the times and locations of their work, women are better able to compete with men for career advancement. With financial assistance for childcare, women can reduce the time they spend on domestic tasks. And, with generous maternity leave, family assistance, and effective reentry programs, women's time off from their careers would have far less of a discriminatory impact. Women will benefit from these policies *if there is no stigma* attached to their use. This will only be the case if these policies are available to *and used by* both women and men.

> Women will benefit from these policies *if there is no stigma* attached to their use. This will only be the case if these policies are available to *and used by* both women and men.

Decision-makers need to ensure that homelife policies are designed, administered, and used on a gender-neutral basis. Apart from eliminating any stigma attached to use of these personal policies, when these benefits are universal and made equally available to women and men, they can operate to "promote productivity, reduce turnover, and improve employees' mental and physical health."[26]

> Andie: When I started my previous law firm's Gender Diversity Committee, we wrote our mission statement referring to gender equity for all of our colleagues, not just for the women. It was a tough sell to get people to understand that we had a broader mission than simply advancing women. Our mission became clear when we successfully rolled out our firm's reduced time policy for capital partners. Our first colleague who relied on the policy was a man. That showed the way for both women and men to follow suit.

Research conducted by Alexandra Kalev and Frank Dobbin, has confirmed that policies to help employees with their responsibilities at home also increase workforce diversity. In looking at data from over 800 U.S. companies, Kalev and Dobbin found, "when companies had universal policies for family leave time, flexible scheduling, and help with childcare, the percentage of Black, Hispanic, and Asian American male and female managers increased significantly."[27]

When companies had universal policies for family leave time, flexible scheduling, and help with childcare, the percentage of Black, Hispanic and Asian American male and female managers increased significantly.

—Alexandra Kalev and Frank Dobbin

Flexibility

The COVID-19 pandemic has made all of us aware that new and very different working arrangements can be possible in many workplaces without any loss of employee productivity. We now understand that there are some realistic alternatives to the old "9 to 5," office-centric models that U.S. companies have been tied to for so long. Women and men are both asking for more flexibility in their work hours and locations. Hewlett and Luce found that 64 percent of highly qualified women think that flexible work arrangements are either "extremely" or "very important" to them.[28] And many men are just as interested in flexible working arrangements as are women.[29]

Mitigating the discriminatory workplace impact of women's domestic inequality depends on organizations having multifaceted policies addressing workforce flexibility. Thus, with PATH, organizations are urged to take into account both the different types of jobs and different personal circumstances of employees holding similar jobs. Where feasible, organizations should offer employees several different options for when, where, and how they work.

Some people are at their happiest and most productive if they can work for long periods without interruption. Others prefer to be in regular communication (virtual or in-person) with their team members. And still others need to be engaged in frequent (face-to-face or virtual) meetings, conversations, and brainstorming sessions to do their best work.[30] Employees in the same jobs may have different flexibility needs, depending on where they are in their careers, what their homelife circumstances are like, and who is in their immediate work groups. Their preferences should be addressed, whenever possible, in highly individualized ways.

Obviously, flexibility policies must take into account the needs of the organization. Employees' desires must be balanced against organizational needs to maintain innovation, productivity, efficiency, customer service, regulatory compliance, and profitability. Such a balancing process is probably best done not by a directive from the top but through a participatory process involving the input of senior executives, middle managers, and front-line career employees. Leaders may also benefit from conducting employee surveys, holding focus groups, and interviewing different constituencies before designing and implementing flexibility policies.

Caveats

Studies show that women are about 50 percent more likely than men to want to work remotely on a full-time basis.[31] If, because of this, an organization's flexibility policies inadvertently lead to significant imbalance between women and men working in and out of the office, the entire initiative could prove counterproductive. Therefore, flexibility policies may need to be coupled with two additional actions to prevent stigma and overcome isolation.

1. Preventing Stigma

If women are the primary users of an organization's flexibility policies— or if women take advantage of these policies to a far greater extent than men—there is a risk that these policies may come to be seen as designed to accommodate women's need for work-life balance. Such a reaction can easily result in a stigma attaching to those women working remotely, and to women generally for a need for "special treatment." To avoid such an outcome, organizations must be sure that their flexibility policies apply universally, understood to be for everyone's benefit. Perhaps the most effective way to convey this message is for senior leaders to personally use the policies. For example, at Slack Technologies, the company offering the messaging program used in offices and for personal use, its executives committed to spend no more than three days a week in the office.[32]

2. Overcoming Isolation

If women work remotely significantly more than do men, they risk being *out of sight, out of mind*. It becomes easy for managers to primarily turn to the men they see for career-enhancing assignments, input on tactical and strategic decisions, and service in key management roles. In addition, invitations to participate in informal networking opportunities and career mentoring and advice might only be extended to people who are physically present in the office. Organizational leaders need to make special efforts to be sure women's careers are not adversely affected by using flexibility policies. This can be done in a variety of ways.

- **Contact**. Managers should be in contact with all members of their teams at least several times a week. Current assignments, workloads, issues, and advancement opportunities, should be discussed. The key is visibility—women working from home must be included as much as possible; perhaps even more so than those in the office.
- **Interaction**. Team members should be regularly discussing ongoing projects, ideas for better working arrangements, and needed material support. It doesn't matter that ideas can be shared by email or text, in text. In order to avoid remote workers' sense of isolation and exclusion, team members should regularly connect over the phone, Zoom, Microsoft Teams, or another cloud-based internet platform.
- **Updates**. Organizations should not continue to rely on traditional informal networks to disseminate information about new

projects, new opportunities, and important developments. More structured methods are now needed, perhaps a regular communication identifying workplace changes and formal job postings for all open positions, new responsibilities, or projects.

- **Networking**. Women working from home need to have access to valuable career-enhancing resources, such as personal and professional advice, relevant information, and intellectual and emotional support. Such resources are often available through strong, diverse networks. If more men are in the office, their networks are likely to be active and vibrant, while women working from home are likely to have weaker professional networks. Organizations, therefore, need to have policies that assure women have access to and can participate in all relevant workplace networks. Exclusionary behaviors that limit women's access, whether they are in the office or working out of the office must be clearly prohibited.

- **Periodic check-ins**. Regardless of the nature of an organization's flexibility policies, it must ensure that its managers have a regular practice of having all-hands team meetings. These check-ins should provide everyone with an opportunity to catch up, receive assignments, discuss projects, express concerns, and provide encouragement.

Stigma and isolation are not inevitable, but they can be real perils for women who work remotely or make use of flexible schedules. Women's decisions to use these policies must not harm their careers. Managers must *carefully monitor the consequences* for the careers of *all* employees who take advantage of these policies. They must ensure that these policies do not backfire, exacerbating—rather than ameliorating—the very situations they were designed to address.

Childcare Assistance

Assistance with childcare arrangements and expenses is another way that organizations can address the discriminatory workplace impact of inequality in the home. The United States—unlike every other developed country—does not have federally funded, high-quality, affordable childcare available for everyone who needs it.[33] Such childcare, if available, would provide significant benefits to the American economy as a whole; the great majority of women with young children; and the educational, material, and emotional well-being of children across the country.[34] President Biden's Build Back Better Plan with its American Families Plan would have provided direct support to ensure that low- and middle-income families spend no more than 7 percent of their income on childcare and that the childcare available to them would be of high quality.[35] Quite unfortunately, the plan failed to pass the U.S. Senate in 2021.[36]

> The United States—unlike every other developed country—does not have federally funded, high-quality, affordable childcare available for everyone who needs it. Such childcare, if available, would provide significant benefits to the American economy as a whole; the great majority of women with young children; and the educational, material, and emotional well-being of children across the country.

The absence of government support for childcare means that private organizations are the only reliable sources of financial assistance with childcare assistance. At present, however, only 8 percent of U.S. companies provide such financial assistance to their employees.[37] While it would be unrealistic to demand or require all organizations provide such assistance, PATH strongly encourages leaders to consider putting in place such assistance. Unless organizations provide *some form of childcare assistance*, it will be difficult, if not impossible, to eliminate the discriminatory workplace impacts on mothers. Therefore, PATH strongly recommends that organizations provide childcare assistance to their employees in one of three ways: an on-site childcare facility, access to a third-party childcare facility, or support with backup childcare assistance.

On-Site Day Care

In many parts of the United States, affordable, quality day care is simply not available, or if facilities are available, they cannot meet community demands.[38] A sobering statistic is that about half of all "Americans live in childcare deserts that lack adequate facilities to look after their kids."[39] Therefore, an employer-sponsored, on-site day care facility can make all the difference between mothers' ability to pursue their full-time careers, or being forced to drop out, drop back, or work part-time. Several large organizations now provide on-site facilities, including Aflac (the American Family Life Assurance Company), Carnival, General Mills, Google, Patagonia, Precision Pharmaceuticals,[40] Clif Bar, Cisco, and Home Depot.[41] The convenience of such on-site facilities cannot be overstated. On-site day care, however, is not an employee benefit most organizations can provide their employees. There are just too many costs and regulatory issues associated with such facilities for them to be widely available.[42] With that said, organizations that are in a position to offer on-site childcare can significantly reduce the discriminatory impact of women's unequal childcare responsibilities, and at the same time gain a competitive advantage in recruiting high-performing professionals (women and men) who would find such a program an important and valuable employee benefit.

Subsidized Off-Site Day Care

Organizations can partner with third-party childcare facilities to provide subsidized off-site day care. By entering into a relationship with a childcare provider, organizations can give their employees preferential access to childcare services at subsidized rates. According to Bright Horizons, a large day care provider, many of its 400 sites are sponsored by organizations for the benefit of their employees.[43] The availability of such employer-sponsored childcare facilities reduces the amount of time that working parents spend on unpaid domestic responsibilities, allowing them more time to devote for their careers.

Backup Childcare

The most common employer-supported childcare programs involve organizations providing their employees with a fixed number of days (typically 10 to 50) of free or heavily subsidized access to an approved childcare facility on a backup, or emergency basis. Employees can turn to these facilities when schools are closed or there is an unanticipated disruption in their normal childcare arrangements. A few companies that offer backup childcare arrangements include Amazon, Apple, Facebook, and General Motors.[44]

According to Bright Horizons, if such backup facilities had not been made available to the client companies it serves,

- 50 percent of those employees would have been forced to reduce their work hours,
- 33 percent would have missed key workplace deadlines, and
- 20 percent would have needed to take a leave of absence or quit their jobs.[45]

Company-supported backup childcare is a valuable resource, providing parents with a way to deal with emergencies that would otherwise require them to miss work.

Caveats

The types of employer-sponsored childcare assistance we have been discussing are only available to young children. But older children also need care, supervision, and structure. During the 10 months that U.S. schools are in session, schools are closed an average of 29 days (including holidays and vacations). When you factor in summer vacation and the times children are not in school while their parents are working, older children need far more care than that which is available from schools, recreational districts, and community centers. As a result, many working mothers must seek out supplementary services for their school-age children. These services can be expensive, hard to find, and insufficient to relieve many parents of their childcare responsibilities. To counter the discriminatory workplace impact suffered by mothers in unequal domestic partnerships, organizations need to establish childcare assistance programs to address the needs of older children as well as of younger ones.[46] Without providing such financial assistance, organizations will leave unaddressed the full extent of the discriminatory workplace impact of gender inequality in the home.

Leave Policies

Leave policies are another area where personnel policies can mitigate the discriminatory impact of women's unequal domestic responsibilities. Policies should address leaves of absence for childbirth, adoption, and other family and medical needs. These challenges can be especially difficult for single parents, including the 11 million single mothers in the United States. Once again, absent established legal leave policies, mothers and other family caregivers find themselves severely disadvantaged in the workplace.

Family Leave

The United States is the *only* developed country in the world that does not provide universal paid maternity leave.[47] Only seven U.S. states provide some form of paid family leave.[48] In the rest of the country, however, whether working women have any financial assistance during pregnancy, child birth, and new infant care depends on their employers. The same applies to adoption and paternity leave.

The United States is the only country among 41 OECD nations that lacks paid parental leave (maternity, paternity, and parental leave entitlements).

—Gretchen Livingston and Deja Thomas, Pew Research Center

Birth and Adoption Leave Policies

It is hard to know how many employers provide birth or adoption leave because estimates vary so widely. *The National Compensation Survey–Benefits*, produced by the U.S. Bureau of Labor Statistics, says that as of 2021, only 23 percent of U.S. employees had employer-provided paid family leave (maternity, paternity, or both).[49] The Society for Human Resource Management noted that 55 percent of its *members* offer paid maternity leave, and 45 percent offer paid paternity leave.[50] A national survey by Mercer, a benefits consulting firm, found that about 40 percent of private employers provide some paid parental leave for both birth and non-birth parents.[51] And, the Kaiser Family Foundation's Health Benefits Survey found that 35 percent of American workers had access to some paid parental leave.[52] Among those organizations that provide paid maternity leave, the average length of paid leave is eight weeks—not a generous amount when it is compared to the average of 18 weeks provided by all of the other 38 members of the Organization for Economic Cooperation and Development.[53]

Even at large companies—those with more than 1,000 workers—only 35 percent do offer paid maternity leave.[54] Unfortunately, this grim picture in the United States is becoming worse. Many companies that offer maternity and paternity leave are reported to be *reducing* the number of paid weeks they offer their employees. An August 22, 2022 *Wall Street Journal* article, for example, noted new data showing that the share of employers offering paid maternity leave beyond that which is required by law dropped from 53 percent in 2020 to 35 percent in 2022.[55] At the same time, organizations are also decreasing the availability of paternity leave, and employers that are providing paid paternity leave fell from 44 to 27 percent during the same period.[56] For most working women, therefore, childbirth and adoption pose a difficult dilemma. If they return to work before they have had time to properly care for themselves and their children, poor maternal and infant health can result.[57] If mothers take unpaid leave, they lose not just their current earnings, but they also risk permanently reducing their future earning power.

There are few PATH absolutes with respect to what organizations should do to end workplace gender inequality. One of them, however, is that organizations must provide at least 12 weeks of paid family leave for childbirth or adoption. For workplace gender equality, this is not a "nice to have," it is an imperative.

> There are few PATH absolutes with respect to what organizations should do to end workplace gender inequality. One of them, however, is that organizations must provide at least 12 weeks of paid family leave for childbirth or adoption.

Forty-nine percent of highly paid women business executives are childless while only 19 percent of their male counterparts are.[58] The implication is crystal clear: without paid family leave and childcare assistance, working mothers just don't have a chance to make it to the leadership ranks of their organizations and stay there.

Transitions

Beyond providing paid family leave, organizations should also provide expectant and new mothers with the support they need to manage their workplace departure, leave of absence, and reentry without facing the risk of losing career opportunities and earning potential. Therefore, under PATH, organizations are expected to adopt policies designed to assist in the transfer of work and responsibilities at the start of parental leaves, staying in touch with parents (according to their wishes) during their leaves, and returning responsibilities to them once they are back at work. Organizations need to assure women they will be able to welcome children into their families without facing serious career advancement and earnings losses.

Motherhood Bias

Organizations should carefully monitor how women are treated, related to, and regarded by their managers, peers, and team members while

Used with permission, Gatis Sluka, and Cartoon Movement.

pregnant and after they become mothers. Motherhood bias, an aspect of gender bias, is unfortunately all too common. Such bias falsely labels new mothers as not fully committed to their careers, unwilling to undertake challenging work or extensive travel, and unavailable after the normal workday hours for consultation, collaboration, and brainstorming.[59] Monitoring the treatment of new mothers should be continued for at least the first three years after women become mothers. Organizations should ensure that assignments given, evaluations received, and responsibilities allocated are not influenced by motherhood bias. Otherwise, such bias can be a serious obstacle to career advancement for mothers.[60] New mothers have a hard enough time in reconciling the demands of their careers and the needs of their children without battling motherhood bias as well.

New Parent Support

In addition to being on the alert for motherhood bias, organizations need to have policies that ensure managers check in with new parents to see what help they might need, monitor their workloads for signs of undue stress, and clarify the priorities of open projects. While managers should be doing these things with respect to everyone who reports to them, such attentiveness is particularly important for new parents who may feel overwhelmed and sleep deprived.

Career Interruption

Career interruptions are more common among women than men. Sixty-four percent of working women take a break at some point in their careers.[61] The problem with such career breaks is that 59 percent of people believe that such a career break is a sign of a lack of career commitment.[62] As a result, managers can be reluctant to hire women who have taken a career break. When they do hire women returning to the workforce, they often do so at significantly reduced compensation and at a lower performance rung than they had occupied before their career break.

In our view, organizations that penalize women who have taken a career break are viewing such women in precisely the wrong way. Returning women are likely to be strongly committed to their careers, highly experienced, and newly energized. In fact, 53 percent of women returning to work after a career break report that they are better at their jobs than they were before the break; 69 percent report the career break helped them gain a clearer perspective on what they really want from life; and 68 percent report that the career break improved their well-being.[63] A career break should not be viewed with suspicion. It is not a red flag; it is an opportunity.

Reentry Program

As part of PATH, organizations should have a well-structured reentry program for women returning to work after a career break. Such a program should ensure that a career break does not negatively affect women's ability to apply for and secure open positions. This means that job postings should not imply that career continuity is necessary or even desirable. For example, LinkedIn candidate searches should not exclude women who have taken career breaks, and organizations should use recruiting sources such as Women Back to Work to identify qualified women candidates returning to their careers.

Cartoon by Barry Deutsch, leftycartoons.com

An organization's reentry program should also include adequate support, resources, and encouragement for returning employees. In addition to an organization's normal onboarding programs that are available to all of its new hires, women returning after a career break should be assisted in restarting their careers.[64] This is particularly important because returning employees might have been subjected to a depreciation of their value and status while out of the workforce.[65] As a result, PATH recommends that reentry programs ensure that such women are promptly welcomed by their team members, provided with access to career-enhancing networks, and mentored with respect to achieving their career goals.

In inclusive workplaces these actions should happen as a matter of course. That said, however, there should be a degree of sensitivity in recognizing the particular vulnerabilities of women returning after a career break. Proactive awareness can go a long way, and it can create positive goodwill across the entire organization if special efforts are made to be sure that career reentry is encouraged, welcomed, and supported.

PATH's Approach

PATH involves a multifaceted approach by which organizations should use their personnel policies to counteract the discriminatory impact of unequal domestic responsibilities. The most obvious of these policies address the extent and nature of permitted flexible workplace arrangements; assistance with childcare responsibilities; family, and other extended leaves; and reentry programs for people who have had a career break. There may well be other policies that can help in this regard, such as:

1. work-related networking and social activities designed to accommodate women's more limited time availability
2. programs that inform women about resources to deal with work/home conflicts
3. role models who can help women in navigating the complications of merging a challenging career with responsibilities at home

4. assistance in negotiating after-hours client interactions, extensive travel, and extended project commitments

In sum, organizations need to ensure that women can fully engage in career opportunities. Whatever policies they choose to consider, develop, and adopt, their goal should be to treat gender inequality in the home as a major factor in perpetuating workplace gender inequality. Although there may be nothing organizations can do directly to end inequality in the home, there is a great deal they can do to help counteract the gender inequality that such domestic inequalities cause in their workplaces.

KEY TAKEAWAYS

- The third step in PATH is to *treat* inequality in the home as a workplace problem.
- PATH is designed to *address inequality that results* because social norms and gender stereotypes tend to place a heavier responsibility on women in the home. Home inequality carries over into the workplace in two ways. Women have less time for work in the first place, and they also tend to take more time away from their careers.
- PATH cannot address situations of individual choice between couples that agree to prioritize or de-prioritize a woman's career.
- Leaders can do much to reduce the discriminatory workplace impact of women's typically heavier domestic responsibilities through

  - flexible hours
  - flexible locations
  - financial support for assistance with caregiving
  - generous and less stigmatized family leaves
  - reentry policies

- All policy changes should be offered on a universal basis to all employees to prevent unintentional discriminatory consequences and to acknowledge the value of these policies to men as well as to women.
- For many women, employer assistance with caregiver expenses and arrangements can make the difference between the realistic prospect of career advancement and career stagnation, part-time work, or dropping out of the workforce altogether.
- Organizations must provide at least 12 weeks of paid family leave for childbirth or adoption.
- Employers should provide childcare assistance through on-site childcare facilities (if feasible), employer-subsidized third-party facilities, and backup day care assistance.
- Managers need to ensure that the assignments that returning mothers are given, the evaluations they receive, and the responsibilities with which they are charged are not negatively affected by motherhood bias.
- Organizations must dispel any notion that reentering employees are different or in need of special help not available to others. They should fully integrate these employees into the workforce as quickly as possible.

Chapter 11

Halt Unequal Performance Reviews, Career Advice, and Leadership Opportunities

PERSONNEL PRACTICES DEAL WITH A wide array of issues, ranging from the mundane to those most critical for employees'
career advancement. Personnel practices with respect to three areas
in particular—performance reviews, career advice, and leadership
opportunities—are key to the equality of women's and men's advancement
possibilities.

It is critical for the success of PATH, therefore, that leaders ensure
that women are not disadvantaged by the nature or operation of their personnel practices. This involves not merely the objective fairness of these
practices—the gender neutrality in their administration—but also an
affirmative effort to ensure women are provided the same encouragement,
advice, and support in their efforts to attain the very highest positions possible. Men are routinely advised to reach P&L responsibilities, senior roles,
and positions that can be stepping stones to board membership and—
ultimately—the opportunity to lead an organization; men are encouraged
to do so and they are provided with the comprehensive support they need
to succeed. Achievement of workplace gender equality depends on women
receiving that same advice, encouragement, and support.

Personnel Decisions and Performance Reviews

Personnel decisions are distinct from performance reviews. Personnel decisions concern hiring and changes to employees' job status or responsibilities. They involve the selection of a candidate or candidates from among an appropriate candidate pool. Performance reviews, on the other hand, focus on helping employees recognize their professional strengths and weaknesses and on assisting them to improve their performance in the future. Performance reviews focus on how employees can get better, move up, and identify near- and long-term goals.

Although personnel decisions and reviews are often conflated at many organizations, we treat them as entirely separate processes within PATH. This separation better enables decision-makers to recognize and effectively deal with the different ways in which structural and individual discrimination work in these two areas. In Chapter 9, we looked at ways to assure that personnel decisions are fair, objective, and inclusive. Here, we look at how to effectively control structural and individual discrimination with respect to performance reviews, and the related topics of career advice and leadership development opportunities.

Performance Reviews

A performance review should have a two-fold objective:

1. To provide employees with an accurate, comprehensive, and non-judgmental assessment of the strengths and weaknesses they have displayed in the performance of their tasks and responsibilities, and
2. To provide employees with specific, action-oriented advice as to how they could improve their work performance in the future.[1]

Awareness, care, and focus are needed to guard against the discriminatory influences that can prevent realization of these core objectives in each employee performance review.

1. Performance Assessments

Author Samuel Culbert convincingly argues that the nature of the criteria that should be used in assessing employees' past performance should be determined by the results the organization wants to achieve over the review period. As he puts it in his book, *Get Rid of Performance Reviews!* employees' and managers' eyes need to be "on the prize, the desired corporate result. It's then up to the boss/subordinate to figure out the best way to get there."[2] Of course, the definition of desired organizational group-wide results does not automatically determine the different roles that specific employees should play in attempting to realize them. There are more and less important roles in this regard; more and less challenging opportunities; more and less career-advancing positions; and a limited number of visible high-profile assignments.

The first area of possible discriminatory influence in performance reviews is in identifying the roles that employees are expected to play and the criteria upon which work performance will be assessed. This process is likely to be influenced by structural discrimination: the (unconscious) assumption that men are better than women at tackling the more challenging, difficult competitive tasks; at performing in roles requiring leadership; and in meeting responsibilities demanding sustained commitment.

Under PATH, organizations should take two important steps to prevent discrimination from influencing the allocation of employee roles and responsibilities. First, each manager should identify in writing the role that each employee is expected to play in the achievement of desired organizational or team results. In some cases, this will be simple and relatively discrimination-free because it will involve a straightforward generic task such as planning, designing, implementing, or providing customer or client service. In other cases, however, where employees are singled out to play unique roles, the matter is not at all straightforward. Why has one individual been selected to lead an initiative rather than another? Why is one individual selected to make a client presentation rather than another? Why is one individual rather than another given responsibility for sign-off as to an acceptable proposal? In all such cases, managers should be required to explain the reason for their selections. By needing to explain their justifications and knowing that their justifications will be reviewed, managers are far more likely to use slow thinking. And by using slow thinking, they are far less likely to be influenced by discriminatory factors.

But even when employees are expected to play more generic roles, discriminatory factors can still influence performance reviews unless the assessment criteria are carefully designed to be gender-neutral. Employees should participate in specification of the criteria for four reasons:

1. **Visualization.** When employees participate in the formulation of applicable criteria, they know what is expected of them in relation to their team members. This is particularly important for women who may be unclear as to what constitutes excellent performance, primarily because of the paucity of female role models.

2. **Predictability.** When employees participate in the formulation of applicable criteria, they cannot be surprised by what is expected of them. Again, this can be particularly valuable for women whose networks are less likely than men's to provide them with the information needed to have a clear sense of expectations.

3. **Candor.** Mutual agreement on assessment criteria fosters open and candid discussions between employees and their managers.

4. **Advancement.** When employees participate in the formulation of assessment criteria, they can gain insights into what is expected for long-term career advancement. Moreover, they can learn where they are with respect to their readiness to move up to the next leadership level and how specific projects and management exposure can help them get there.[3] Again, this is particularly important for women because expected future performance is often not as clear to them as it is for men because of the lack of female role models and the likely relative weakness of their information networks.

2. Presentation of Evaluations

Gender-neutral performance reviews also depends on the manner in which managers present the reviews to employees. Research shows that performance reviews are often presented to women and men in very different ways.[4] Women are more likely to receive vague evaluations with few specific details of what they have done well and what they could do to improve and advance in their careers. Studies also show that men are more likely to receive longer, more detailed reviews that focus on their technical skills, compared to shorter reviews for women that are more concerned with their communication skills.[5] Writing in the *Harvard Business Review*, three Stanford researchers found that men are more likely than women to have their performance evaluations presented in terms of specific career guidance—guidance that is directly tied to specific organizational outcomes. Women, on the other hand, are likely to have their evaluations given to them in general terms, without specific, actionable advice as to how they can improve their performance.[6]

"Frankly, your performance has been spotty."

Copyright Andrew Grossman/www.cartoonresource.com

Even when women and men receive equally positive performance evaluations, their results can be shared in ways that are framed by descriptors that are strongly shaped by gender stereotypes. For example, one study found that although there were no differences in the assessments of women's and men's objective job performance, women were still more likely than men to be evaluated as "inept, frivolous, gossipy, excitable, scattered, temperamental, panicky, and indecisive."[7]

Benevolent sexism can also lead to women being disadvantaged by their performance reviews. Women experience benevolent sexism when they are treated with apparent kindness, but are not provided with the same candid criticism and action-oriented advice as men. Benevolent sexism was revealed in a study where participants were asked to rate two reports that were equally poorly written. When the reviewers had no information about the gender of the authors of the reports, they presented their results in very similar ways. When the reviewers were told the supposed gender of the authors, however, feedback they gave to the woman and man was very different. The man received straightforward specific information as to where the report was of poor quality and what he needed to make it better. When it came to the woman, however, the reviewers shaded their true assessment, telling her that the work product was almost a full letter grade higher than they had actually evaluated it. In other words, the reviewers were reluctant to be direct and candid with the woman. As a result, they flat-out lied to her about the quality of her work product.[8] Often, women do not receive crucial information they need to better understand personal performance shortcomings, or the information they need to address those deficiencies, improve, and make progress. What triggers benevolent sexism?

1. Evaluators may believe women are too emotionally fragile to deal with critical reviews.
2. Evaluators may feel a need to protect women and to shield them from the harsh realities of their own shortcomings.
3. Evaluators may want to "go easy" on women because they think women need greater support.

Whether it is because of gender bias or benevolent sexism, women often do not receive the same straightforward, accurate, and action-oriented advice that men get as to why, where, and how they need to improve their performance. Candid advice gives men an advantage, allowing them to correct and adjust their performance. Women cannot advance on equal terms with men unless their performance reviews are equally straightforward, unbiased, candid, and task-based. Unless they do, women will inevitably fall behind men in terms of career advancement.

> Candid advice gives men an advantage, allowing them to correct and adjust their performance. Women cannot advance on equal terms with men unless their performance reviews are equally straightforward, unbiased, candid, and task-based.

PATH and Performance Reviews

Women and men must receive equally direct, complete, and accurate assessments of their past performance (the first aspect of a performance review). They must also receive equally helpful, action-oriented, and future-oriented suggestions for improvement (the second aspect of a performance review). Both of these requirements are essential to eliminate gender inequality. To ensure both aspects of performance reviews are gender-neutral under PATH, organizations are advised to both train their managers, and to make several structural changes in the review process.

Training

Managers need to be trained to effectively provide performance reviews. They should be provided with information about the hurtful consequences of bias-influenced evaluations; the subtle dangers of benevolent sexism; the myth of women's emotional frailty; and the importance of women and men both receiving complete and accurate information about the quality of their performance. Training alone, however, is not likely to result in gender neutrality in all aspects of the performance review process. Little progress can be made at ending gender inequality by relying solely on *training* to change individual behavior.

First, to build truly inclusive workplaces, managers and the employees who report to them need to have a positive working relationship based on mutual respect. With mutual respect, a straight-talking relationship becomes possible. We are not suggesting a personal friendship. Rather, there should be a working relationship that involves candid, direct, and action-oriented advice. In such relationships, both parties are likely to feel psychologically safe enough to be direct and honest with the other, so that "mistakes can be acknowledged, learned from, and rectified."[9]

Second, organizations should not leave the manner, timing, and content of performance reviews to the personal discretion of individual managers. There must be accountability. Reviews should be required upon the completion of major projects and assignments. And such reviews should follow a three-part format:

1. Identify the employee's specific performance strengths and weaknesses in relation to specified criteria.
2. Advise the employee on how they can improve performance in a helpful and action-oriented way.
3. Discuss the employee's likely next steps to ensure their career progression.

Third, after conducting a performance review, each manager should be required to complete a standardized form summarizing both the assessment given of the employee's performance and the future-looking advice that was provided to the employee. The written reports should be periodically reviewed by a third party. These forms should provide a summary of the performance assessment; the advice given; the date of the review; its length and location; and any comments, complaints, or concerns expressed by the employee in the review. The fact that these reports will be reviewed by a third party is likely to make the managers attentive to the quality and completeness of their performance reviews.

A review of the reports by a third party also provides a way to iden-tify whether there are unequal patterns revealed as to the reviews that women and men receive.

A possible objection that might be raised to such a formalized per-formance review process is that it will overburden managers and distract them from their other responsibilities. This should not be the case. Perfor-mance reviews should be conversations, not formal presentations. They can and should naturally follow the completion of major projects and assignments. They can take place anywhere, over a cup of coffee or at a shared lunch. They should be thought of as occasions for two-way discus-sions. The prescribed format of performance reviews is intended to ensure that all of a manager's performance reviews are basically similar, with no advantage in terms of content given to either women or men. And, the written reports should be standardized so they can be quickly completed.

Career Advice

Organizations need to take steps beyond ensuring the gender neutrality of performance reviews to also ensure women and men receive equiva-lent advice, coaching, and encouragement with respect to their career trajectories. This means that managers need to explicitly address career goals with women and men, and discuss how employees can achieve those goals. These discussions should address employees' existing tal-ents; the sorts of assignments and responsibilities they need to move to the next career level; the goals they seek to reach each year over the next five years; and the support, training, and monitoring that they need to get there. These discussions should be designed to set goals and provide ongoing feedback about progress toward those goals.[10]

Even when conversations about career advice take place, however, they tend to proceed very differently for women than they do for men. For example, the dramatic underrepresentation of women in stepping-stone and P&L positions is due in large part to the fact that men are encour-aged to pursue such positions but women are not. In a 2018 study of 3,038

U.S. professionals, only 14 percent of women as opposed to 46 percent of men were encouraged to consider P&L roles, and more than three times as many men had received detailed information on career paths leading to P&L jobs within the two years preceding the survey's data collection.[11]

As we also saw in Chapter 1, women are also held back from stepping-stone positions because of gender stereotypes. In a 2017 study of more than 2,600 senior executives, women were found to be just as likely as men to possess the kind of skills and charisma that are predictive of success as a future CEO.[12] Yet, women CEO candidates were 28 percent *less likely* than their male peers to actually secure these top spots.[13]

Thus, simply providing objective and straightforward performance reviews will not improve women's chances of advancing into senior leadership *unless* they are coupled with career advice, counseling, and encouragement that is as likely to point women toward the C-suite and NEO positions as it does men.

> Simply providing objective and straightforward performance reviews will not improve women's chances of advancing into senior leadership *unless* they are coupled with career advice, counseling, and encouragement that is as likely to point women toward the C-suite and NEO positions as it does men.

This will not happen unless organizations develop formal career advice processes in which there is both an unbiased assessment of potential and an unbiased indication of future goals. As always under PATH, the process must be in writing and reviewed by a third party. This calls for candid conversations involving not only unfiltered assessment of current strengths and weaknesses but also honest, unbiased appraisals of where employees are in their careers, and what they need to do to keep advancing toward the top of their organization. As Peter Capelli and Anna Tavis note, these sorts of conversations need to "keep revisiting two basic questions: What am I doing that I should keep doing? and

What am I doing that I should change?[14] Organizational leaders need to be focused not just on a fair performance review process but also on a career advice process that is specifically designed to ensure that equivalently talented, high-potential women are put on precisely the same leadership tracks as men, and that they receive the support, encouragement, and opportunities they require to reach the top.

Leadership Development

In addition to ensuring that women and men receive specific, focused, and helpful performance reviews and similar career advancement advice, women also need leadership development opportunities that are comparable to men's. This must be done if organizations are finally to see women moving into P&L positions, NEO roles, and C-suite stepping-stone positions at rates comparable to men. Therefore, with PATH, organizations are expected to develop workplace practices that ensure women receive the same leadership development opportunities, advice, and recognition as men.

Affinity bias is a major obstacle to achieving this result. Because most senior leaders are men—indeed, only 15 percent of senior executives at Fortune 500 companies are women[15]—they are far more comfortable assigning responsibilities to, relying on, and sharing ideas, advice, and opportunities with other men. As a result, even without any purposeful discriminatory intent, junior men naturally receive more leadership opportunities, more frequent advice on behavioral expectations, and more recognition of their legitimacy in performing in those roles than do comparably situated women.[16]

If affinity bias is left unchecked, when it comes time for organizations to fill leadership positions, men will inevitably be seen as stronger candidates than their female counterparts. They will have had greater and more varied leadership experiences; more interactions with other workplace leaders; and a greater number of occasions to practice, adjust, and try out new leadership skills.[17] For men, therefore, affinity bias creates a *virtuous* circle. Men receive more leadership development opportunities than women, so they are more likely to advance into increasingly senior leadership positions. In turn, this increases the likelihood that they will obtain even more opportunities for leadership development. For women, however, affinity bias creates a *vicious* circle. Because women receive fewer leadership development opportunities than men, they also receive fewer advancement opportunities than men. This, in turn, reduces the likelihood that the women will receive more leadership development opportunities in the future.[18]

In addition to affinity bias, women face several other serious obstacles to advancing into the higher and more challenging ranks of senior leadership and to being accepted and fully supported when they do:

- the paucity of female role models *from whom to learn effective female leadership styles, behaviors, and identities*[19]
- being more frequently tracked into positions that are not stepping stones for senior leadership (that is, line and operations positions)[20]
- having networks that are weaker and less capable of opening leadership opportunities, providing visibility, and generating recognition[21]
- being increasingly seen as outsiders, exceptions, and "others" as they move up the leadership ladder
- increasingly being subjected to greater scrutiny, criticism, and isolation than their male counterparts[22]

> To overcome these obstacles—affinity bias, lack of role models, being differently tracked, having weaker networks, being seen as outsiders, and receiving unmerited scrutiny—organizations need a program that is designed to provide women with the same leadership development opportunities, support, and recognition of their contributions as men receive.

To overcome these obstacles—affinity bias, lack of role models, being differently tracked, having weaker networks, being seen as outsiders, and receiving unmerited scrutiny—organizations need a program that is designed to provide women with the same leadership development opportunities, support, and recognition of their contributions as men receive. Under PATH, we refer to this as gender-conscious leadership development.

Liza Donnelly

Gender-Conscious Leadership Development

There are four specific areas where organizational management must focus to ensure that women and men have truly equal and realistic opportunities to ascend to the top of the most senior leadership roles in the organization:

1. Leadership Experience: Attend specific occasions to perform as leaders at increasingly senior levels.
2. Leadership Advice: Give coaching, mentoring, and advice that is specific and appropriate for their career aspirations.
3. Women-Only Communities: Offer occasions to participate in safe women-only spaces where sensitive concerns, frustrations, and aspirations can be discussed.
4. Career Coaching: Give recognition as legitimate leaders.

With PATH, all entry-level career professionals should be included in such a gender-conscious leadership development program. As women and men gain seniority, organizations need to identify their high-potential performers, that is, those who should be prepared for senior leadership positions.[23] Nevertheless, one study found that only 16 percent of organizations have a formal process for doing so and a shocking 85 percent of organizations rely on informal manager feedback to make their selections.[24]

The identification of such high-potential individuals who will receive structured leadership preparation is highly likely to be influenced by gender stereotypes, status beliefs, and individual biases. There is often an unconscious assumption that (most) men have and (most) women don't have the commitment, qualities, and characteristics needed to perform well in challenging, highly demanding senior leadership positions.[25] Therefore, this identification process needs to be carefully monitored to assure it is being administered in a gender-neutral manner. Organizations should not mandate gender parity in their leadership development programs. It would be a clear sign of the presence of discrimination if women were less than 30 percent of the employees identified as high potential for advancement into senior leadership. However, leadership development program will not be able to assure women's successful participation in senior leadership.[26]

1. Leadership Experience

The key to assuring that women and men have comparable opportunities to display and develop their leadership abilities is a gender-neutral process by which visible responsibilities, challenging projects, and team leadership roles are assigned.

As a first step, organizations need to track the frequency and nature of the assignments that women are given (in comparison to comparably situated men) to exercise leadership responsibilities. Leadership, like any other complex skill, rarely comes naturally and usually takes a great deal of practice.[27] As Frank Caspedes writes, "work experience (job

"Could I be allowed to fulfill my potential ...
please?"

www.CartoonStock.com

assignments, organizational relationships, and especially performance feedback) accounts for about 70% of the professional-development learning relevant to career advancement, with about 15% each for formal training courses and life experiences (hobbies, interests, family: the other things you do and love outside work)."[28] Unless organizations track the leadership development opportunities provided to women and men, the likelihood is that men—but not women—will receive the sorts of leadership experience, exposure, and acceptance they need to step into ever increasingly senior leadership roles.

2. Leadership Advice

Beyond assuring that women have opportunities to exercise and display their leadership abilities on equal terms to those of men, organizations need to provide women with advice, criticism, and encouragement about their leadership performance that is comparable to those that men receive. This advice, like that in the context of performance reviews must be non-judgmental, action-oriented, and supportive.

Beyond focusing on the acquisition or strengthening of specific behavioral characteristics valuable for leaders, women should also receive advice designed to help them develop a clear idea of their inner strengths so they can perform convincingly and effectively as leaders.

> Beyond focusing on the acquisition or strengthening of specific behavioral characteristics valuable for leaders, women should also receive advice designed to help them develop a clear idea of their inner strengths so they can perform convincingly and effectively as leaders.

Becoming a leader requires employees to integrate "the leader identity into their core self."[29] For women, leadership also requires them to acquire a leadership style that will be effective, authentic, and accepted. A style that avoids the too soft, too hard double bind of the Goldilocks Dilemma and finds a "just right" style. It is not something men are likely to consider. An organization's gender-conscious leadership development program, therefore, should specifically focus on helping women internalize their own identity as a leader and overcome the gender stereotypes that they may have previously internalized.

> In our experience, the gender of a mentor (or adviser, coach, or counselor) is far less important than the mentor's empathy, wisdom, and practical commitment to the overall process.

A further, but highly important aspect of leadership advice should come in the form of mentoring. More men than women have workplace mentors.[30] And, because of affinity bias, this mentoring advice is likely to come from senior leaders. An organization's gender-conscious leadership development program, therefore, must overcome this male advantage through a formal mentorship process available to women and men. While there is a good deal of discussion about the desirability of women having other women as mentors,[31] in our experience, the gender of a mentor (or adviser, coach, or counselor) is far less important than the mentor's empathy, wisdom, and practical commitment to the overall process. In the mentorship program that we offer through www.AndieandAl.com to women interested in advancing in their careers,[32] we have seen some great successes with men mentoring women and some disappointing progress in some relationships where women mentor women. We have found that the key to successful mentoring is effective training of the mentors;[33] that only individuals who are sincerely committed to the mentoring process are selected as mentors, and that both mentors and mentees understand their responsibilities and the ongoing need to actively engage with each other.[34] There also needs to be a formal process by which high potential women have regular access to senior executives who are knowledgeable about their organizations' existing norms, processes, and practices; and display different leadership styles. These leaders should be working with women on how to leverage one opportunity into others that span important, visible objectives, including moving into new ones that can lead to P&L, NEO, board, and organizational ownership positions.

3. Women-Only Communities

No matter how fair and unbiased an organization's leadership opportunities and career advice activities are, women's paths to senior leadership will inevitably be far more fraught than men's. Therefore, notwithstanding our indifference as to the gender of women's mentors, we feel strongly that women need to be provided with an opportunity to interact with other women without men being present. Such opportunities are occasions for women to reflect candidly on their successes and setbacks; discuss their experiences in dealing with gendered obstacles; develop a sense of community: consider their shared values, and similar objectives; and offer each other encouragement and advice. Regular women-to-women interactions should be free from judgment, without any pressure to conform to male norms, and without expectations that there is only one way to lead.[35] In women-only communities, women are more likely to feel comfortable in letting their hair down and candidly expressing their concerns and anxieties than they might in mixed-gender environments.[36]

4. Career Coaching

With PATH, organizations should recognize that the transition from a valued and productive team member to become a manager of other people is a major career transition that can be difficult. And each time a person moves up the leadership ladder, there is yet another difficult career transition. These transitions typically involve the need to acquire and display new sets of skills and attitudes, and build new relationships.[37]

At each step of the way through successive leadership roles, therefore, an individual must reexamine the professional identity that was successful in the past but might not be appropriate in the new role.[38] Women can be especially hesitant to abandon the comfort of their existing identities that have taken them to where they are now. But those identities might not be effective going forward. In increasingly high leadership roles, women are likely to face increasing pressure to adopt a masculine leadership style; increased scrutiny, attention, and criticism; and greater risks from mistakes or missteps. As a consequence, organizations need to structure their gender-conscious leadership development so that women receive strong support, encouragement, and coaching at each progressive stage of their leadership ascent.

Organizations need to structure their gender-conscious leadership development so that women receive strong support, encouragement, and coaching at each progressive stage of their leadership ascent.

Organizations need gender-conscious leadership development programs to effectively counteract the structural discrimination that systemically disadvantages women in their efforts to attain senior leadership positions and the individual discrimination that systematically disadvantages women by making this pursuit often unpleasant, isolating, and lacking in support. A key indication of the presence of gender inequality in a workplace is the disparity between women and men in senior leadership positions. Therefore, a gender-conscious leadership development program should focus on assuring women's abilities to fill positions with P&L responsibilities, which will lead to NEO roles, and serve in stepping-stone roles to the C-suite. Women need to be just as supported, and accepted for these important roles are the men. This means organizations must design, administer, and continuously monitor these programs so that women no less than men obtain the experiences, advice, and acceptance to climb to the highest levels of leadership. PATH does not aim to reduce men's leadership opportunities but rather to ensure that women's opportunities are just as great—which they most definitely are not at the present time. This will only happen if organizations carefully monitor the responsibilities women and men are assigned; the coaching, training, and mentoring they receive; and the encouragement, support, and recognition they are afforded as they develop and perform as leaders.

> PATH does not aim to reduce men's leadership opportunities but rather to ensure that women's opportunities are just as great— which they most definitely are not at the present time.

KEY TAKEAWAYS

- The fourth step in PATH is to *halt* the unequal performance reviews, career advice, and leadership development opportunities for women and men.

- We focus on three specific areas that must change if we are to achieve and sustain gender equality in the workplace:

  1. the nature and frequency of performance evaluations and feedback
  2. the content and availability of training, coaching, and mentoring
  3. sponsorship opportunities for leadership development

- Women are overlooked or held back because of personnel practices that do not prevent affinity bias, which inevitably exist when senior leaders (mostly men) are far more likely to support, advise, and seek to advance those who are like them (typically other men).
- Organizations can also make meaningful strides toward gender equality by introducing steps to eliminate unconscious bias in their feedback and evaluation processes, such as putting in place the following actions:

  - Clearly define criteria, with no ambiguities or contradictory requirements.
  - Offer no opportunity for open-ended comments.
  - Establish and agree to evaluation criteria, in advance of the evaluation period.
  - Offer women the same direct feedback and opportunity to improve as they offer to men.

- Organizations should take affirmative steps to establish leadership development programs specifically designed to counter the discriminatory situations women face as they seek to climb the leadership leader. These include:

  - opportunities for women to develop and exercise their leadership abilities comparable to the opportunities men now have
  - mentoring from a senior leader on a regular, consistent basis

  - participation in women-only communities where they are comfortable in reflecting on gendered obstacles to leadership opportunities, exchanging experiences, and providing advice for dealing with these obstacles
  - explicit career counseling

- It is important that women be assigned senior leaders as mentors. To ensure active engagement and successful mentorships, leadership should provide effective training for mentors; choose individuals who are committed to mentoring; and create direct, detailed responsibilities for mentors and mentees.

PART IV

PUTTING IT ALL TOGETHER

Chapter 12

Making The PATH Changes

THE FOUR PRINCIPAL CHANGES THAT are called for by PATH are separate but interdependent changes that work together to effectively address all aspects of workplace gender inequality:

- Prioritize elimination of exclusionary behavior.
- Adopt discrimination-resistant methods of personnel decision-making.
- Treat inequality in the home as a workplace problem.
- Halt unequal performance reviews, career advice, and leadership opportunities.

PATH targets structural discrimination by ensuring that personnel systems, processes, and practices operate without the influence of gender stereotypes or their embedded status beliefs. In doing so, PATH also targets individual discrimination by transforming the workplace culture within which individuals judge, deal with, and interact with one another. There is, thus, a positive, mutually reinforcing interaction between the structural changes PATH recommends and the behavioral changes that result from those changes. As Jessica Nordell writes in *The End of Bias: A Beginning*, "Individuals create the processes, structures, and organizational cultures" that form the context within which personnel decisions are made, and these processes, structures, and cultures "in turn shape individuals' thoughts and actions."[1]

> Mounting a successful assault on gender inequality depends on a well-conceived, properly resourced, and imaginatively led initiative to bring about the PATH changes.

Although PATH recommends specific, practical, and realistic workplace changes to eliminate both structural discrimination and individual discrimination, these changes are not self-executing. An organization cannot simply announce its support of PATH and expect to see any reduction in gender inequality. Mounting a successful assault on gender inequality depends on a well-conceived, properly resourced, and imaginatively led initiative to bring about the PATH changes.

PATH is, therefore, similar to other efforts to transform important aspects of an organization's operations—say, to improve its customer service, increase its profitability, or transition to a digital environment.[2] Major organizational changes of this kind are notoriously difficult to successfully pull off. McKinsey & Company, for example, found that only 37 percent of companies that had launched a major change initiative were successful in achieving their desired results.[3] McKinsey also found that the most common reason that change initiatives fail is employee resistance to the proposed change.[4] Employee resistance is hardly surprising. As we saw in Chapter 2, status quo bias is a powerful obstacle to getting employees to change the ways they perform their jobs, to adopt new behaviors, and to accept new methods for performance evaluations. For that reason, successful implementation of the PATH changes depends, in large part, on managers' abilities to overcome employee resistance and persuade them to actively support PATH's implementation.[5]

There is likely to be another source of resistance to the PATH changes, and that is men's suspicion of, concern with, and outright hostility to workplace changes they see as designed to reduce their leadership dominance; undermine masculine norms, values, and expectations; and challenge long-accepted male privilege.

Successful PATH implementation depends on organizations overcoming *both* status quo bias *and* men's resistance to changes they perceive to be contrary to their self-interest. Let's examine the most effective ways leaders can overcome status quo bias, and then turn to how they can overcome men's concern that PATH may reduce their current power, resources, or status.

Overcoming Status Quo Bias

Status quo bias leads to very stubborn resistance to change. When asked to adopt new ways of doing jobs, adjust to new practices, or revisit the very basis upon which relationships with colleagues have been built, employees can behave (subtly or not so subtly) in ways that clearly convey, "I don't want to," or "I prefer not to."

Something makes me feel you aren't comfortable with change.

www.CartoonStock.com

Successful PATH implementation, therefore, depends on the ability of leaders to change attitudes from "Not on my watch," to "Sounds like a good idea. Let's do it!"

So how can organization do this? In our view, fostering the needed changes in employee's attitudes all comes down to strong leadership capable of motivating employees to do things that they initially don't want to do.[6] As David Shore, director of two Harvard Professional Development Programs focused on strategies for leading change, puts it, managing organizational change "has a cornerstone leading human capital (people) in a way that facilitates the next outcome. If you can't change your people, you can't change anything."[7]

To be successful, therefore, we believe organizations need to place that leadership of the PATH initiative in the hands of a carefully composed team—the PATH Team—with the power, resources, and influence to motivate employees—particularly middle managers—*to want to* support and make the recommended changes. First, let's consider the desirable attributes of the PATH Team members who will be responsible for steering and implementing the program.

The PATH Team

The composition of the PATH team is of paramount importance in overcoming an "I prefer not" attitude. It must be seen as broadly representative of all employee constituencies, supported fully by senior management, and with the ultimate authority to effect PATH's recommended changes. This means that PATH Team members need to be diverse, and drawn from at least three different groups:

- individuals in executive positions with such formal authority that their membership is seen as a clear indication of the organization's strong commitment to PATH
- experienced managers with widely recognized knowledge of the company's operations, well-earned reputations for getting things done, and without suspicion they are "yes men" for senior management
- rank-and-file career-track employees with wide and highly trusted informal influence

This last group is particularly important. These employees are what have been called "hidden influencers,"[8]—individuals who may not hold senior managerial positions or formal authority but who have earned deep respect among the organization's workforce and are very familiar with day-to-day operations. They should be capable of strongly influencing the viewpoints, attitudes, and behaviors of a significant number of other employees. In other words, they should generally by seen as role models and attitude leaders. Organizations might identify these individuals by surveying employees, asking such questions as "Whom do you go to for advice?" and "Whose perspective on workplace issues do you seek out?" Or, the organization might ask managers to identify the most highly respected individuals on their teams.

An effective PATH Team will include executives with extensive formal authority; managers with deep knowledge of personnel practices and how to effect change; and members of the rank and file who command wide respect and influence. Its size and structure will depend on the size and structure of the organization. Some organizations will have a single team whose purview is the entire company, while other organizations might have multiple teams with specific regional or divisional responsibilities. Regardless of its size, however, the PATH Team should have a comparable number of women and men among its members.

> An effective PATH Team will include executives with extensive formal authority; managers with deep knowledge of personnel practices and how to effect change; and members of the rank and file who command wide respect and influence.

Once team members are chosen, they will need to select a strong leader, establish clear rules of deliberation and decision-making, and agree on methods of taking related actions. These preliminary discussions should provide the team with valuable ways for members to get to know one another, come to grips with the extensive nature of their responsibilities and powers, and gain a sense of shared ownership for PATH's successful implementation.

Formulating a PATH Statement

The first substantive undertaking for the PATH Team should be the formulation of a statement as to why the organization is choosing PATH, the objectives it seeks to accomplish through PATH's implementation, and why those objectives will benefit the organization, its teams, and employees. This PATH Statement should address four key considerations.

1. The nature and operation of both structural and individual discrimination.
2. Why *not making the recommended changes* and maintaining the status quo would be contrary to the best interests of the organization, its teams, and its employees.
3. How PATH's four principles work in combination to end workplace gender inequality resulting from both structural and individual discrimination.
4. How and by whom PATH's recommended changes will be made to the organization's systems, processes, and practices.

The PATH Statement should be relatively brief, cogent, and compelling. Most importantly, it needs to be clearly grounded in the organization's core values, including its aspiration to be a true meritocracy. It should also make it clear that PATH is *not* an affirmative action program designed to advance women but a program to ensure that a workplace's decisions, practices, and policies operate in a fair, objective, and inclusive manner for everyone.

> The PATH Statement should be relatively brief, cogent, and compelling. Most importantly, it needs to be clearly grounded in the organization's core values, including its aspiration to be a true meritocracy.

By emphasizing that the PATH changes are designed to ensure that everyone's talents, achievements, and potentials are accurately evaluated and fairly rewarded, the PATH Team will have taken the first important step toward overcoming the "I prefer not to" attitude. It will have also opened the door for the PATH Team to undertake more direct, focused efforts to persuade middle managers that they will find it personally rewarding to serve as PATH's front-line change agents.

Selling the PATH Statement

Once the PATH Statement is released, the organization's CEO or most senior leader should publicly announce her or his full, unconditional, and active support for implementing all aspects of the PATH program. This announcement is the first step in what should become an active, focused campaign to sell the PATH Statement to key workplace participants—its middle managers.[9]

Middle managers are key to PATH's successful implementation because they will, ultimately, be the individuals actually responsible for making the recommended changes.[10] They will be changing the ways personnel decisions are made, the personnel policies that are adopted, and personnel practices that are followed. As MIT professor Jonathan Byrnes observes, "Regardless of what high-potential initiative the CEO chooses for the company, the middle management team's performance will determine whether it is a success or a failure."[11]

> "Regardless of what high-potential initiative the CEO chooses for the company, the middle management team's performance will determine whether it is a success or a failure."
>
> —Jonathan Byrnes

Undoubtedly, the initial reaction of many middle managers to release of the PATH Statement will be "What's this mean for me?"[12] In anticipation of this reaction, the PATH Team members need to formulate a convincing case for why PATH will be good for them personally; by increasing their authority and responsibility; assisting in creating high performance teams that are more productive, effective and collaborative, and reducing complaints about unfair treatment.

In order to convince middle managers that PATH will be good for them and for the organization, the PATH Team needs to transform their mindsets from "I prefer not to" to "I want to make this happen." McKinsey & Company found that "70 percent of the reason change doesn't happen is due to people's mindsets and beliefs."[13] Logic, reason, and data will not change people's mindsets. This can only be done by engaging with their emotions. Therefore, the PATH Team must find ways to engage emotionally with middle managers to get them invested in PATH's success, and excited about its benefits.

The most effective way the PATH Team can engage emotionally with the middle managers, in our view, is to establish active coaching and mentoring relations with them that are focused on the responsibilities they will have for PATH's implementation. As author Scott Edinger writes in the *Harvard Business Review*, "Coaching and developing others is…among the strongest connections a leader has at their disposal for inspiring people to achieve high levels of performance."[14] Through coaching, mentoring, and advising, the PATH Team can build the emotional bonds with middle managers that are needed to persuade them to change their mindsets. These emotional bonds can also be used to help middle managers, "transition from one emotional state to another—from reacting to the loss of the status quo to being creative about the future."[15]

The PATH Team can also forge strong emotional bonds with middle managers through open dialogue about these managers' concerns, difficulties, fears, objections, and disagreements. With frequent, no-holds-barred conversations, the PATH Team can strengthen these managers' sense of being part of a community effort to create a workplace that functions effectively to advance the organization's interests, their teams' interests, their direct reports' interests, and their personal interests. This dialogue can help middle managers come to see not only what needs to change, but why it needs to change. By fostering frequent, candid, honest conversations, the PATH Team will help middle managers work through their discomfort, realize that such discomfort is a necessary component of change, and come to see enormous benefits to be realized by effecting the recommended changes.

With coaching, development efforts, and active dialogue, the PATH Team should be able to generate the emotional energy and focus the middle managers need to move them away from the status quo and toward full embrace of the recommended changes. Once the PATH Team is confident that the middle managers are ready to positively engage with the contemplated changes, it is time to begin the actual implementation process. Not all middle managers need to be convinced of the need for or value of PATH, but their attitudes and mindsets need to be, at a minimum, open to working for PATH's implementation. Until the PATH Team is certain that this is the case, it is pointless to begin implementation efforts.

The inevitable question is what should the PATH Team do about managers who can't be moved away from the "Not on my watch" mindset, who obstinately refuse to change, and who are firmly wedded to the status quo. If there are managers who remain intransigent, the Team might decide these managers do not belong in an inclusive organization and need to move on from the organization.

Implementing the PATH Plan

When the PATH Team believes the workplace is ready to positively engage with the PATH changes, it should announce when, where, and how these changes will begin to be made. In other words, the PATH Team should present a plan for implementation of recommended changes—the PATH Plan. Although all of PATH's changes need to be made before workplace gender inequality is finally and completely eliminated, changes cannot and should not be initiated at the same time. Some can occur relatively quickly; others will take longer to become a reality; while still others will require far more resources, managerial effort, and employee engagement before they can be effected. For example, an organization can take concrete steps to prevent exclusionary behavior in its workplaces relatively quickly, but it will take much longer for it to establish an appropriate gender-conscious leadership development program.

The PATH Plan needs to be explicit about how employees and particularly middle managers will be persuaded to abandon their shared everyday habits about how to do personnel management and to adopt new habits in this regard.[16]

As John Kotter writes, "Change sticks when it...seeps into the bloodstream of the corporate body. Until new behaviors are rooted in social norms and shared values, they are subject to degradation as soon as the pressure for change is removed."[17]

> "Change sticks when it...seeps into the bloodstream of the corporate body. Until new behaviors are rooted in social norms and shared values, they are subject to degradation as soon as the pressure for change is removed."
>
> —John Kotter

Personnel-management habits are not unlike a long-followed route a driver takes to get to work. If that driver *can be convinced* that a different route is faster with less chance of delays and accidents, the driver is likely to change routes—establishing over time a new driving habit. Likewise, if middle managers *can be convinced* that the new, different approaches to personnel management will lead to a more productive workplace, less prone to the influence of discrimination, they are likely to change their habits in this regard.

Managers are far more likely *to be convinced* that they should adopt new personnel-management habits if the PATH Team can "materialize" for them what the new habits will look like, how they will feel, and how they can be acquired. As Emily Balcetis, associate professor of psychology at New York University, explains in *Clearer, Closer, Better: How Successful People See the World*,[18] when individuals can materialize new ways of behaving—can form a picture of the new behavior that is clear,

Managers are far more likely *to be convinced* that they should adopt new personnel-management habits if the PATH Team can "materialize" for them what the new habits will look like, how they will feel, and how they can be acquired.

specific, and concrete—they are far more likely to be successful in working that new behavior up into a new habit. And, indeed, the acquisition of new habits is the most effective way to overcome their status quo bias.

The critical roles middle managers must play in PATH's implementation, and the methods by which their personnel-management habits are changed, should be common features of all PATH Plans. Beyond those commonalities, however, the PATH Plans will differ from organization to organization. Such plans must take into consideration the specific features of each organization's culture; the most problematic areas of its personnel-management practices, and what other change initiatives are going on at the organization at the same time. With that said, however, every PATH Plan should address:

- The process by which the PATH Team will receive feedback, reactions, criticisms, and expressions of support or opposition. In other words, every organization needs to have a process by which anyone affected by the PATH changes can offer comments on, criticism of, and suggestions for improving the implementation process.[19]
- The reasons each step in the implementation process is being taken; the benefits expected to be realized by taking it; and how that step fits in with other steps to make the organization's workplaces more fair, objective, and inclusive. Such reasons are essential to ensuring that employees have confidence that the PATH Team knows what it is doing, recognizes the intended benefits of the changes, and is comfortable that the changes will not endanger their psychological safety. As Professor Kanter notes, if employee

are to support a major change initiative, they need a sense of psychological safety "as well as an inspiring vision."[20]

- The process by which middle managers will regularly keep the members of their teams informed about the progress being made; the setbacks that have been encountered; and any shifts in direction that may be needed. This informational process needs to be two-way—managers need to keep their team members informed about developments; and team members need to keep their managers informed about reactions, complaints, and suggestions for improving the implementation process.

- The process by which to ensure there is a steady series of "small wins"—tangible, incremental advances in eliminating gender inequality. Workplace engagement increases if people see evidence that their projects are moving forward, even if that is only by incremental amounts. A series of small wins often has a surprisingly strong positive effect, because it begins to reveal a pattern that attracts allies, deters opponents, and lowers resistance to subsequent changes.

- A change process involving "small steps." As Bill Taylor, cofounder of *Fast Company*, writes, "The best way to get people to change something big, or do something hard, is to first ask them to change something small or do something easy."[21] Once managers have taken small steps and have achieved positive results, they are far more likely to be willing to take increasingly bigger steps the next time.

- How the organization will provide support, reassurance, and counseling to employees who are disoriented by the changes. As we have seen, it is difficult for organizations to accomplish major changes, and one of the reasons this is so difficult is because people are often uncertain as to their ability to play their expected part in effecting change. As a result, the PATH Team should, as Professor Kantor writes "over-invest in structural reassurance, providing abundant information, education, training, mentor, and support systems."[22] In this regard, a PATH Plan should specify the process by which the PATH Team will monitor managers' moods, attitudes, and level of engagement. When engagement lags, discouragement is apparent, or resistance increases, the PATH Team needs to have a ready plan to provide needed encouragement and support to help employees get back on track.

A strong PATH Team will formulate a compelling PATH Statement, that effectively "sells" the need for and value of the recommended changes, and develops an effective, comprehensive PATH Plan for implementing those changes. If a PATH Team can do this, it will be successful in overcoming status quo bias and employees' "not on my watch" mindsets. Employees will come to appreciate the full extent to which workplace gender inequality is hurting their organization's productivity, its teams' performance, and their personal engagement, satisfaction, and sense of value.

Dealing with Men's Self-Protective Instincts

In Chapter 6, we looked at men's lack of involvement in efforts to end workplace gender inequality. But beyond being reluctant to participate in DEI efforts, men can also be active opponents of such efforts. There are basically three reasons men might oppose the implementation of PATH's workplace changes: zero-sum thinking, gender bias, and fear of losing power. Let's look at each of these reasons and how a PATH Team can best to deal with them.

> There are basically three reasons men might oppose the implementation of PATH's workplace changes: zero-sum thinking, gender bias, and fear of losing power.

1. Zero-Sum Thinking

Zero-sum thinking is an assumption people commonly make that situations involve either their winning or their losing. In other words, zero-sum thinking assumes one person's gain must come at the expense of another person's loss. When men think in this way, they see women's workplace advance as implying their workplace retreat. They believe that in order for women's workplace situation to get better, their situation must get worse.[23]

At a certain level, zero-sum thinking is unquestionably correct: if a C-suite has 12 members, eight of whom are now men, and women increase their C-suite representation from four to six, there will be two fewer men in the C-suite. This, however, is not the normal focus of men's zero-sum thinking. Rather, their thinking in this respect operates at a more general, abstract level, independent of any specific, concrete experience. Zero-sum thinking assumes that economic opportunities are finite and fixed. Thus, if women get more opportunities, men must get less; a status gain for women must involve a status loss for men; and women's increase in power, must necessarily mean men's loss of power.[24]

> Zero-sum thinking assumes that economic opportunities are finite and fixed. Thus, if women get more opportunities, men must get less; a status gain for women must involve a status loss for men; and women's increase in power, must necessarily mean men's loss of power.

Zero-sum thinking is wrong as a matter of economic reality. Economic opportunities are not fixed but can be increased. Therefore, to overcome zero-sum thinking, the PATH Team needs to attack it both intellectually and emotionally. Intellectually, the PATH Team needs to assemble data on the economy as a whole, as well as on stand-out companies that make it clear that *increasing women's participation in leadership increases, not decreases, everyone's career opportunities.* The PATH Team's presentation in this regard needs to show not only that women's advancement does not require men to lose ground, but also that men are better off when women advance. Men gain increased access to information, greater exposure to diverse ideas and networks, and more opportunities to develop enhanced interpersonal skills.

Zero-sum thinking must also be confronted psychologically by engaging employees in productive, collaborative mixed-gender team projects. By structuring work teams so that men work with strong, capable women, they can experience women's ascent without loss of their own status or authority. In addition, men need to hear from other men about positive career developments that resulted from working with or reporting to women. Moreover, when women and men work together to achieve common goals, they often have positive experiences of increased effectiveness, improved job satisfaction, and greater career engagement.[25]

2. Gender Stereotypes

Men also resist efforts to increase women's leadership opportunities because they hold the status beliefs inherent in gender stereotypes. Because of such status beliefs, men can regard women—in comparison to men—as less competent performers, weaker leaders, poorer competitors, and less able negotiators. As we have seen throughout this book, such beliefs are not true.[26] So again, the PATH Team needs to counter this source of opposition to PATH both intellectually and emotionally.

- Intellectually, the PATH Team needs to present persuasive data demonstrating that women are just as ambitious, competitive, competent, and committed to their careers as are men.[27] Moreover, the PATH Team needs to convincingly show that women are just as likely to want to continue to pursue challenging careers after becoming a parent as men.[28]
- Psychologically, men's status beliefs can be undermined by exposing them to strong, committed, and highly skilled women. Such status beliefs can also be discredited when men observe other men praising, promoting, and choosing to work with women; when they observe other men intervening to interrupt biased judgment about or disparagement of women's accomplishments, abilities, and potential; and when they see other men supporting, rewarding, and standing up for women. Such personal experiences should give men a strong nudge to reject gender stereotypes with their embedded status beliefs.[29]

3. Power

Another source of men's potential opposition to PATH's implementation is their fear of losing power in relation to women. Power in this instance is equated with control,[30] and being in control—whether at home, at work, or in social relationships—is often the way men define themselves as men. In other words, being in control is the essence of their masculinity and the core of their personal identity.[31] Therefore, for men who think this way, initiatives to increase women's workplace power are a direct attack on their defining who they are.[32]

The PATH Team needs to undermine this equation of being a man with being in control in situations involving women. This can be done, for example, by the PATH Team structuring workgroups so that men are put into situations in which they share power and control with women. Such experiences are likely to foster a sense that women's exercise of power does not necessarily come at the cost of men's power—that power and control can be shared. The PATH Team's objective, therefore, should be to show men that their power is not a function of their gender but of their competence and accomplishments.

> The PATH Team needs to undermine this equation of being a man with being in control in situations involving women.

KEY TAKEAWAYS

- The PATH Program recommends effective techniques for eliminating both structural discrimination and individual discrimination. It is not self-executing.
- Transformational change is notoriously difficult, and eliminating gender inequality is a transformational change. To be successful,

the PATH Plan will require the same leadership and resources as any other major organizational transformation effort.

- We identify two specific types of employee resistance that can impede successful PATH implementation: general employee resistance and specifically men's suspicion of workplace changes likely to reduce their long-accepted male privilege.

- Successful PATH implementation will come down to the organization's ability to change each employee's attitude from "I prefer not to" to one of "I think this is a good idea."

- We believe the best way to do this is to create the PATH Team with the vision, power, resources, and influence to motivate employees—particularly middle managers—to want to support and make recommended changes.

- The PATH Team will include executives with extensive formal authority; managers with deep knowledge of personnel practices and how to effect change; and people who command wide respect and influence.

- We identify three key steps the PATH Team must go through to be successful: (1) Formulate a compelling and inspiring vision statement that includes the company's reasons for seeking to establish the PATH Program; (2) Sell the vision statement, specifically to middle managers; and (3) Develop a strategic plan for PATH's implementation.

- The PATH Team must be prepared to act to overcome or, at least, address possible opposition from (some) male managers. There are three reasons men might oppose establishment of the PATH Principles: zero-sum thinking, gender bias, and fear of losing power.

- If organizations realize that the benefits they will reap from ending workplace gender inequality are just as great as those they would obtain from direct efforts to increase their productivity, innovation, employee retention, and gain new customers or clients, there is real hope that workplace gender inequality can be ended in the foreseeable future. PATH is a practical, effective, and realistically achievable way for companies to achieve this goal.

Chapter 13

The Promise of PATH

DESPITE THE ENORMOUS PROGRESS WOMEN have made in entering, advancing, and excelling in previously all-male career fields, America's workplaces remain persistently and severely unequal for women and men. Current DEI initiatives have made little progress over recent years in reducing this inequality. With the best of intentions and the expenditure of great amounts of time, effort, and resources, DEI initiatives have made little difference in the gender makeup of organizational leadership, or in women's sense of workplace inclusion, engagement, and satisfaction.

The promise of PATH is a way out of this unproductive, wasteful, and discouraging situation. PATH is a new, different, and effective way to finally put an end to workplace gender inequality. Women are ready to move up but they are frustrated by the resistance they experience; they are capable of leading but discouraged by the gendered obstacles to their doing so; and they are positioned to make major contributions to their organizations, but are angry because they are not appropriately recognized when they do. PATH offers these women and their organizations a clear, achievable, and realistic way forward. It offers a way to transform our workplaces from places in which gender matters for achievement, acceptance, and recognition to inclusive places where gender is irrelevant and meritocracies are a reality.

This book reflects our long history of battling gender inequality. It presents how, when, and where organizations can effect a transition to equality. There will, of course, be opposition, resistance, and skepticism. But PATH works; it can reenergize existing DEI initiatives, give them a new focus, and set them on a new, more sharply defined and effective path forward.

PATH does not attempt to end workplace gender inequality by training people to behave in less biased and more inclusive ways. Individuals' current biased workplace behavior is a symptom of the structural inequality in their workplace. PATH shows organizations how to change their workplace systems, processes, and practices so that instead of systemically fostering unequal career outcomes for women and men, they operate in fair, equal, and gender-neutral ways. PATH provides organizations with the tools and techniques they need to ensure that their workplaces are inclusive, supportive, and resistant to individual discrimination.

The promise of PATH lies in the practical, effective, and realistic ways in which its recommended changes can transform gendered workplaces to workplaces characterized by true inclusion because their participants feel both fairly treated and able to be their authentic selves because of psychological safety. The promise of PATH is the promise of workplace gender equality.

PATH's promise is bold but attainable: it is a promise that workplaces can function in better, fairer, and more inclusive ways for everyone. But beyond the workplace, PATH also holds out the promise of significant benefit in many other areas as well. Because workplaces are an important source of individuals' power, resources, and status in our society, PATH will lead to greater equality between women and men, at large. By association, this should have a positive effect on the media, the public sphere, and the home.

PATH and the Media

Workplace gender equality will make it much less likely that movies, television, and advertising will depict women and men in traditionally stereotypical ways. If business, professional, and nonprofit leadership is far more gender diverse than it is now, there will be far less credibility in depicting women as primarily concerned with domestic matters, happy to devote themselves to childcare to the exclusion of career advancement, comfortable leaving the breadwinning role to their partners, or simply serving as the love interest of a movie hero. Moreover, as we begin to progress toward more inclusive, respectful, harassment-free workplaces, characterizing women in sexually objectified ways will come to be seen as incongruous and inappropriate.

PATH and the Public Sphere

In the Introduction we called attention to the intensified assault on women's rights and ambitions. With increased power, resources, and status, women will be in a position to better defend their rights and challenge disparaging comments about their ambitions and achievements. This is not to say that forces that stand in opposition to equal social and domestic status will fold their tents and slink away. They will not, but it will become increasingly apparent that these forces are fighting a losing battle. As more women ascend to leadership roles, the credibility of the claim that their place is in the home will dwindle. With equal opportunities to acquire power, resources, and status, women will cease to be such easy targets when they demonstrate strength, confidence, and leadership abilities, and it will come to be less easy for anyone to spout misogynistic nonsense that women don't belong in prominent public roles.

PATH and the Home

Unquestionably, gender inequality in the home—unequal responsibilities for childcare and eldercare, unequal authority over finances and fundamental life choices, and unequal career and lifestyle priorities—is the most intransigent of all manifestations of gender inequality. Nevertheless, the greatest hope for its elimination lies in the increase in women's career opportunities and meritocratic advancements on a par with men in the workplace. Gender inequality in the home is a direct reflection of pervasive gender stereotypes and their accompanying status beliefs. Eliminating gender inequality in the workplace will strike a blow against these stereotypes and status beliefs. When that happens, homelife should also begin to change, and as gender stereotypes and status beliefs fade; so, too, will patterns of domestic gender inequality.

PATH and the Future

PATH provides organizations with the realistic possibility of ending both structural and individual discrimination—the twin sources of workplace gender inequality. Organizational leaders' recognition of the benefits that PATH can bring will mark the beginning of the end of workplace gender inequality. With PATH, organizations can make their workplaces true meritocracies: diverse, inclusive, and satisfying places for everyone. The promise of PATH is a richer, more creative, and more productive life for us all.

GLOSSARY

This glossary of key terms we use in this book is designed to provide a useful reference guide and aid in avoiding misunderstandings or confusion.

Affinity bias: An implicit or explicit preference to associate with people who share one's own social identity (often thought of as in-group members) over people of different social identities (often thought of as out-group members). It is a tendency to favor the familiar over the different. Affinity bias systematically disadvantages women in their careers simply because they are not "like" the men who make up the overwhelming majority of leaders in their workplaces. Affinity bias causes those leaders to prefer to assign work to, socialize with, and provide more support to other men.

Agentic: Derived from the word *agency*, this term describes a person who exhibits stereotypically masculine traits, such as being assertive, competitive, independent, self-confident, proactive, strong, forceful, loud, rational, unemotional, and risk taking. Leaders are stereotypically seen as agentic. See *communal* for characteristics attributed to women.

Backlash: A catchall term that refers to the negative consequences women often experience when they act in agentic ways, and men experience when they act in communal ways. These negative consequences include being excluded from important meetings, networks, and events; being stigmatized for behaviors; being criticized for lacking in social sensitivity; or discriminated against for acting contrary to stereotypical expectations. Men also fear backlash from other men when they support efforts to end gender inequality.

Benevolent bias: An attitude most often expressed by senior men (but which can also be expressed by senior women) who believe that traditional gender stereotypes correctly characterize women's capacities and appropriate roles. As a consequence, these leaders behave toward women who work for them in benevolent ways—solicitous, kind, considerate, concerned, helpful, protective, and patronizing. But they do not provide these women with the same career opportunities and responsibilities as the men that work for them. Benevolent bias is also seen in the annual reviews given to women, where women are not given feedback on ways they can improve their performance. It is a form of sexism.

Bias: We use the word *bias* to refer to the predisposition to engage in discriminatory behavior toward members of a social identity group as the result of stereotypes of one sort or another that are held about members of that group. Bias can be manifested in treating people in one social identity group less favorably than people in another, or by preferentially advancing, providing more opportunities for, or compensating more generously those people in one group over another. It can also be demonstrated negatively by refusing to hire, interact with, or consider for particular tasks or projects a person from a social identity group. It is also displayed by viewing people in a different social identity group as having decidedly unpleasant or objectionable personal qualities.

Communal: Derived from *community* and *communion*, the term *communal* describes a person with characteristics and traits that are stereotypically feminine, such as being nurturing, kind, sympathetic, concerned with the needs of others, socially sensitive, warm, approachable, understanding, solicitous of others' feelings, emotional, sentimental, gentle, domestic, family-focused, good with children, modest, and friendly. A communal person is stereotypically seen as a good assistant or helper, not as a good leader. See *agentic* for characteristics attributed to men.

Double bind: A psychological state in which a person receives conflicting messages and faces a negative outcome, no matter which of two available behaviors that person adopts. For an example, see *Goldilocks dilemma*.

Explicit bias: A negative attitude or preconception that is held about the characteristics of people in a particular social identity group.

Feminine stereotypes: The traditional, often unconscious, belief that women are and should be communal and should not be (very) agentic. See *communal* and *agentic*.

Gender: The socially constructed different identities women and men have in the context of social interactions. The term *feminine* refers to women's socially approved norms, attitudes, and characteristics, and *masculine* refers to men's socially approved norms, attitudes, and characteristics. Gender is to be contrasted to women and men by biological sex differences.[1] Not all individuals and groups of people, however, "fit established gender norms." In this book, we attempt to be sensitive to individuals and

groups with gender identities other than female and male, such as nonbi-
nary, gender nonconforming, queer, and gender-fluid individuals.

Gender bias: The manifestation of the status beliefs as to the superiority of
men over women, the masculine over the feminine; agentic behavior over
communal behavior. These status beliefs are embedded in our society's
pervasive gender stereotypes. This is the underpinning for beliefs that men
will lead more effectively, perform more competently, behave more competitively, negotiate more forcefully, and display stronger career commitment than women. Gender bias consists of two distinct forms: sexism and
misogyny.

Gender stereotypes: Reflexive, automatic, often unconscious beliefs, expectations, and preconceptions that people (women and men) hold about the
qualities, capacities, and characteristics of other people (and themselves)
because of their gender.

Goldilocks dilemma: The double bind women face because they suffer by being
dismissed as effective leaders when they conform to communal stereotypes
but being disliked and thought to be too unpleasant to be effective leaders when they behave in accordance with agentic stereotypes. We refer to
this double bind as the Goldilocks dilemma because women are frequently
viewed as too soft (too communal) or too hard (too agentic) but rarely just
right. See *double bind*.

Greedy jobs: Jobs that pay substantially more compensation than other jobs.
They provide little flexibility and require people in greedy jobs to always be
available, requiring long, "heroic" hours of work.

Implicit bias: A person's automatic, unconscious attribution of stereotypical
characteristics to members of particular social identity groups.

Inclusion: A sense of being welcomed, valued, and listened to on one's team
and in one's workplace.

In-group bias: Favoring the people in your social identity group or more limited circle of people of similar status. Members of a dominant in-group
can display favoritism toward other in-group members, without feeling or
behaving in negative ways toward out-group members.

Incivility: Rude or discourteous behavior that can be experienced in a variety of
ways, including receiving condescending comments or microaggressions;
having one's competence disparaged; enduring social and professional
snubs; being excluded from valuable networks and work-related social
activities; being ignored or dismissed; dealt with sarcastically; interrupted
or talked over; contradicted rudely; or treated with disregard. Incivility
is a relatively mild form of what is often referred to as counterproductive

workplace behavior. More severe forms of such behavior include interpersonal aggression, bullying, and deliberate social and professional undermining. These hostile behaviors are typically undertaken with the unambiguous intent to harm another person. Workplace incivility, by contrast, is not necessarily designed to harm someone else as much as it is to express disapproval, displeasure, or distaste at another person.

Individual discrimination: Individual discrimination leads to systematic exclusion, treatment, and expectation of women as less important, less valuable, or less important than men.

Intersectionality: The intersection of distinct social identities with gender. Such identities include race, age, abilities, education, ethnicity, gender identity, religion, sexual orientation, LGBTQ+ identification, socioeconomic status, and so on. A woman's intersectional characteristics contribute to her unique experiences and perspectives. It complicates the nature of the workplace discrimination she faces. As a result, gender equality may remove all forms of workplace discrimination for some women but not others.

Masculine stereotypes: The traditional, often unconscious, assumption that men are and should be agentic and that they should not be (very) communal.

Microaggressions: A form of incivility involving a comment or action (often unconscious or unintentional) that expresses a prejudiced attitude toward someone who is a member of a marginalized group (such as a woman, a racial or ethnic minority, or an LGBTQ+ person). Microaggressions are slights that convey a derogatory or negative view or opinion about a marginalized person or group. See *incivility*.

Out-group bias: Disparagement of persons who are not in one's in-group. It is often expressed through (intentional or unintentional) exclusion, incivility, or harassment. There is a very thin line between feeling comfortable with other in-group members and feeling uncomfortable with out-group members. There is another very thin line between feeling uncomfortable with out-group members and disparaging or expressing hostility toward them.

PATH Program: A two-pronged approach to end workplace gender inequality. It is based on the premise that the inequalities from structural discrimination and individual discrimination can only be eliminated through changes to a company's personnel-management systems, processes, and practices. PATH has four components: (1) **Prioritize** elimination of exclusionary behavior; (2) **Adopt** bias-free methods of decision-making; (3) **Treat** inequality in the home as a workplace problem; and (4) **Halt** unequal performance evaluations and leadership development opportunities.

Sexism: The (implicit or explicit) assumption that women should be caregivers and assistants, without comparable roles, responsibilities, and opportunities that are available to men.

Social identity: A person's self-identified membership in a social identity group or groups—such as race, ethnicity, gender, social class, sexual orientation, gender identification, LGBTQ+ identification, physical ability, or religion.

Status quo bias: Resistance to change. Similar to affinity bias, status quo bias expresses a preference for, or greater comfort with, the familiar. Status quo bias can be thought of as a preference for "the devil you know," rather than "the devil you don't." While there is considerable variation among people in their aversion to change, status quo bias is often a powerful force generating significant resistance to social change. Status quo bias is a powerful obstacle to getting employees to change the ways they perform their jobs, to adopt new behaviors, and to accept new methods for performance evaluations. Status quo bias also reinforces male leaders' resistance to making fundamental changes in established practices.

Stepping-stone positions: CEOs, CFOs, and P&L positions are the stepping-stone positions that lead to ever greater advancement and election to the board of directors at another public company. They are the positions that also lead to C-suite positions.

Stereotypes: We use the word *stereotype* to refer to a characteristic or set of characteristics that people ascribe to people (including themselves) based on their distinctive social identities, such as gender, sexual orientation, gender identity, LGBTQ+ identity, race, ethnicity, age, and motherhood. When people believe (consciously or unconsciously) without actual credible information that a person of a particular social group has the stereotypical characteristics associated with that group, they are making a biased or prejudiced evaluation that can lead to discriminatory consequences. Stereotypes are overly broad and unsupported generalizations about characteristics supposedly shared by members of the stereotyped group. Stereotypes function as scripts for behavior—prescribing how people should be evaluated and regarded and how others should relate to them. Such scripts frequently result in discriminatory behavior.

Systemic problem: Results from the operation of a system—an established way in which an organization operates, the interconnected set of norms, values, and expectations that define its culture. Workplace gender inequality is a systemic problem because women's and men's unequal career outcomes result from the ways in which their workplace systems function.

Unconscious bias: See *implicit bias*.

NOTES

Introduction

1. Janet L. Yellen, "The History of Women's Work and Wages and How It Has Created Success for Us All," *The Brookings Institution,* May 2020, https://www.brookings.edu/essay/the-history-of-womens-work-and-wages-and-how-it-has-created-success-for-us-all/.
2. Andrea S. Kramer and Alton B. Harris, *Breaking Through Bias: Communication Techniques for Women to Succeed at Work,* 2nd ed. (Boston & London: Nicholas Brealey, 2020).
3. Teresa M. Amabile and Steven J. Kramer, "The Power of Small Wins," *Harvard Business Review,* May 2011, https://hbr.org/2011/05/the-power-of-small-wins.
4. Rosabeth Moss Kanter, "The Interplay of Structure and Behavior: How System Dynamics Can Explain or Change Outcomes by Gender or Social Category," Harvard Business School, https://www.hbs.edu/faculty/Shared%20Documents/conferences/2013-w50-research-symposium/kanter.pdf.
5. Kimberlé W. Crenshaw, *On Intersectionality: Essential Writings* (New York: The New Press, 2017).
6. *Roe v. Wade,* 410 US 113 (1973).
7. *Dobbs v. Jackson Women's Health Organization,* 945 F. 3d 265.
8. Sheryl Gay Stolberg "In Missouri, Battles Over Birth Control Foreshadow a Post-Roe World," *New York Times,* June 25, 2022, https://www.nytimes.com/2022/06/13/us/politics/birth-control-roe-v-wade.html.
9. Rachel Sun, "UI Employees Say Memo on Abortion, Contraception Creating Chill Effect in Classroom," *NWPB,* October 3, 2022, https://www.nwpb.org/2022/10/03/ui-employees-say-memo-on-abortion-contraception-creating-chilling-effect-in-classroom/. *Also, see Celeste Huang-Menders, "The Fight to Protect Contraception Rights After Dobbs," Women's Media*

Center, August 4, 2022, https://womensmediacenter.com/fbomb/the-fight -to-protect-contraceptive-rights-after-dobbs.

10. Sara Edwards, "What To Do if CVS, the Nation's Largest Pharmacy, Refuses To Fill Your Birth Control," *USA Today,* July 29, 2022, https:// www.usatoday.com/story/money/retail/2022/07/27/pharmacist-wont-fill -birth-control-because-faith/10154078002/.

11. María Luisa Paúl, "14-year-old's Arthritis Meds Denied After Arizona Abortion Ban, Doctor Says," *The Washington Post,* October 5, 2022, https:// www.washingtonpost.com/nation/2022/10/05/abortion-arizona-arthritis -prescription-refill/.

12. Right to Contraception Act, H.R. 8373, 117th Cong. (2022), https://www .congress.gov/bill/117th-congress/house-bill/8373/text.

13. Kramer and Harris, *Breaking Through Bias,* 47.

14. "When Women Are the Enemy: The Intersection of Misogyny and White Supremacy," Anti-Defamation League, July 20, 2018, https://www.adl .org/resources/reports/when-women-are-the-enemy-the-intersection-of -misogyny-and-white-supremacy.

15. Kristin Kobes du Mez, *Jesus and John Wayne: How White Evangelicals Corrupted a Faith and Fractured a Nation* (New York: Liveright Publishing Corporation, 2020).

16. Kramer and Harris, *Breaking Through Bias*, Chapter 5.

Chapter 1

1. "Class of 2020 National Summary Report," National Association for Law Placement, Inc. (NALP), August 26, 2021, https://www.nalp.org/uploads /NationalSummary Report_Classof2020.pdf.

2. "Degrees Conferred by Race/Ethnicity and Sex," U.S. Department of Education. Institute of Education Sciences, National Center for Education Statistics, https://nces.ed.gov/fastfacts/display.asp?id=72.

3. Mary Biekert and Bloomberg, "MBA Programs Have Record High Female Enrollment This Year—but It's Still Only 41%," November 21, 2021, https://fortune.com/2021/11/12/mba-programs-record-high-female -enrollment/.

4. "2020 Vault/MCCA Law Firm Diversity Survey Report," Vault and the Minority Corporate Counsel Association (MCCA), 2020, https://mcca .com/wp-content/uploads/2021/02/2020-Vault_MCCA-Law-Firm -Diversity-Survey-Report-FINAL.pdf.

5. "Women in the Workplace 2022," LeanIn.Org and McKinsey & Company, October 18, 2022, https://www.mckinsey.com/~/media/mckinsey/featured%20insights/diversity%20and%20inclusion/women%20in%20the%20workplace%202022/women-in-the-workplace-2022.pdf.
6. Dan Marcec, "Q1 2021 Equality Gender Diversity Index," Equilar, May 20, 2021, https://www.equilar.com/reports/81-q1-2021-equilar-gender-diversity-index.
7. David F. Larcker and Brian Tayan, "Diversity in the C-Suite: The Dismal State of Diversity Among Fortune 100 Senior Executives," *Rock Center for Corporate Governance at Stanford University Closer Look Series: Topics, Issues, and Controversies in Corporate Governance* No. CGRP-82, April 1, 2020, https://www.gsb.stanford.edu/faculty-research/publications/diversity-c-suite.
8. Larcker and Tayan, "Diversity in the C-Suite."
9. Maggie McGrath, "You Won't Believe How Many All-Female CEO-CFO Duos Run The 500 Largest Public U.S. Companies," *Forbes*, October 17, 2022, https://www.forbes.com/sites/maggiemcgrath/2022/10/17/you-wont-believe-how-many-all-female-ceo-cfo-duos-run-the-500-largest-public-us-companies/?sh=74bb17996679.
10. Jackie Cook, "What Will It Take to Close the Gender Pay Gap for Good?" *Morningstar*, February 22, 2021, https://www.morningstar.com/articles/1025601/what-will-it-take-to-close-the-gender-pay-gap-for-good.
11. Cook, "What Will It Take."
12. Larcker and Tayan, "Diversity in the C-Suite."
13. Larcker and Tayan, "Diversity in the C-Suite."
14. Dan Kaplan and Jane Stevenson, "Women C-Suite Ranks Nudge Up—A Tad," Korn Ferry, https://www.kornferry.com/insights/this-week-in-leadership/women-in-leadership-2019-statistic.
15. Erin Lehr, "Why Are So Few Women in the C-Suite?" Equilar, December 8, 2020, https://www.equilar.com/blogs/492-why-are-so-few-women-in-the-c-suite.html.
16. Vanessa Fuhrmans, "Where Are All the Women CEOs?" *Wall Street Journal*, February 6, 2020, https://www.wsj.com/articles/why-so-few-ceos-are-women-you-can-have-a-seat-at-the-table-and-not-be-a-player-11581003276.
17. Steven N. Kaplan and Morten Sorensen, "Are CEOs Different? Characteristics of Top Managers," No. w23832, *National Bureau of Economic Research*, September 2017, https://www.nber.org/papers/w23832.
18. Kaplan and Sorensen, "Are CEOs Different?"

19. Ahu Yildirmaz, Christopher Ryan, and Jeff Nezaj, "2019 State of the Work-force Report," ADP Research Institute, April 16, 2019, https://www.adpri .org/assets/2019-state-of-the-workforce-report/.

20. Yildirmaz, Ryan, and Nezaj, "2019 State of the Workforce."

21. "Women in the Workplace 2022," LeanIn.Org and McKinsey & Company.

22. Audrey Williams June, "Despite Progress, Only 1 in 4 College Presidents Are Women," *The Chronicle of Higher Education*, March 16, 2015, https:// www.chronicle.com/article/despite-progress-only-1-in-4-college-presidents -are-women/.

23. Linda Searing, "The Big Number: Women Now Outnumber Men in Medical Schools," *Washington Post*, December 23, 2019, https://www .washingtonpost.com/health/the-big-number-women-now-outnumber -men-in-medical-schools/2019/12/20/8b9eddea-2277-11ea-bed5-880264cc 91a9_story.html.

24. Amy Paturel, "Where Are All the Women Deans?" Association of American Medical Colleges ("AAMC"), June 11, 2019, https://www.aamc.org/news -insights/where-are-all-women-deans.

25. "What Is It Like for Women in Consulting?" Consultiful, https://www .consultiful.com/women-in-consulting/.

26. Alison Rogish, Stacy Sandler, and Neda Shemluck, "Within Reach? Achiev-ing Gender Equity in Financial Services Leadership," *Deloitte Insights,* November 19, 2019, https://www2.deloitte.com/us/en/insights/industry/ financial-services/women-in-financial-services-leadership-roles.html.

27. Brian Martucci, "Where Are All the Women Architecture Leaders?" *Finance & Commerce*, February 27, 2020, https://finance-commerce.com /2020/02/where-are-all-the-women-architecture-leaders/.

28. "Women in STEM Statistics to Inspire Future Leaders," *BigRentz*, Febru-ary 23, 2021, https://www.bigrentz.com/blog/women-in-stem-statistics/.

29. Martha M. Lauzen, "The Celluloid Ceiling: Behind-the-Scenes Employment of Women on the Top U.S. Films of 2020," 2021, *The Center for Women in Television and Film*, https://womenintvfilm.sdsu.edu/wp-content/uploads /2021/01/2020_Celluloid_Ceiling_Report.pdf.

30. "2019 Statistics," Women and Hollywood, 2019, https://womenand hollywood.com/resources/statistics/2019-statistics/#:~:text=Females %20accounted%20for%2037%25%20of,had%2010%20or%20more %20females.

31. "Report Card on Female Representation in Hollywood Shows Few Women at the Top," *Variety* online, December 13, 2017, https://variety.com/2017 /biz/news/women-in-leadership-roles-hollywood-1202638260/.

32. Kim Parker, Juliana Menasce Horowitz, and Renee Stepler, "On Gender Differences, No Consensus on Nature vs. Nurture," Pew Research Center, Washington, D.C., December 5, 2017, https://www.pewresearch.org/social-trends/2017/12/05/on-gender-differences-no-consensus-on-nature-vs-nurture/.

33. Marianne Cooper, "The False Promise of Meritocracy," *The Atlantic*, December 1, 2015, https://www.theatlantic.com/business/archive/2015/12/meritocracy/418074/.

34. Shannon K. McCoy and Brenda Major, "Priming Meritocracy and the Psychological Justification of Equality," *Journal of Experimental Social Psychology* 43, no. 3 (May 2007): 341-351, https://www.sciencedirect.com/science/article/abs/pii/S0022103106000904?via%3Dihub.

35. McCoy and Major, "Priming Meritocracy."

36. McCoy and Major, "Priming Meritocracy."

37. Michelle King, "The Authority Gap: Why Women Are Still Taken Less Seriously Than Men," *Forbes*, October 26, 2021, https://www.forbes.com/sites/michelleking/2021/10/26/the-authority-gap-why-women-are-still-taken-less-seriously-than-men/?sh=636c6cd3634d.

38. Richard Martell, David Lane, and Cynthia Emrich, "Male-Female Differences: A Computer Simulation," *American Psychologist* 51, no. 2 (1996): 157-158.

39. Martell, "Male-Female Differences."

40. Yuhao Du, Jessica Nordell and Kenneth Joseph, "Insidious Nonetheless: How Small Effects and Hierarchical Norms Create and Maintain Gender Disparities in Organizations," *Socius: Sociological Research for a Dynamic World*, 8: 1–12.August 13, 2022,

    The 2022 simulation considered six ways in which gender bias manifests itself: i. women's errors and failures on projected are penalized more than men's; ii. women's successes on projects are valued less than men's; iii. women are penalized for behaviors that depart from stereotypically feminine behaviors; iv. women receive fewer assignments that allow them to develop new skills and report having less access to challenging assignments; v. women receive more blame when a mixed-gender team fails, than do men; and vi. women receive less credit in mixed-gender teams than do men.

41. Tracy Certo, "Lenore Blum Shocked the Community with Her Sudden Resignation from CMU. Here She Tells Us Why," *Next Pittsburgh*, September 6, 2018, https://nextpittsburgh.com/features/lenore-blum-speaks-out-about-sexism-in-the-workplace/.

42. Certo, "Lenore Blum Shocked the Community."

43. Janel Sutkus, "Findings from the Spring 2016 Discriminatory and Sexual Harassment Study," Carnegie Mellon University Institutional Research and Analysis, https://www.cmu.edu/student-diversity/dash-study-findings.pdf.

44. Kim Parker and Cary Funk, "Gender Discrimination Comes in Many Forms for Today's Working Women," Pew Research Center, Washington, D.C. December 14, 2017, https://www.pewresearch.org /fact-tank/2017/12/14/gender-discrimination-comes-in-many-forms-for -todays-working-women/.

45. Victoria Mars and Christine Svarer, "We Asked Thousands of Women What's Holding Them Back. Here's What They Had to Say," *Fortune,* November 10, 2021, https://fortune.com/2021/11/10/whats-holding-women-back-gender -inequality/.

46. "COVID Data Tracker," Centers for Disease Control and Prevention, March 21, 2022, https://covid.cdc.gov/covid-data-tracker/#datatracker-home.

47. Richard Fry, "Some Gender Disparities Widened in the U.S. Workforce During the Pandemic," Pew Research Center, Washington, D.C. January 14, 2022, https://www.pewresearch.org/fact-tank/2022/01/14/some-gender -disparities-widened-in-the-u-s-workforce-during-the-pandemic/.

48. Misty L. Heggeness et al., "Tracking Job Losses for Mothers of School-Age Children During a Health Crisis," U.S. Census Bureau, March 3, 2021, https://www.census.gov/library/stories/2021/03/moms-work-and-the -pandemic.html.

49. Kate Chesley, "Survey Reveals COVID-19's Significant Stress on Stanford Faculty," *Stanford Report,* February 26, 2021, https://news.stanford.edu /report/2021/02/26/survey-reveals-covid-19s-significant-stress-stanford -faculty/.

50. Jennifer March Augustine and Kate Prickett, "Gender Disparities in Increased Parenting Time During the COVID-19 Pandemic: A Research Note," *Demography* 59, no. 4 (2022): 1233-1247.

51. Augustine and Prickett, "Gender Disparities."

52. Caitlyn Collins et al., "COVID-19 and the Gender Gap in Work Hours," *Gender, Work & Organization* 28, no. S1 (2021): 101-112.

53. Collins et al., "COVID-19."

Chapter 2

1. Naomi Cahn, "Women's Status and Pay in the C-Suite: New Study," *Forbes,* February 19, 2021, https://www.forbes.com/sites/naomicahn/2021/02/19 /womens-status-and-pay-in-the-c-suite--new-study/?sh=34e54e753762.

2. "Women in the Workplace 2022," LeanIn.Org and McKinsey & Company, October 18, 2022, https://www.mckinsey.com/featured-insights/diversity-and-inclusion/women-in-the-workplace.

3. Michael Rosander et al. "Gender Matters: Workplace Bullying, Gender, and Mental Health," *Frontiers in Psychology* 11, (October, 2022): 1-13.

4. Janet Shibley Hyde, "The Gender Similarities Hypothesis," *American Psychological Association* 60, no. 6 (2005): 590.

    Essentialists regard cognitive differences between women and men as natural, fixed, deep-seated, discrete, and related to biological sex (Haslam et al., 2000; Skewes et al., 2018). Seen through an evolutionary lens, two possibilities arise if a cognitive trait is heritable; the trait can either be transmitted equally to both sexes or unequally. This gives rise to two hypotheses; the gender similarity hypothesis (Hyde, 2005, 2014) or a sexual difference hypothesis (e.g., Buss and Schmitt, 1993; Miller, 2000; Kimura, 2004; Baron-Cohen et al., 2005; Cahill, 2006).

    Mikkel Wallentin, 'Sex Differences in Neurology and Psychiatry,' Handbook of Clinical Neurology, 2020, https://www.sciencedirect.com/topics/psychology/gender-similarities-hypothesis. See also, Goldberg, The Inevitability of Patriarchy).

5. Catherine H. Tinsley and Robin J. Ely, "What Most People Get Wrong About Men and Women," *Harvard Business Review*, May-June 2018, https://hbr.org/2018/05/what-most-people-get-wrong-about-men-and-women.

6. Hyde, "The Gender Similarities Hypothesis."

7. Zlatan Krizan and Angie Hunt, "Gender Roles: Men and Women Are Not So Different After All," *Iowa State University News*, January 29, 2015, https://www.news.iastate.edu/news/2015/01/29/genderdifferences. *Men do appear to be more prone to violence than women: Laura O'Toole, Jessica R. Schiffman, and Rosemary Sullivan, "Preface: Conceptualizing Gender Violence," in Gender Violence: Interdisciplinary Perspectives (New York: New York University Press, 2020), xi.*

8. Margo Wilson and Martin Daly, "Competitiveness, Risk Taking, and Violence: The Young Male Syndrome," *Ethology and Sociobiology* 6, no. 1 (1985): 59-73.

9. Tinsley and Ely, "What Most People."

10. Anna Fels, "Do Women Lack Ambition?" *Harvard Business Review*, April 2004, https://hbr.org/2004/04/do-women-lack-ambition.

11. Fels, "Do Women Lack Ambition?"

12. Agneta H. Fischer, "Sex Differences in Emotionality: Fact or Stereotype?" *Feminism & Psychology* 3, no. 3 (1993): 304.

13. Catherine Hakim, "Women, Careers, and Work-Life Preferences," *British Journal of Guidance & Counseling* 34, no. 3 (2006): 282.

14. Ellen Lenney, "Women's Self-Confidence in Achievement Settings," *Psychological Bulletin* 84, no. 1 (1977): 1.

15. Lenney, "Women's Self-Confidence."

16. Stephen Goldberg, *The Inevitability of Patriarchy* (William Morrow and Company, New York), 1973.

17. Sheryl Sandberg, *Lean In: Women, Work, and the Will to Lead* (New York: Alfred A. Knopf, 2013), 8.

18. Dina Gerdeman, "How Gender Stereotypes Kill a Woman's Self-Confidence," *Harvard Business Review*, February 25, 2019, https://hbswk.hbs.edu/item/how-gender-stereotypes-less-than-br-greater-than-kill-a-woman-s-less-than-br-greater-than-self-confidence.

19. Darren T. Baker and Juliet Bourke, "How Confidence is Weaponized Against Women," *Harvard Business Review*, October 20, 2022, https://hbr.org/2022/10/how-confidence-is-weaponized-against-women. *See also: Deepa Purushothaman, Lisen Stromberg, and Lisa Kaplowitz, "5 Harmful Ways Women Feel They Must Adapt in Corporate America," Harvard Business Review, October 31, 2022, https://hbr.org/2022/10/5-harmful-ways-women-feel-they-must-adapt-in-corporate-america.*

20. Baker and Bourke, "How Confidence is Weaponized."

21. Katie Abouzahr et al., "Dispelling the Myths of the Gender 'Ambition Gap,'" BCG Perspectives, April 5, 2017, https://www.bcg.com/publications/2017/people-organization-leadership-change-dispelling-the-myths-of-the-gender-ambition-gap/.

22. Megan Mackenzie, *Beyond the Band of Brothers: The US Military and the Myth that Women Can't Fight* (Cambridge: Cambridge University Press, 2015).

23. Luisa Alemany, Mariarosa Scarlata, and Andrew Zacharakis, "How the Gender Balance of Investment Teams Shapes the Risks They Take," *Harvard Business Review*, December 24, 2020, https://hbr.org/2020/12/how-the-gender-balance-of-investment-teams-shapes-the-risks-they-take.

24. Lisa Belkin "The Opt-Out Revolution," *New York Times*, October 26, 2003, https://www.nytimes.com/2003/10/26/magazine/the-opt-out-revolution.html. See also, Gretchen Livingston, "More than One-in-Ten U.S. Parents are Also Caring for an Adult," Pew Research Center, Washington, D.C., November 29, 2018, https://www.pewresearch.org/fact-tank/2018/11/29/more-than-one-in-ten-u-s-parents-are-also-caring-for-an-adult/.

25. Robin J. Ely and Irene Padavic, "What's Really Holding Women Back?" *Harvard Business Review*, March-April 2020, https://hbr.org/2020/03/whats-really-holding-women-back.

26. Wendy J. Fox, "Women Aren't 'Opting Out' of the Work Force. They Are Being Forced Out," *Ms. Magazine*, October 22, 2020, https://msmagazine.com/2020/10/22/jobs-women-work-workforce-opt-out-forced-out-wage-gap-gender/.

27. Allan G. Johnson, "Patriarchy, the System: An It, Not a He, a Them, or an Us," in *Women's Lives: Multicultural Perspectives*, eds. Gwyn Kirk and Margo Okazawa-Rey Emerita (Boston: McGraw-Hill, 2004).

28. Sapna Cheryan and Hazel-Rose Markus, "Rooting Out the Masculine Defaults in Your Workplace," *Harvard Business Review*, October 21, 2022.

29. Cheryan and Markus, "Rooting Out."

30. Cheryan and Markus, "Rooting Out."

31. Fred L. Pincus, "From Individual to Structural Discrimination" in *Race and Ethnic Conflict: Contending Views on Prejudice, Discrimination, and Ethnoviolence*, eds. Fred L. Pincus and Howard J. Ehrlich, (New York: Routledge, 1999).

32. Victoria L. Brescoll, "Leading with Their Hearts? How Gender Stereotypes of Emotion Lead to Biased Evaluations of Female Leaders," *The Leadership Quarterly* 27 no. 3, (2016): 415-428.

33. Cecilia Ridgeway, *Framed by Gender: How Gender Inequality Persists in the Modern World* (Oxford: Oxford University Press, 2011).

34. Ridgeway, *Framed by Gender.*

35. Rhea E. Steinpreis, Katie A. Anders, and Dawn Ritzke, "The Impact of Gender on the Review of the Curricula Vitae of Job Applicants and Tenure Candidates: A National Empirical Study," *Sex Roles* 41, (1999): 509-528.

36. Martha Foschi, "Double Standards for Competence: Theory and Research," *Annual Review of Sociology* 26, (2000): 21-42.

37. Corine A. Moss-Racusin, et al., "Science Faculty's Subtle Gender Biases Favor Male Students," *Proceedings of the National Academy of Sciences,*109, no. 41 (2012): 16474-16479.

38. Amanda Barroso, and Anna Brown, "Gender Pay Gap in U.S. Held Steady in 2020," Pew Research Center, Washington, D.C. May 25, 2021, https://www.pewresearch.org/fact-tank/2021/05/25/gender-pay-gap-facts/.

39. Herminia Ibarra, Robin J. Ely, and Deborah M. Kolb, "Women Rising: The Unseen Barriers," *Harvard Business Review*, September 2013, https://hbr.org/2013/09/women-rising-the-unseen-barriers.

40. Walter Lipmann, *Public Opinion* (San Diego: Harcourt, Brace & Co., 1922).

41. Lipmann, *Public Opinion*.

42. Edward C. Stewart, "Culture of the Mind: On the origins of meaning and emotion," in *Culture in the Communication Age, ed. James Lull* (London and New York: Routledge, 2001), 9.

43. Lippman, *Public Opinion*.

44. Jeffrey Davis, "The Bias Against Difference and How it Gets in the Way of Creativity and Collaboration," *Psychology Today,* June 25, 2020, https://www.psychologytoday.com/us/blog/tracking-wonder/202006/the-bias-against-difference.

45. Laura Ross, "Similarity Bias in Hiring and How to Avoid It," *Vervoe,* May 2, 2022, *https://vervoe.com/similarity-bias-in-hiring/.*

46. Janice D. Yoder, and Patricia Aniakudo, "Outsider Within the Firehouse: Subordination and Difference in the Social Interactions of African American Women Firefighters," *Gender & Society* 11, no. 3 (1997): 324-341.

47. Miller McPherson, Lynn Smith-Lovin, and James M. Cook, "Birds of a Feather: Homophily in Social Networks," *Annual Review of Sociology* 27, no. 1 (2001): 415-444.

48. Herminia Ibarra, "Paving an Alternative Route: Gender Differences in Managerial Networks" *Social Psychology Quarterly* 60, no. 1 (1997): 91.

49. McPherson, "Birds of a Feather."

50. McPherson, "Birds of a Feather."

51. Sundiatu Dixon-Fyle et al., "Diversity Wins: How Inclusion Matters," McKinsey & Company, May 19, 2020, https://www.mckinsey.com/featured-insights/diversity-and-inclusion/diversity-wins-how-inclusion-matters.

52. "Women in the Workplace 2022," LeanIn.Org and McKinsey & Company.

53. "Women in the Workplace 2022," LeanIn.Org and McKinsey & Company.

54. Adrian J. Villicana, Donna M. Garcia, and Monica Biernat, "Gender and Parenting: Effects of Parenting Failures on Evaluations of Mothers and Fathers," *Group Processes & Intergroup Relations* 20, no. 6 (2015): 867-878.

55. Timothy Frawley, "Gender Bias in the Classroom: Current Controversies and Implications for Teachers," *Childhood Education* 81, no. 4 (2005): 221-227.

56. Catherine Hakim, "Women, Careers, and Work-Life Preferences," *British Journal of Guidance & Counselling* 34, no. 3 (2006): 279-294.

57. Maria Minor, "Women in the Workplace: Why They Don't Get Recognized as Much as Men," *Forbes,* December 5, 2020, https://www.forbes.com/sites/mariaminor/2020/12/05/women-in-the-workplace-why-they-dont-get-recognized-as-much-as-men/?sh=5511902057df.

58. Joni Hersch and W. Kip Viscusi, "Gender Differences in Promotions and Wages," *Industrial Relations: A Journal of Economy and Society* 35, no. 4 (1996): 461-472.
59. Inga Minelgaite Snaebjornsson et al., "Cross-Cultural Leadership: Expectations on Gendered Leaders' Behavior," *SAGE Open* 5 (2015): 2.
60. Shruti Jolly et al., "Gender Differences in Time Spent on Parenting and Domestic Responsibilities by High-Achieving Young Physician-Researchers," *Annals of Internal Medicine* 160, no. 5 (2014): 344-353.
61. Jerome Bruner, *Acts of Meaning: Four Lectures on Mind and Culture (The Jerusalem-Harvard Lectures)* (Cambridge: Harvard University Press, 1990).
62. Alicia Ako-Brew, "Recognition of Gender Microaggressions in the Workplace: The Case of Predisposition and Propensity to Recognize," PhD diss., 982, (University of Missouri–St. Louis, 2020).
63. Friederike Mengel, "Gender Differences in Networking," *The Economic Journal* 130, no. 630 (2020): 1842-1873.
64. Charlie Cobb, and William Peters, "A Class Divided," *Frontline,* Public Broadcasting Service, March 26, 1985, https://www.pbs.org/wgbh/pages/frontline/shows/divided/etc/script.html.
65. Britt Frank, *The Science of Stuck: Breaking Through Inertia to Find Your Path Forward* (New York: Penguin Random House, 2022).
66. Helena R. M. Radke, Matthew J. Hornsey, and Fiona Kate Barlow, "Changing Versus Protecting the Status Quo: Why Men and Women Engage in Different Types of Action on Behalf of Women," *Sex Roles* 79, no. 9 (2018): 505-518.
67. Daniel Kahneman and Amos Tversky, "Prospect Theory: An Analysis of Decision Under Risk," *Econometrica* 47, no. 2, (1979) 263-292.
68. Kahneman and Tversky, "Prospect Theory."
69. Kahneman, *Thinking, Fast and Slow* (New York: Farrar, Straus and Giroux, 2011).
70. Richard H. Thaler and Cass R. Sunstein, *Nudge: Improving Decisions about Health, Wealth, and Happiness* (New Haven and London: Yale University Press), 34.
71. Thaler and Sunstein, *Nudge.*

Chapter 3

1. Brian Amble, "Collaboration and Gender," *Management-Issues,* June 1, 2012, https://www.management-issues.com/news/6495/collaboration-and-gender/.

2. Sangeeta Bharadwaj Badal, "The Business Benefits of Gender Diversity,"
    Gallup, January 20, 2014, https://www.gallup.com/workplace/236543/
    business-benefits-gender-diversity.aspx.

3. Sylvia Ann Hewlett, Melinda Marshall, and Laura Sherbin, "How Diver-
    sity Can Drive Innovation," *Harvard Business Review*, December 2013,
    https://hbr.org/2013/12/how-diversity-can-drive-innovation.

4. Astrid C. Homan and Lindred L. Greer, "Considering Diversity: The Posi-
    tive Effects of Considerate Leadership in Diverse Teams," *Group Processes
    & Intergroup Relations* 16, no. 1 (2013): 105-125.

5. David Rock and Heidi Grant, "Why Diverse Teams Are Smarter," *Harvard
    Business Review*, November 4, 2016, https://hbr.org/2016/11/why-diverse
    -teams-are-smarter.

6. Michael Chui and Anna Bernasek, "Forward Thinking on Economic Recov-
    ery and Gender Equality with Laura Tyson," McKinsey & Company, July
    28, 2021, https://www.mckinsey.com/featured-insights/gender-equality
    /forward-thinking-on-economic-recovery-and-gender-equality-with
    -laura-tyson.

7. "Men as Allies: Engaging Men to Advance Women in the Workplace,"
    Center for Women and Business at Bentley University, Spring 2017, https://
    www.ceoaction.com/media/1434/bentley-cwb-men-as-allies-research
    -report-spring-2017.pdf.

8. Katherine W. Phillips, "How Diversity Makes Us Smarter," *Greater Good
    Magazine*, September 18, 2017, https://greatergood.berkeley.edu/article
    /item/how_diversity_makes_us_smarter.

9. Anna Johansson, "Why Workplace Diversity Diminishes Groupthink
    and How Millennials Are Helping," *Forbes*, July 20, 2017, https://
    www.forbes.com/sites/annajohansson/2017/07/20/how-workplace
    -diversity-diminishes-groupthink-and-how-millennials-are-helping
    /?sh=2657e77a4b74.

10. Alison Reynolds and David Lewis, "Teams Solve Problems Faster When
    They're More Cognitively Diverse," *Harvard Business Review*, March 30, 2017,
    https://hbr.org/2017/03/teams-solve-problems-faster-when-theyre-more
    -cognitively-diverse.

11. Reynolds and Lewis, "Teams Solve."

12. Sundiatu Dixon-Fyle et al., "Diversity Wins: How Inclusion Matters,"
    McKinsey & Company, May 19, 2020, https://www.mckinsey.com/featured
    -insights/diversity-and-inclusion/diversity-wins-how-inclusion
    -matters. *See also, "Critical Mass: What Happens When Women Start to
    Rule the World," course led by Jay Newton-Small, offered by Institute of*

Politics (IOP) at the Harvard Kennedy School, https://iop.harvard.edu/get -involved/study-groups/critical-mass-what-happens-when-women-start -rule-world-led-jay-newton.

13. Andre P. Audette, "Gender Equality Supports Happiness and Well-Being," *The Gender Policy Report,* September 13, 2019, https://genderpolicyreport .umn.edu/gender-equality-supports-happiness/.

14. Audette, "Gender Equality Supports Happiness."

15. Hewlett, "How Diversity Can Drive Innovation."

16. "Why Diversity and Inclusion Matter," Catalyst, June 24, 2020, https:// www.catalyst.org/research/why-diversity-and-inclusion-matter/.

17. Rocío Lorenzo et al., "The Mix That Matters: Innovation Through Diversity," Boston Consulting Group, April 26, 2017, https://www.bcg.com /publications/2017/people-organization-leadership-talent-innovation -through-diversity-mix-that-matters.

18. Lorenzo et al., "The Mix That Matters."

19. Stephen Turban, Dan Wu, and Letian (LT) Zhang, "When Gender Diversity Makes Firms More Productive," *Harvard Business Review,* February 11, 2019, https://hbr.org/2019/02/research-when-gender-diversity-makes -firms-more-productive.

20. Robin J. Ely and David A. Thomas, "Getting Serious About Diversity: Enough Already with the Business Case" *Harvard Business Review,* November-December 2020, https://hbr.org/2020/11/getting-serious-about -diversity-enough-already-with-the-business-case.

21. Dixon-Fyle, "Diversity Wins."

Chapter 4

1. Bryce Covert, "The Secret to Getting More Women on Corporate Boards: The $100,000 Threat," *Politico,* February 25, 2022, https://www.politico .com/news/magazine/2022/02/25/california-companies-women-boards -quotas-00010745.

2. Ceilidh Kern, "EU Parliament Passes Directive on Gender Quotas for Boards," *Euractiv,* November 23, 2022, https://www.euractiv.com/section /economy-jobs/news/eu-parliament-passes-directive-on-gender-quotas-on -corporate-boards/.

3. California Secretary of State, *Women on Boards (SB 826),* California Secretary of State 2018, https://www.sos.ca.gov/business-programs/women-boards.

4. Lori A. Oliver and Jessica M. Norris, "Corporate Governance Emerging Best Practices Series: Gender-Diverse Boards," *The National Law Review,* August

18, 2020, https://www.natlawreview.com/article/corporate-governance
-emerging-best-practices-series-gender-diverse-boards.

5. *Regents of the University of California v. Allan Bakke.* 438 U.S. 265 98 S. Ct.
    2733 57 L.Ed.2d 750.

6. Kimberly Houser, "Board Gender Diversity A Path to Achieving Substan-
    tive Equality in the U. S." *William and Mary Review* 63, (2021): 529.

7. Charles C. Fawcett, Securities Exchange Act Release No. 56770, 91 S.E.C.
    Docket 2594 (November 8, 2007); *D.L. Cromwell Invs., Inc. v. NASD Regu-
    lation, Inc.,* 279 F.3d 155, 162 (2d Cir. 2002); *Desiderio v. National Ass'n of
    Secs. Dealers, Inc.,* 191 F. 3d 198, 206-07 (2d Cir. 1999); *Jones v. SEC,* 115
    F. 3d 1173, 1183 (4th Cir. 1997); *First Jersey Secs., Inc. v. Bergen,* 605 F. 2d
    690, 698 (3d Cir. 1979); *Blum v. Yaretsky,* 457 U.S. 991, 1004 (1982). *See also,
    Desiderio, 191 F.3d at 207 (The SEC's approval of FINRA's Form U-4).*

8. Billy Culleton, "State Lawmakers Continue Push To Increase Diversity in
    Corporate Boardrooms," *Multistate,* March 17, 2021, https://www.multi
    state.us/insider/2021/3/17/state-lawmakers-continue-push-to-increase
    -diversity-in-corporate-boardrooms.

9. Levi Sumagaysay, "Not a 'Woke Mission': Nasdaq, SEC Say Push for Diversity
    on Corporate Boards is What Investors Want," *MarketWatch,* August 29, 2022,
    https://www.marketwatch.com/story/not-a-woke-mission-nasdaq-sec
    -push-for-diversity-on-corporate-boards-is-what-investors-want-11661821759.

10. Richard Thompson Ford, "Perverse Effects of Antidiscrimination Law,"
    New York Times, June 30, 2015, https://www.nytimes.com/roomfordebate
    /2014/03/24/if-gays-can-marry-and-be-fired-for-doing-so/perverse
    -effects-of-antidiscrimination-law.

11. Lauren Weber, "How to Expand Diversity in the Workplace," *Wall Street
    Journal,* January 9, 2021, https://www.wsj.com/articles/how-to-expand
    -diversity-in-the-workplace-11610204183.

12. *But see our discussion about the Nasdaq's disclosure rule where the Nasdaq's
    rules are being challenged as a state action because the SEC approves the
    Nasdaq's rules.*

13. Weber, "How to Expand Diversity."

14. Weber, "How to Expand Diversity."

15. Lydia Beyoud and Andrew Ramonas, "Shareholders Up Demands for
    Workforce Diversity Data Seen by Few," Daily Labor Report, June 7,
    2021, https://news.bloomberglaw.com/esg/shareholders-up-demands-for
    -workplace-diversity-data-seen-by-few.

16. Beyoud and Ramonas, "Shareholders Up Demands."

17. Beyound and Ramonas, "Shareholders Up Demands."

18. Sarah Krouse, "BlackRock: Companies Should Have at Least Two Female Directors," *Wall Street Journal*, February 2, 2018, https://www.wsj.com /articles/blackrock-companies-should-have-at-least-two-female -directors -1517598407/.

19. Joann S. Lublin and Sarah Krouse, "State Street to Start Voting Against Companies That Don't Have Women Directors," *Wall Street Journal*, March 7, 2017, https://www.wsj.com/articles/state-street-says-it-will- start-voting-against-companies-that-dont-have-women- directors-1488862863.

20. Kim Elsesser, "Goldman Sachs Won't Take Companies Public If They Have All-Male Corporate Boards," *Forbes*, January 23, 2020, https:// www.forbes.com/sites/kimelsesser/2020/01/23/goldman-sachs -wont-take-companies-public-if-they-have-all-male-corporate-boards /?sh=1475a1b19475/.

21. Ellen Milligan and Todd Gillespie, "Diversity at Elite Law Firms is so Bad Clients Are Docking Fees," October 5, 2021, https://news.bloom berglaw.com/business-and-practice/diversity-at-elite-law-firms -is-so-bad-clients-are-docking-fees.

22. David O'Connor, "Increasing Law Firm Diversity" in *Diversity & Inclusion Committee Newsletter*, Winter 2020, https://www.americanbar.org/groups /tort_trial_insurance_practice/publications/committee-newsletters /increasing_law_firm_diversity/.

23. "Executives," Media Gallery, Meta Platforms, accessed April 2, 2022, *https://about.facebook.com/media-gallery/executives/*.

24. "Executive Officers," Leadership, Goldman Sachs, accessed April 2, 2022, https://www.goldmansachs.com/about-us/people-and-leadership /leadership/executive-officers//.

25. Dawn Lim, "BlackRock Must Hit ESG Targets or Pay More to Borrow Money," *Wall Street Journal*, April 7, 2021, https://www.wsj.com/articles /blackrock-must-hit-esg-targets-or-pay-more-to-borrow-money -11617769833#:~:text=The%20firm%20struck%20a%20financing, Latino%20employees%20in%20its%20workforce./.

26. "Intersection: Delivering on Diversity, Gender Equality, and Inclusion," McKinsey & Company, last modified 2020, https://www.mckinsey.com/~ /media/McKinsey/Email/Intersection/2020/12/2020-12-02.html?cid =other-eml-dni-mip-mck&hlkid=70fd350403c64c0e8d518beb3d801299 &hctky=11360948&hdpid=e0a58a6c-14cb-43fa-959c-cbafe7b1ee24.

27. Rachel Feintzeig, "More Companies Say Targets Are the Key to Diversity," *Wall Street Journal,* September 30, 2015, https://www.wsj.com/articles /more-companies-say-targets-are-the-key-to-diversity-1443600464.

28. Siri Chilazi, Iris Bohnet, and Oliver Hauser, "Achieving Gender Balance at All Levels of Your Company," *Harvard Business Review,* November 30, 2021, https://hbr.org/2021/11/achieving-gender-balance-at-all-levels-of -your-company.

29. Chilazi, Bohnet, and Hauser, "Achieving Gender Balance."

30. Chilazi, Bohnet, and Hauser, "Achieving Gender Balance."

31. Joyce He and Sarah Kaplan, "The Debate About Quotas," *Gender and the Economy,* October 26, 2017, https://www.gendereconomy.org/the-debate -about-quotas//.

32. Zulekha Nathoo, "Why Diverse Hires Can't Always Escape Tokenism," BBC, September 6, 2021, https://www.bbc.com/worklife/article/20210902-why -diverse-hires-cant-always-escape-tokenism/.

33. Feintzeig, "More Companies Say Targets."

34. *Regents of the University of California v. Allan Bakke,* 438 U.S. 265 98 S. Ct. 2733 57 L.Ed.2d 750.

Chapter 5

1. Matt Krentz et al, "Fixing the Flawed Approach to Diversity," Boston Consulting Group online, January 17, 2019, https://www.bcg.com /publications/2019/fixing-the-flawed-approach-to-diversity.

2. "Diversity and Inclusion (D&I) Global Market Report 2022" GlobeNewswire, https://www.globenewswire.com/news-release/2022/08/09/2494604/0/en /Diversity-and-Inclusion-D-I-Global-Market-Report-2022-Diverse-Com panies-Earn-2-5-Times-Higher-Cash-Flow-Per-Employee-and-Inclusive -Teams-Are-More-Productive-by-Over-35.html and source research at https://www.strategyr.com/market-report-diversity-and-inclusion-fore casts-global-industry-analysts-inc.asp.

3. Jim Tyson, "Most Companies Increase Spending on Diversity Training: Survey," *CFO Dive,* May 13, 2021, https://www.cfodive.com/news/most -companies-increase-spending-diversity-training-survey/600149/.

4. "Women in the Workplace 2022," LeanIn.Org and McKinsey & Company, October 18, 2022, https://www.mckinsey.com/featured-insights/diversity -and-inclusion/women-in-the-workplace.

5. U.S. Equal Employment Opportunity Commission, "Sex-Based Discrimination," https://www.eeoc.gov/sex-based-discrimination. *The law forbids*

discrimination when it comes to any aspect of employment, including hiring, firing, pay, job assignments, promotions, layoff, training, fringe benefits, and any other term or condition of employment.

6. Elizabeth Levy Paluck and Donald P. Green, "Prejudice Reduction: What Works? A Review and Assessment of Research and Practice," *Annual Review of Psychology* 60, (2009): 339-367.

7. Paluck and Green, "Prejudice Reduction."

8. Katerina Bezrukova et al., "A Meta-Analytical Integration of over 40 Years of Research on Diversity Training Evaluation," *Psychological Bulletin* 142, no. 11 (2016): 1227.

9. Calvin K. Lai et al., "Reducing Implicit Racial Preferences: A Comparative Investigation of 17 Interventions" *Journal of Experimental Psychology: General* 143, no.4 (2014): 1765.

10. Patrick S. Forscher et al., "A Meta-Analysis of Procedures to Change Implicit Measures," *Journal of Personality and Social Psychology* 117, no. 3, 522-559.

11. Doyin Atewologun, Tinu Cornish, and Fatima Tresh, "Unconscious Bias Training: An Assessment of the Evidence for Effectiveness," *Equality and Human Rights Commission Research Report 113*, March 2018, https://www.equalityhumanrights.com/sites/default/files/research-report-113-unconcious-bais-training-an-assessment-of-the-evidence-for-effectiveness-pdf.

12. Carol T. Kulik et al., "The Rich Get Richer: Predicting Participation in Voluntary Diversity Training," *Journal of Organization Behavior* 28, no. 6, 753-769.

13. Rohini Anand and Mary-Frances Winters, "A Retrospective View of Corporate Diversity Training from 1964 to the Present," *Academy of Management Learning & Education* 7, no. 3 (2008): 357.

14. Frank Dobbin and Alexandra Kalev, "Why Diversity Programs Fail," *Harvard Business Review* 94, no.7 (2016): 14.

15. Carol T. Kulik et al., "The Rich Get Richer."

16. "Guide: Raise Awareness About Unconscious Bias," Rework with Google, *https://rework.withgoogle.com/print/guides/5079604133888000/.*

17. "Managing Unconscious Bias," Facebook, *https://managingbias.fb.com/.*

18. "Microsoft Inclusion Journey," Microsoft, *https://www.microsoft.com/en-us/inclusion-journey.*

19. Frank Dobbin and Alexandra Kalev, "Why Doesn't Diversity Training Work? The Challenge for Industry and Academia," *Anthropology Now* 10, no. 2 (2018): 48-55.

20. Edward H. Chang et al., "The Mixed Effect of Online Diversity Training," *Proceedings of the National Academy of Sciences* 116, no. 16 (2019): 7778-7783.

21. Chang et al., "The Mixed Effect."

22. Alex Lindsey et al., "Two Types of Diversity Training that Really Work," *Harvard Business Review*, July 28, 2017, https://hbr.org/2017/07/two-types-of-diversity-training-that-really-work.

23. Lindsey et al., "Two Types of Diversity."

24. Joelle Emerson, "Don't Give Up on Unconscious Bias Training – Make It Better," *Harvard Business Review*, April 28, 2017, https://hbr.org/2017/04/dont-give-up-on-unconscious-bias-training-make-it-better.

25. Emerson, "Don't Give Up."

26. Jesse Singal, "Awareness Is Overrated," *The Cut* online, July 17, 2014, https://www.thecut.com/2014/07/awareness-is-overrated.html/.

27. Milenko Martinovich, "Many Americans Still Underestimate the Risks of Smoking, Stanford Scholars Say," Stanford News Service, August 22, 2017, https://news.stanford.edu/press-releases/2017/08/22/americans-misinformed-smoking/.

28. Scott O. Lilienfeld and Hal Arkowitz, "Why 'Just Say No' Doesn't Work," *Scientific American*, January 1, 2014, https://www.scientificamerican.com/article/why-just-say-no-doesnt-work/.

29. Dobbin and Kalev, "Why Sexual Harassment."

30. Krentz et al, "Fixing the Flawed."

31. Lyn Denend et al., "Analysis of Gender Perceptions in Health Technology: A Call to Action," *Analysis of Biomedical Engineering* 48, no. 5 (2020): 1573-1586.

32. Lyn Denend, Paul Yock, and Dan Azagury, "Research: Small Wins Can Make a Big Impact on Gender Equality," *Harvard Business Review*, November 6, 2020, https://hbr.org/2020/11/research-small-wins-can-make-a-big-impact-on-gender-equality.

33. Elisabeth Kelan, "Why Aren't We Making More Progress Towards Gender Equity?" *Harvard Business Review*, December 21, 2020, https://hbr.org/2020/12/why-arent-we-making-more-progress-towards-gender-equity/.

34. Michelle King, "We Need to Stop Fixing Women and Start Fixing Workplaces," *Evoke* online, October 10, 2019, https://www.evoke.org/articles/october-2019/big-ideas/we-need-to-stop-fixing-women-start-fixing-workplaces.

35. King, "We Need to Stop."

36. Rosalind Gill and Shani Orgad, "Confidence Culture and the Remaking of Feminism," New Formations 91, no. 91 (2017): 16-34.

37. Gill and Orgad, "Confidence Culture."

38. Sandberg, Lean In: Women, Work, and the Will. To Lead (New York: Knopf, 2013), 8.

39. Michelle Mone, My Fight to the Top (New York: Blink Publishing, 2015), 14.

40. Courtney E. Martin, "Arianna Huffington: The Visionary," Glamour online, October 31, 2011, https://www.glamour.com/story/arianna-huffington#:~:text =%22If%20my%20daughters%2C%20and%20women,simply%20 sticking%20your%20neck%20out.%22.

41. Grainne Fitzsimons, Aaron Kay, and Jae Yun Kim, "'Lean In' Messages and the Illusion of Control," Harvard Business Review, July 30, 2018, https://hbr.org/2018/07/lean-in-messages-and-the-illusion-of-control.

42. Fitzsimons, Kay, and Kim, "'Lean In' Messages."

43. Avivah Wittenberg-Cox, "Gender Initiatives Are Culture Change Initiatives," Harvard Business Review, October 14, 2015, https://hbr.org/2015/10 /gender-initiatives-are-culture-change-initiatives.

44. Tiffany L. Green and Nao Hagiwara, "The Problem with Implicit Bias Training," Scientific American, August 28, 2020, https://www.scientific american.com/article/the-problem-with-implicit-bias-training/.

45. Dobbin and Kalev, "Why Doesn't Diversity Training Work?"

46. Jena McGregor "How Most Leadership Training Programs Fail Women," The Washington Post, October 23, 2017, https://www.washingtonpost .com/news/on-leadership/wp/2017/10/23/how-most-leadership-training -programs-fail-women//.

47. Toni Schmader, Tara C. Dennehy, and Andrew S. Baron, "Why Antibias Interventions (Need Not Fail)," Perspectives on Psychological Science 17, no. 5 (2022): 1381-1403.

Chapter 6

1. We discuss these types of programs in Chapter 5.

2. Jackie Cook, "What Will It Take to Close the Gender Pay Gap for Good," Morningstar, February 22, 2021, https://www.morningstar.com /articles/1025601/what-will-it-take-to-close-the-gender-pay-gap- for-good.

3. Michael Flood, "Men and Gender Equality," in Engaging Men in Building Gender Equality, eds. Michael Flood and Richard Howson (Newcastle: Cambridge Scholars Publishing, 2016), 3-4.

4. Promundo-US, "So You Want to be a Male Ally for Gender Equality? (And You Should): Results of a National Survey, and a Few Things You Should Know," 2019, https://www.equimundo.org/resources/male-allyship/.

5. Promundo-US, "So You Want."

6. Juliana Menasce Horowitz and Ruth Igielnik, "A Century After Women Gained the Right to Vote, Majority of Americans See Work to Do on Gender Equality," Pew Research Center, Washington, D.C. July 7, 2020, https://www.pewresearch .org/social-trends/2020/07/07/a-century-after-women-gained-the -right-to-vote-majority-of-americans-see-work-to-do-on-gender-equality/.

7. Julia Taylor Kennedy, and Pooja Jain-Link, "What Majority Men Really Think About Diversity and Inclusion (And How to Engage Them in It)," *Coqual,* August 2020, https://coqual.org/wp-content/uploads/2020/09 /CoqualMajorityMenBelongingKeyFindings090720.pdf.

8. Elad N. Sherf, Subrahmaniam Tangirala, and Katy Connealy Weber, "It's Not My Place! Psychological Standing and Men's Voice and Participation in Gender-Parity Initiatives," *Organization Science* 28, no. 2 (2017): 193-210.

9. Lily Zheng, "How to Show White Men That Diversity and Inclusion Efforts Need Them," *Harvard Business Review,* October 28, 2019, https://hbr.org/2019/10/how-to-show-white-men-that-diversity-and -inclusion-efforts-need-them.

10. Bill Leonard, "Don't Exclude White Males from Diversity and Inclusion Programs," *Society for Human Resource Management,* February 12, 2013, https:// www.shrm.org/resourcesandtools/hr-topics/behavioral-competencies /global-and-cultural-effectiveness/pages/whitemales-diversity-inclusion .aspx.

11. Jamillah Bowman Williams and Jonathan M. Cox, "The New Principle-Practice Gap: The Disconnect Between Diversity Beliefs and Actions in the Workplace," *Sociology of Race and Ethnicity* 8, no. 2 (2022): 301.

12. Rebecca K. Ratner and Dale T. Miller, "The Norm of Self-Interest and Its Effects on Social Action," *Journal of Personality and Social Psychology* 81, no. 1 (2001): 14.

13. Kelly Paul, "The Benefits of Taking Time to Tackle Unconscious Bias," *E&T Engineering & Technology,* August 17, 2020, https://eandt.theiet.org/content /articles/2020/08/the-benefits-of-taking-time-to-tackle-unconscious-bias/.

14. Adam Grant, "Why So Many Men Don't Stand Up for Their Female Colleagues," *The Atlantic,* April 29, 2014, https://www.theatlantic.com/business /archive/2014/04/why-men-dont-stand-up-for-women-to-lead/361231/.

15. Grant, "Why So Many Men."

16. Zheng, "How to Show White Men."

17. Bob Pease, "Disengaging Men from Patriarchy: Rethinking the Man Question in Masculinity Studies," in *Engaging Men in Breaking Gender Equality,* eds. Michael Flood and Richard Howson (Newcastle: Cambridge Scholars Publishing, 2015), 56.

18. Jeanine Prime and Corinne A. Moss-Racusin, "Engaging Men in Gender Initiatives: What Change Agents Need to Know," *Catalyst,* May 4, 2009, https://www.catalyst.org/research/engaging-men-in-gender-initiatives -what-change-agents-need-to-know/.

19. *We discuss women's employee resource groups in our book, It's Not You, It's the Workplace.*

20. Anne E. Collier, *Men in the Mix: How to Engage Men on Issues Related to Gender in the Legal Profession* (Chicago: American Bar Association, Commission on Women in the Profession, 2021), 3.

21. Collier, *Men in the Mix*, 4.

22. Debora L. Spar, "Good Fellows: Men's Role & Reason in the Fight for Gender Equality," *Daedalus, Journal of the American Academy of Arts & Sciences* 149, no.1, (2020): 227.

23. Spar, "Good Fellows," 227.

24. Meera Jagannathan, "Want to Support Your Female Colleagues—Particularly in a Male-Dominated Field? Do This One Thing," *Market Watch,* August 11, 2021, https://www.marketwatch.com/story/want-to-support -your-female-colleagues-particularly-in-a-male-dominated-field-do-this -one-thing-11628697541.

25. Bourke and Dillon, "The Diversity and Inclusion Revolution."

26. Deanna deBara, "Gender Diversity: Benefits, Challenges & Strategies," Hourly, September 26, 2022, https://www.hourly.io/post/gender-diversity.

27. Jennifer Mueller, Sarah Harvey, and Alec Levenson, "How to Steer Clear of Group Think," *Harvard Business Review,* March 7, 2022, https://hbr .org/2022/03/how-to-steer-clear-of-groupthink.

28. Katherine W. Phillips, "How Diversity Makes Us Smarter," *Scientific American,* October 1, 2014, https://www.scientificamerican.com/article/how -diversity-makes-us-smarter/.

29. Jeanine Prime and Corinne A. Moss-Racusin, and Heather Foust-Cummings, "Engaging Men in Gender Initiatives: Stacking the Deck for Success," *Catalyst,* May 4, 2009, https://www.catalyst.org/research /engaging-men-in-gender-initiatives-what-change-agents-need -to-know/.

Chapter 7

1. Sheen S. Levine, David Stark, and Michèle Lamont, "Is Your DEI Progress Undermined by Attention Inequality?" *Harvard Business Review*, October 24, 2022, https://hbr.org/2022/10/is-your-dei-progress-undermined-by -attention-inequality.
2. Bob Pease, *Undoing Privilege: Unearned Advantage in a Divided World* (London: Zed Books, 2010).
3. Alexandra Kalev and Frank Dobbin, "How Companies Should Set—and report DEI Goals," *Harvard Business Review*, September 29, 2022, https:// hbr.org/2022/09/how-companies-should-set-and-report-dei-goals.
4. "EEO-1 Component 1 Data Collection," U.S. Equal Employment Opportunity Commission, accessed March 3, 2022, https://www.eeocdata.org /EEO1/home/index.

Chapter 8

1. Ron Friedman, "High-Performing Teams Don't Leave Relationships to Chance," *Harvard Business Review*, September 14, 2022, https://hbr .org/2022/09/high-performing-teams-dont-leave-relationships-to-chance.
2. Pilar Rivera-Torres, Rafael Angel Araque-Padilla, and María José Montero-Simó, "Job Stress Across Gender: The Importance of Emotional and Intellectual Demands and Social Support in Women," *International Journal of Environmental Research and Public Health* 10, no. 1 (2013): 375.
3. Paolo Gaudiano, "Women's Equality in the Workplace Requires Greater Inclusion," *Forbes*, March 8, 2022, https://www.forbes.com/sites/paologaudiano /2022/03/08/womens-equality-in-the-workplace-requires-greater-inclusion /?sh=50819dd02eb4.
4. Resa E. Lewiss et al., "Stop Protecting 'Good Guys'," *Harvard Business Review*, August 1, 2022.
5. Darrell Norman Burrell et al., "Sexual Harassment Training Focusing Solely on Protecting Organizations From Lawsuits Won't Change a Toxic Culture for Women to an Inclusive One," *International Journal of Public Sociology and Sociotherapy* 1, no. 1 (2021): 12-25.
6. *Williams v. Saxbe*, 413 F. Supp. 654 (D.D.C. 1976).
7. *Burlington Industries v. Ellerth*, 524 U.S. 742 (1998); *Faragher v. City of Boca Raton*, 524 U.S. 775 (1998).
8. Frank Dobbin and Alexandra Kalev, "Training Programs and Reporting Systems Won't End Sexual Harassment. Promoting More Women Will,"

Harvard Business Review, November 15, 2017, https://hbr.org/2017/11
/training-programs-and-reporting-systems-wont-end-sexual-harassment
-promoting-more-women-will.

9. Chai R. Feldblum and Victoria A. Lipnic, "EEOC Select Task Force on the
Study of Harassment in the Workplace," Equal Employment Opportunity Commission, June 6, 2016, https://www.eeoc.gov/sites/default/files
/migrated_files/eeoc/task_force/harassment/report.pdf.

10. Caitlin Flanagan "The Problem with HR," *The Atlantic,* July 2019, https://
www.theatlantic.com/magazine/archive/2019/07/hr-workplace-harrassment
-metoo/590644/.

11. Flanagan, "The Problem with HR."

12. Donald Sull and Charles Sull, "How to Fix a Toxic Culture," MIT Sloan
Management Review, September 28, 2022.

13. Sull and Sull, "How to Fix."

14. U.S. Department of Health and Human Services, Office of the U.S. Surgeon
General, "The Surgeon General's Framework for Workplace Mental Health
and Well-Being [in The Workplace]," October 20, 2022. https://www.hhs
.gov/surgeongeneral/priorities/workplace-well-being/index.html.

15. Mallika Marshall, "Toxic Workplaces Can Take a Toll on Your Mental and
Physical Health, Surgeon General Says," CBS News, October 24, 2022, https://
www.cbsnews.com/boston/news/toxic-workplaces-mental-physical-health
-surgeon-general-report-vivek-murthy/.

16. Marshall, "Toxic Workplaces."

17. Ellen Gabler et. al., "NBC Fires Matt Lauer, the Face of 'Today.'" *New York
Times,* November 9, 2017, https://www.nytimes.com/2017/11/29/business
/media/nbc-matt-lauer.html.

18. Kim Barker and Ellen Gabler, "Charlie Rose Made Crude Sexual Advances,
Multiple Women Say," *New York Times,* November 20, 2017, https://www
.nytimes.com/2017/11/20/us/charlie-rose-women.html.

19. Jenny Singer, "How Many Men at CBS Had Heard That Eliza Dushku Was
Sexually Threatened on Tape?" *Forward,* December 19, 2018, https://for
ward.com/schmooze/416342/cbs-sexual-harassment-scandal-implicates
-top-execs-showrunner-actors-and.

20. Emily Steel, "Fox Establishes Workplace Culture Panel After Harassment
Scandal," *New York Times,* November 20, 2017, https://www.nytimes.com
/2017/11/20/business/media/fox-news -sexual-harassment.html.

21. Emily Steel, "How Bill O'Reilly Silenced His Accusers," *New York Times,*
April 4, 2018, https://www.nytimes.com/2018/04/04/business/media/how
-bill-oreilly-silenced-his-accusers.html.

22. Sarah Ellison, "Inside the Final Days of Roger Ailes's Reign at Fox News" *Vanity Fair*, September 22, 2016, https://www.vanityfair.com/news/2016/09 /roger-ailes-fox-news-final-days.

23. Gabriel Sherman, "The Revenge of Roger's Angels," *New York Times*, September 5, 2016, http://nymag.com/intelligencer/2016/09/how-fox-news-women -took-down-roger-ailes.html.

24. *See discussion of out-group bias in Chapter 3.*

25. Andrea S. Kramer and Alton B. Harris, "How Do Your Workers Feel About Harassment? Ask Them," *Harvard Business Review*, January 29, 2018, https://hbr.org/2018/01/how-do-your-workers-feel-about-harassment-ask -them.

26. Cailin S. Stamarski and Leanne S. Son Hing, "Gender Inequalities in the Workplace: The Effects of Organizational Structures, Processes, Practices, and Decisions Makers' Sexism," *Frontiers in Psychology* 6, (2015): 1400.

27. Francesca Gino, "Why It's So Hard to Speak Up Against a Toxic Culture," *Harvard Business Review*, May 21, 2018, https://hbr.org/2018/05 /why-its-so-hard-to-speak-up-against-a-toxic-culture.

28. Amy Edmondson, "Psychological Safety and Learning Behavior in Work Teams," *Administrative Science Quarterly* 44, no. 2 (1999): 350-383.

29. Laura Delizonna, "High-Performing Teams Need Psychological Safety. Here's How to Create It, Six Ways to Build Trust," *Harvard Business Review*, August 24, 2017, https://hbr.org/2017/08/high-performing-teams -need-psychological-safety-heres-how-to-create-it.

30. Delizonna, "High-Performing Teams."

31. Susan Peppercorn, "How to Tell If a Prospective Employer values Psychological Safety," *Harvard Business Review*, September 1, 2022, https://hbr .org/2022/09/how-to-tell-if-a-prospective-employer-values-psychological -safety.

32. Sujin K. Horwitz and Irwin B. Horwitz, "The Effects of Team Diversity on Team Outcomes: A Meta-Analytic Review of Team Demography," *Journal of Management* 33, no. 6 (2007): 989.

33. Henrik Bresman and Amy C. Edmondson, "Research: To Excel, Diverse Teams Need Psychological Safety," *Harvard Business Review*, March 17, 2022, https:// hbr.org/2022/03/research-to-excel-diverse-teams-need-psychological -safety.

34. Bourke and Dillon, "The Diversity and Inclusion Revolution."

35. Stefanie K. Johnson et al., "Has Sexual Harassment at Work Decreased Since #MeToo?" *Harvard Business Review*, July 18, 2019, https://hbr .org/2019/07/has-sexual-harassment-at-work-decreased-since-metoo.

36. Johnson et al., "Has Sexual Harassment."

37. Sofia Kluch and Megan Brenan, "U.S. Women Feel Less Respected Than European, Canadian Peers," *Gallup,* March 8, 2019, https://news.gallup .com/poll/247205/women-feel-less-respected-european-canadian-peers.aspx.

38. Sheila Brassel, Tara Van Bommel, and Kathrina Robotham, "Three Inclusive Team Norms That Drive Success," *Catalyst,* https://www.catalyst.org /reports/inclusive-team-norms-success.

39. Melissa Quinn, "Sotomayor Says Supreme Court Adjusted Argument Format Partly Over Interruptions of Female Justices," CBS News online, October 14, 2021, https://www.cbsnews.com/news/supreme-court-justice -sonia-sotomayor-oral-arguments-female-justices-interruptions/.

40. Quinn, "Sotomayor Says."

41. Gino, "Why It's So Hard."

42. Bresman and Edmondson, "Exploring the Relation."

43. Nuala Walsh, "How to Encourage Employees to Speak Up When They See Wrongdoing," *Harvard Business Review,* February 4, 2021, https://hbr .org/2021/02/how-to-encourage-employees-to-speak-up-when-they-see -wrongdoing.

44. Peter Bailinson et al., "Understanding Organizational Barriers to a More Inclusive Workplace," McKinsey & Company, June 23, 2020, https://www .mckinsey.com/~/media/McKinsey/Business%20Functions/Organiza tion/Our%20Insights/Understanding%20organizational%20barriers%20 to%20a%20more%20inclusive%20workplace/Understanding-organiza tional-barriers-to-a-more-inclusive-workplace.pdf.

45. W. Brad Johnson and David G. Smith, "How Men Can Confront Other Men About Sexist Behavior," *Harvard Business Review,* October 16, 2020, https://hbr.org/2020/10/how-men-can-confront-other-men-about-sexist -behavior.

46. Jamie L. Gloor, Gudrun Sander, and Alyson Meister, "What to Do about Employees Who Consciously Exclude Women," *Harvard Business Review*, November 8, 2021, https://hbr.org/2021/11/what-to-do-about-employees -who-consciously-exclude-women.

47. Kim Elsesser, *Sex and the Office: Women, Men and the Sex Partition That's Dividing the Workplace* (Taylor Trade Publishing, 2015), 171.

48. Dobbin and Kalev, "Training Programs."

49. Frank Dobbin and Alexandra Kalev, "Why Sexual Harassment Programs Backfire," *Harvard Business Review,* May-June 2020, https://hbr .org/2020/05/why-sexual-harassment-programs-backfire.

50. Dobbin and Kalev, "Why Sexual Harassment."

Chapter 9

1. Hadas Mandel, "The Individual and Structural Aspects of Gender Inequality At Work," *Oxford Human Rights Hub,* May 2, 2017, https://ohrh.law.ox .ac.uk/the-individual-and-structural-aspects-of-gender-inequality- at-work/.
2. Mahzarin R. Banaji, Max H. Bazerman, and Dolly Chugh, "How (Un)Ethical Are You?" *Harvard Business Review,* December 2003, https://hbr.org /2003/12/how-unethical-are-you.
3. Banaji, Bazerman, and Chugh, "How (Un)Ethical Are You."
4. Desmond Charles Sergeant and Evangelos Himonides, "Orchestrated Sex: The Representation of Male and Female Musicians in World-Class Symphony Orchestras," *Frontiers in Psychology,* August 16, 2019, https://www .frontiersin.org/articles/10.3389/fpsyg.2019.01760/full.
5. Christina Hoff Sommers, "Blind Spots in the 'Blind Audition' Study," *Wall Street Journal,* October 20, 2019, https://www.wsj.com/articles/blind -spots-in-the-blind-audition-study-11571599303.
6. Claire Cain Miller, "Is Blind Hiring the Best Hiring?" *New York Times Magazine,* February 25, 2016, https://www.nytimes.com/2016/02/28/magazine /is-blind-hiring-the-best-hiring.html.
7. Miller, "Is Blind Hiring."
8. Julian Kolev, Yuly Fuentes-Medel, and Fiona Murray, "Is Blinded Review Enough? How Gendered Outcomes Arise Even Under Anonymous Evaluation," National Bureau of Economic Research, *Working Paper 25759,* April 2019, https://www.nber.org/papers/w25759.
9. Andrea S. Kramer and Alton B. Harris, *Breaking Through Bias: Communication Techniques for Women to Succeed at Work,* 2nd Edition (Boston & London: Nicholas Brealey 2020), 202-204.
10. Kramer and Harris, *Breaking Through Bias.*
11. *A 2017 study of the effects of "de-identifying" the gender of applications to the Australian Public Service initially seems to do precisely that. The study found when women's gender was not identified they were hired less frequently than they were when it was. The Australian researchers found, however, that the reason women fared better when APS officers knew their gender than when they didn't was because these officers then were able to discriminate in favor of women.*
12. Michael J. Hiscox et al., "Going Blind to See More Clearly: Unconscious in Australian Public Service (APS) Shortlisting Processes" *Behavioral Economics Team of the Australian Government,* June, 2017, https://

behaviouraleconomics.pmc.gov.au/projects/going-blind-see-more
-clearly-unconscious-bias-australian-public-service-aps-shortlisting.

13. Kate Glazebrook, "What Is Blind Hiring? A Guide to Blind Recruitment," *Be Applied*, October 5, 2022, https://www.beapplied.com/post
/what-is-blind-hiring.

14. "Performance over Privilege & Pedigree," GapJumpers, https://www
.gapjumpers.me/.

15. "Unitive Enhances Blind Resume Review with TalentSonar Acquisition,"
Cision, https://www.prnewswire.com/news-releases/unitive-enhances-blind
-resume-review-with-talentsonar-acquisition-300392584.html.

16. Miller, "Is Blind Hiring."

17. Aaron Holmes, "AI Could Be the Key to Ending Discrimination in Hiring, but Experts Warn It Can Be Just as Biased as Humans," *Business
Insider,* October 8, 2019, https://www.businessinsider.com/ai-hiring-tools
-biased-as-humans-experts-warn-2019-10.

18. Zahira Jaser et al., "Where Automated Job Interviews Fall Short" *Harvard
BusinessReview,*January27,2022,https://hbr.org/2022/01/where-automated
-job-interviews-fall-short.

19. Shelley Correll et al., "Inside the Black Box of Organizational Life: The
Gendered Language of Performance Assessment," *American Sociological
Review* 85, no. 6 (2020): 1022-1050.

20. Tyler Cowen, "Of Course Stereotypes Are Holding Women Back," *The
Malasian Reserve, https://themalaysianreserve.com/2021/11/24/of-course-
stereotypes-are-holding-women-back/.*

21. Correll et al., "Inside the Black Box."

22. *We discuss the goldilocks dilemma in Breaking Through Bias, 14-17.*

23. "University of California Performance Management for Senior Administrators," University of California, accessed March 2022, https://regents
.universityofcalifornia.edu/policies/smgperfform.pdf.

24. University of California, "Performance Management for Senior
Administrators."

25. University of California, "Performance Management for Senior
Administrators."

26. Holly Quinn, "Are Your Job Descriptions as Inclusive as You Think They
Are?" *Technically,* April 29, 2022, https://technical.ly/company-culture
/how-to-write-inclusive-job-descriptions/.

27. Frank Dobbin and Alexandra Kalev, *Getting to Diversity: What Works and
What Doesn't* (Cambridge: Harvard University Press, 2022).

28. Dobbin and Kalev, *Getting to Diversity*, 44-47.

29. Peter Cappelli and Anna Tavis, "The Performance Management Revolution: The Focus is Shifting from Accountability to Learning," *Harvard Business Review,* October 2016, https://hbr.org/2016/10/the-performance-management-revolution.

30. Dobbin and Kalev, *Getting to Diversity,* 161.

31. Ben Slater, "Recruiting, Fast and Slow: Lessons from Human Psychology," *Beamery,* March 8, 2017, https://beamery.com/resources/blogs/recruiting-fast-and-slow-lessons-from-human-psychology.

32. Pamela Fuller, Mark Murphy, and Anne Chow, *The Leader's Guide to Unconscious Bias: How to Reframe Bias, Cultivate Connection, and Create High-Performing Teams,* (New York: Simon & Schuster, 2020).

33. Daniel Kahneman, *Thinking, Fast and Slow* (New York: Macmillan, 2011).

34. Betsy Mason, "Curbing implicit bias: what works and what doesn't. Psychologists have yet to find a way to diminish hidden prejudice, but they do have strategies for thwarting discrimination," Knowable Magazine, June 6, 2020, https://knowablemagazine.org/article/mind/2020/how-to-curb-implicit-bias.

35. Andreea Gorbatai, Smaranda Boroș, and Katherine Ullman, "Why Middle Managers Struggle to Implement DEI Strategies," *Harvard Business Review,* October 13, 2022, https://hbr.org/2022/10/why-middle-managers-struggle-to-implement-dei-strategies.

36. Andreea Gorbatai, Smaranda Boros, and Katherine Ullman, "Why Middle Managers Struggle Minority Candidates, its Effectiveness and Criticism," *The Sporting News,* March 28, 2022, https://www.sportingnews.com/us/nfl/news/what-is-rooney-rule-nfl-minority-candidates-effectiveness-criticisms/1k4m7oilxr8nv1xjs9f9bw2k7d.

37. Brakkton Booker, "NFL Announces New Rules to Tackle Lack of Diversity in its Coaching, Executive Ranks," *NPR,* May 19, 2020, https://www.npr.org/2020/05/19/858702029/nfl-announces-new-rules-to-tackle-lack-of-diversity-in-its-coaching-executive-ra.

38. Dave Sheinin et al., "How the NFL Blocks Black Coaches," *The Washington Post,* September 21, 2022, https://www.washingtonpost.com/sports/interactive/2022/nfl-black-head-coaches/.

39. Jeff Green, "Corporate America Loves the Rooney Rule. But Does It Work?" *Financial Post,* March 21, 2022, https://financialpost.com/pmn/business-pmn/corporate-america-loves-the-rooney-rule-but-does-it-work.

40. Green, "Corporate America."

41. Stefanie K. Johnson, David R. Hekman, and Elsa T. Chan, "If There's Only One Woman in Your Candidate Pool, There's Statistically No Chance She'll be Hired," *Harvard Business Review*, April 26, 2016, https://hbr .org/2016/04/if-theres-only-one-woman-in-your-candidate-pool-theres -statistically-no-chance-shell-be-hired.

42. Google, "Action #1 Hiring," accessed April 3, 2022, https://about.google /belonging/diversity-annual-report/2022/hiring.

43. David Rock and Paulette Gerkovich, "Why Diverse Teams Outperform Homogeneous Teams," *Neuroleadership Institute,* June 10, 2021, https:// neuroleadership.com/your-brain-at-work/why-diverse-teams-outperform -homogeneous-teams/.

44. Anna Johansson, "Why Workplace Diversity Diminishes Groupthink and How Millennials Are Helping," *Forbes,* July 20, 2017, https://www.forbes.com /sites/annajohansson/2017/07/20/how-workplace-diversity-diminishes -groupthink-and-how-millennials-are-helping/?sh=1406aa7c4b74.

45. Ellyn Shook, "How to Set—and Meet—Your Company's Diversity Goals," *Harvard Business Review,* June 25, 2021, https://hbr.org/2021/06/how-to-set -and-meet-your-companys-diversity-goals.

46. Joan C. Williams, Rachel M. Korn, and Asma Ghani, "To Build a DEI Program That Works, You Need Metrics," *Harvard Business Review,* October 12, 2022, https://hbr.org/2022/10/to-build-a-dei-program-that-works-you-need-metrics.

47. Kim Parker and Cary Funk, "Gender Discrimination Comes In Many Forms For Today's Working Women," Pew Research Center, Washington, D.C., December 14, 2017, https://www.pewresearch.org/fact-tank/2017/12/14/ gender-discrimination-comes-in-many-forms-for-todays-working-women/.

Chapter 10

1. Brigid Schulte and Stavroula Pabst, "How Companies Can Support Single Parents," *Harvard Business Review,* June 28, 2021, https://hbr .org/2021/06/how-companies-can-support-single-parents.

2. Beth Kowitt, "Are Women on a Collision Course with the COVID Ceiling?" *Fortune* online, October 4, 2021, https://fortune.com/longform/covid -women-in-leadership-corporate-maerica-pandemic-effects/.

3. "Young Goldman Sachs Bankers Ask for 80-Hour Week Cap," BBC News, March 19, 2021, https://www.bbc.com/news/business-56452494.

4. Claudia Goldin, *Career and Family: Women's Century-Long Journey Toward Equity* (Princeton: Princeton University Press, 2021).

5. Jason Aten, "Xerox's Former CEO Made a Controversial Statement About Work-Life Balance. Why She's Not Wrong," *Inc.*, March 17, 2022, https://www.inc.com/jason-aten/xeroxs-former-ceo-made-a-controversial-statement-about-work-life-balance-why-shes-not-wrong.html.

6. Audrey Goodson Kingo, "Is a Stay-at-Home Spouse the Secret to Executive Success?" Chief, June 29, 2021, https://chief.com/articles/stay-at-home-spouse.

7. Naz Beheshti, "How 'Greedy' Jobs and Inflexible Schedules Impact the Gender Pay Gap," *Forbes,* December 5, 2019, https://www.forbes.com/sites/nazbeheshti/2019/12/05/how-greedy-jobs-and-inflexible-schedules-impact-the-gender-pay-gap/?sh=30875fdf6707.

8. Robin J. Ely, Pamela Stone, and Colleen Ammerman, "Rethink What You 'Know' About High-Achieving Women: A Survey of Harvard Business School Graduates Sheds New Light on What Happens to Women—and Men—After Business School," *Harvard Business Review,* December2014,https://hbr.org/2014/12/rethink-what-you-know-about-high-achieving-women.

9. Gretchen Gavett, "The Problem with 'Greedy Work'," *Harvard Business Review,* September 28, 2021, https://hbr.org/2021/09/the-problem-with-greedy-work.

10. Barbara Ortutay "Women Say They Do Most Chores, Child Care: AP-NORC Poll," *AP News,* December 14, 2021, https://apnews.com/article/coronavirus-pandemic-business-lifestyle-health-us-news-21e5e959e9f53c0f3060cabf8c521ff1.

11. Lois M. Collins, "Who's Helping Around the House? It's a He Said, She Said Situation," *Deseret News,* October 12, 2021, https://www.deseret.com/2021/10/12/22698901/do-men-or-women-help-more-around-the-house-american-family-survey-childcare-cleaning-chores?fr=operanews.

12. "For Both Moms and Dads, More Time Spent on Child Care," Pew Research Center, Washington, D.C. June 15, 2017, https://www.pewresearch.org/ft_17-06-14_fathers_1965_2015/.

13. "Caregiving in the US 2020," The National Alliance for Caregiving (NAC) and AARP, May 2020, https://www.caregiving.org/research/caregiving-in-the-us/caregiving-in-the-us-2020/.

14. Andrea Shalal, "Aging Population to Hit U.S. Economy Like a 'Ton of Bricks' -U.S. Commerce Secretary," Reuters, July 12, 2021, https://www.reuters.com/world/us/aging-population-hit-us-economy-like-ton-bricks-us-commerce-secretary-2021-07-12/.

15. Victoria Masterson, "Here's What Women's Entrepreneurship Looks Like Around the World," July 20, 2022, https://www.weforum.org /agenda/2022/07/women-entrepreneurs-gusto-gender/.

16. Goldin, *Career and Family*.

17. Bianca Bax et al., "Working Women and the War for Talent," Bain & Company, 2022, https://www.bain.com/insights/working-women-and -the-war-for-talent/.

18. "Women in the Workplace 2022," LeanIn.Org and McKinsey & Company, p. 18.

19. "Women in the Workplace 2022," LeanIn.Org and McKinsey & Company, p. 18.

20. Ivona Hideg et al., "Do Longer Maternity Leaves Hurt Women's Careers?" *Harvard Business Review*, September 14, 2018, https://hbr.org/2018/09 /do-longer-maternity-leaves-hurt-womens-careers.

21. Goldin, *Career and Family*.

22. Goldin, *Career and Family*.

23. Hideg et al., "Do Longer Maternity Leaves."

24. Heather Gillin, "How Career Interruptions Affect Women," *Texas A&M Today*, March 9, 2020, https://today.tamu.edu/2020/03/09/how-career- interruptions-affect-women/.

25. Sylvia Ann Hewlett and Carolyn Buck Luce, "Off-Ramps and On-Ramps: Keeping Talented Women on the Road to Success," *Harvard Business Review*, March 2005, https://hbr.org/2005/03/off-ramps-and-on-ramps -keeping-talented-women-on-the-road-to-success.

26. Alexandra Kalev and Frank Dobbin, "The Surprising Benefits of Work/ Life Support", *Harvard Business Review*, September-October 2022, https:// hbr.org/2022/09/the-surprising-benefits-of-work-life-support.

27. Kalev and Dobbin, "The Surprising Benefits."

28. Hewlett and Luce, "Off-Ramps and On-Ramps."

29. Brigid Schulte, "Survey: Majority of Men Want Flexible Work," *Washington Post*, October 21, 2014, https://www.washingtonpost.com/news/local /wp/2014/10/21/survey-majority-of-men-want-flexible-work/.

30. Lynda Gratton, "How to Do Hybrid Right," *Harvard Business Review*, May-June 2021, https://hbr.org/2021/05/how-to-do-hybrid-right.

31. Peter Cappelli, "In a Hybrid Office, Remote Workers Will Be Left Behind," *Wall Street Journal*, August 13, 2021, https://www.wsj.com /articles/hybrid-workplace-promotions-11628796072.

32. Sylvia Ann Hewlett, "Off-Ramps and On-Ramps."

33. Claire Cain Miller, "How Other Nations Pay for Child Care. The U.S. Is an Outlier," *New York Times,* October 6, 2021, https://www.nytimes.com/2021/10/06/upshot/child-care-biden.html.

34. Robert Paul Hartley et al., "A Lifetime Worth of Benefits; The Effect of Affordable, High-Quality Childcare on Family Income, the Gender Earnings Gap, and Women's Retirement Security," Center on Poverty & Social Policy and National Women's Law Center, March 2021, https://nwlc.org/wp-content/uploads/2021/04/A-Lifetimes-Worth-of-Benefits-_FD.pdf.

35. "Fact Sheet: The American Families Plan," The White House, April 28, 2021, https://www.whitehouse.gov/briefing-room/statements-releases/2021/04/28/fact-sheet-the-american-families-plan/.

36. Austin Ahlman, "Build Back Better Dies…Again." *The American Prospect*, April 28, 2022, https://prospect.org/politics/build-back-better-dies-again/. *See also, Kelly Anne Smith, "Biden's Build Back Better Plan Is Dead. Now What?" Forbes, March 2, 2022. https://www.forbes.com/advisor/personal-finance/ build-back-better-plan-dead/.*

37. Brigid Schulte and Stavroula Pabst, "How Companies Can Support Single Parents," *Harvard Business Review,* June 28, 2021, https://hbr.org/2021/06/how-companies-can-support-single-parents.

38. Steven Jessen-Howard, Rasheed Malik, and MK Falgout, "Costly and Unavailable: America Lacks Sufficient Child Care Supply for Infants and Toddlers," *Center for American Progress,* August 4, 2020, https://www.americanprogress.org/article/costly-unavailable-america-lacks-sufficient-child-care-supply-infants-toddlers/.

39. Greg Rosalsky, "The Case for Revolutionizing Child Care in America," NPR, August 15, 2022, https://www.npr.org/sections/money/2022/05/17/1098524454/the-case-for-revolutionizing-child-care-in-america.

40. Nicole Dew, "These 17 Companies Help Employees with Child Care," *The Penny Hoarder,* August 15, 2022, https://www.thepennyhoarder.com/make-money/career/companies-with-child-care/.

41. Amel Zahid, "Onsite Childcare—How to Get Started, Lessons from the Pioneers," *Medium.com*, July 31, 2018, https://medium.com/@amelzhd/onsite-childcare-how-to-get-started-lessons-from-the-pioneers-c21baedb44e2. *We discuss motherhood bias in Breaking Through, 17-20.*

42. Gwen Moran, "What Will It Take for Employers to Offer On-Site Day Care," *Fast Company,* February 16, 2016, https://www.fastcompany.com/3056440/what-will-it-take-for-employers-to-offer-on-site-day-care.

43. Camila Beiner, "Child Care Is Getting More Support from Some Private Companies," NPR, January 4, 2022, https://www.npr.org/2022/01/

04/1064124004/child-care-is-getting-more-support-from-some-private-companies.

44. Beiner, "Child Care."

45. Nadine El-Bawab, "Employers Offer Stipends for Babysitting and Tutoring to Sweeten Child-Care Benefits and Win Over Workers," CNBC, July 9, 2021, https://www.cnbc.com/2021/07/09/employers-sweeten-child-care-benefits-to-win-over-workers-.html.

46. Alicia Sasser Modestino et al., "Childcare Is a Business Issue," *Harvard Business Review,* April 29, 2021, https://hbr.org/2021/04/childcare-is-a-business-issue.

47. Gretchen Livingston and Deja Thomas, "Among 41 Countries, only U.S. Lacks Paid Parental Leave," Pew Research Center, Washington, D.C., December 16, 2019, https://www.pewresearch.org/fact-tank/2019/12/16/u-s-lacks-mandated-paid-parental-leave/.

48. Benjamin Bennett et al., "Paid Leave Pays Off: The Effects of Paid Family Leave on Firm Performance," National Bureau of Economic Research, December 2020, https://www.nber.org/papers/w27788.

49. "What Data Does the BLS Publish on Family Leave?" U.S. Bureau of Labor Statistics, September 23, 2021, https://www.bls.gov/ebs/publications/pdf/family-leave-benefits-fact-sheet.pdf.

50. Allen Smith, "SHRM Research: More Employers Are Offering Paid Leave," *The Society for Human Resource Management,* September 15, 2020, https://www.shrm.org/resourcesandtools/legal-and-compliance/employment-law/pages/more-paid-leave-offered.aspx.

51. Emily Ferreira and Rich Fuerstenberg, "The Pressure is on to Modernize Time-off Benefits: 6 Survey Findings," *Mercer Health News,* January 16, 2019, https://www.mercer.us/our-thinking/healthcare/the-pressure-is-on-to-modernize-time-off-benefits-6-survey-findings.html.

52. "Paid Leave in the U.S.," Kaiser Family Foundation, December 17, 2021, https://www.kff.org/womens-health-policy/fact-sheet/paid-leave-in-u-s/.

53. Chris Kolmar, "Average Paid Maternity Leave in the U.S," Zippia, Inc., September 12, 2022, https://www.zippia.com/advice/average-paid-maternity-leave/

54. "Paid Leave," Kaiser Family Foundation.

55. Kathryn Dill and Angela Yang, "Companies Are Cutting Back on Maternity and Paternity Leave: Many Employers Dial Down How Much Paid Time Off They Give New Moms and Dads," *Wall Street Journal,* August 22, 2022, https://www.wsj.com/articles/the-surprising-benefit-some-companies-are-taking-awayparental-leave-11661125605.

56. Dill and Yang, "Companies Are Cutting Back."

57. Michelle Moniz, Ryan Howard, and Michael Englesbe, "How U.S. Employers Can Support Women's Health," *Harvard Business Review,* June 2, 2022, https://hbr.org/2022/06/how-u-s-employers-can-support-womens-health.

58. Sylvia Ann Hewlett, "Executive Women and the Myth of Having It All," *Harvard Business Review,* April 2002, https://hbr.org/2002/04/executive-women-and-the-myth-of-having-it-all.

59. Mita Mallick, "Maternity Leave Isn't Enough to Retain New Moms," *Harvard Business Review,* November 30, 2020, https://hbr.org/2020/11/maternity-leave-isnt-enough-to-retain-new-moms.

60. Mary Beth Ferrante, "Before Breaking the Glass Ceiling, Women Must Climb the Maternal Wall," *Forbes,* October 31, 2018, https:www.forbes.com/sites/marybethferrante/2018/10/31/before-breaking-the-glass-ceiling-women-must-climb-the-maternal-wall/?sh=85338c7c5194, *See also, Joan [...] it is.* C. Williams and Kate Massinger, "Need a Good Parental Leave Policy? Here It Is," *Harvard Business Review,* November 23, 2015, https://hbr.org/2015/11/need-a-good-parental-leave-policy-here-it-is.

61. Camilla Han-He, "Why It's Time to Rewrite the Narrative on Career Breaks," LinkedIn, February 28, 2022 https://www.linkedin.com/pulse/why-its-time-rewrite-narrative-career-breaks-camilla-han-he/.

62. Carol Fishman Cohen, "A New Way to Explore the Pause in Your Career," *Harvard Business Review,* March 23, 2022, https://hbr.org/2022/03/a-new-way-to-explain-the-pause-in-your-career.

63. "A New Way to Represent Career Breaks on LinkedIn," LinkedIn, March 1, 2022, https://news.linkedin.com/2022/march/new-way-to-represent-career-breaks-on-linkedin.

64. Ron Carucci, "To Retain New Hires, Spend More Time Onboarding Them," *Harvard Business Review,* December 3, 2018, https://hbr.org/2018/12/to-retain-new-hires-spend-more-time-onboarding-them.

65. Carol Fishman Cohen, "Return-to-Work Programs Come of Age," *Harvard Business Review,* September-October 2021, https://hbr.org/2021/09/return-to-work-programs-come-of-age.

Chapter 11

1. Frank V. Cespedes, "How to Conduct a Great Performance Review," *Harvard Business Review,* July 8, 2022, https://hbr.org/2022/07/how-to-conduct-a-great-performance-review.

2. Samuel A. Culbert, *Get Rid of the Performance Review! How Companies Can Stop Intimidating, Start Managing—and Focus on What Really Matters* (New York: Grand Central Publishing, 2010), 217.

3. Bryan Hancock, Elizabeth Hioe, and Bill Schaninger, "The Fairness Factor in Performance Management," *McKinsey Quarterly,* April 5, 2018, https://www.mckinsey.com/business-functions/people-and-organizational-performance/our-insights/the-fairness-factor-in-performance-management.

4. Paola Cecchi-Dimeglio, "How Gender Bias Corrupts Performance Reviews, and What to Do About It," *Harvard Business Review,* April 12, 2017, https://hbr.org/2017/04/how-gender-bias-corrupts-performance-reviews-and-what-to-do-about-it.

5. Lori Nishiura Mackenzie, JoAnne Wehner, and Shelley J. Correll, "Why Most Performance Evaluations Are Biased, and How To Fix Them," *Harvard Business Review,* January 11, 2019, https://hbr.org/2019/01/why-most-performance-evaluations-are-biased-and-how-to-fix-them.

6. Shelley J. Correll and Caroline Simard, "Research: Vague Feedback Is Holding Women Back," *Harvard Business Review,* April 29, 2016, https://hbr.org/2016/04/research-vague-feedback-is-holding-women-back.

7. David G. Smith, Judith E. Rosenstein, and Margaret C. Nikolov, "How Performance Evaluations Hurt Gender Equality," *Behavioral Scientist,* June 26, 2018, https://behavioralscientist.org/how-performance-evaluations-hurt-gender-equality/.

8. Leah Asmelash, "Women Are Told More Lies Than Men in Workplace Reviews, New Research Suggests. And That Can Prevent Gender Equality," *CNN,* May 25, 2020, https://www.cnn.com/2020/05/25/us/women-workplace-gender-bias-study-trnd/index.html.

9. Culbert, *Get Rid*, 175.

10. Cespedes, "How to Conduct."

11. Fuhrmans, "Where Are All."

12. Kaplan and Sorensen, "Are CEOs Different?"

13. Kaplan and Sorensen, "Are CEOs Different?"

14. Peter Cappelli and Anne Tavis, "The Performance Management Revolution," *Harvard Business Review,* October 2016, https://hbr.org/2016/10/the-performance-management-revolution.

15. Katharina Buchholz, "How Has the Number of Female CEOs in Fortune 500 Companies Changed Over the Last 20 Years?" World Economic Forum, March 10, 2022, https://www.weforum.org/agenda/2022/03/ceos-fortune-500-companies-female/.

16. Herminia Ibarra, Nancy M. Carter, and Christine Silva, "Why Men Still Get More Promotions Than Women," *Harvard Business Review,* September 2010, https://hbr.org/2010/09/why-men-still-get-more-promotions-than-women.

17. Ibarra, Carter, and Silva, "Why Men Still Get More."

18. Melissa Wheeler and Victor Sojo, "One Unconscious Bias Is Keeping Women Out of Senior Roles," *Business Insider,* March 8, 2017, https://www.businessinsider.com/women-in-senior-roles-workplace-equality-2017-3.

19. Robert J. Ely, "The Effects of Organizational Demographics and Social Identity on Relationships Among Professional Women," *Administrative Science Quarterly* 39, no. 2, (1994): 203-238.

20. Joan Acker, "Hierarchies, Jobs, Bodies: A Theory of Gendered Organizations," *Gender & Society* 4, no. 2 (1990): 140.

21. "Research: Women in Management (Quick Take)," *Catalyst,* March 1, 2022, https://www.catalyst.org/research/women-in-management/.

22. Kathy E. Kram and Marion McCollom Hampton, "When Women Lead: The Visibility-Vulnerability Spiral" in *Reader in Gender, Work and Organization,* eds. Robin J. Ely, Erica Gabrielle Foldy, and Maureen A. Scully (Hoboken: Wiley-Blackwell, 2003), 211-223.

23. Navio Kwok and Winny Shen, "Leadership Training Shouldn't Just Be for Top Performers," *Harvard Business Review,* January 20, 2022, https://hbr.org/2022/01/leadership-training-shouldnt-just-be-for-top-performers.

24. Elizabeth Weingarten and Liz Kofman-Burns, "Is Your Leadership Development Program Undermining Your DEI Goals?," *Harvard Business Review,* October 6, 2022, https://hbr.org/2022/10/is-your-leadership-development-program-undermining-your-dei-goals.

25. Alice H. Eagly and Steven J. Karau, "Role Congruity, Theory of Prejudice Toward Female Leaders," *Psychological Review* 109, no. 3 (2002): 573.

26. Jay Newton-Small, "Critical Mass: What Happens When Women Start to Rule the World," *Harvard Kennedy School, Institute of Politics,* https://iop.harvard.edu/get-involved/study-groups/critical-mass-what-happens-when-women-start-rule-world-led-jay-newton.

27. Colleen Ammerman and Boris Groysberg, "How to Close the Gender Gap," *Harvard Business Review,* May 2021, https://hbr.org/2021/05/how-to-close-the-gender-gap.

28. Cespedes, "How to Conduct."

29. Douglas T. Hall, "Self-awareness, Identity, and *Leader Development,*" in *Leader Development for Transforming Organization: Growing Leaders for*

Tomorrow, eds. David V. Day, Stephen J. Zaccaro, and Stanely M. Halpin (Mahway: Lawrence Erlbaum Associates, 2004), 153-176.

30. Herminia Ibarra, "A Lack of Sponsorship Is Keeping Women from Advancing into Leadership," *Harvard Business Review*, August 19, 2019, https://hbr.org/2019/08/a-lack-of-sponsorship-is-keeping-women-from -advancing-into-leadership.

31. Maryann Bruce, "Mentoring Matters: The Importance of Female Mentorship," *Forbes*, October 26, 2021, https://www.forbes.com/sites/committeeof200/ 2021/10/26/mentoring-matters-the-importance--of-female- mentorship/?sh=6989105bccaa.

32. Angelica Cesario, "Andie Kramer and Al Harris: Empowering Women and Engaging Men to Deal With Gender Bias," *Above the Law*, May 8, 2017, https://abovethelaw.com/lawline-cle/2017/05/08/andie-kramer-and-al -harris-empowering-women-and-engaging-men-to-deal-with-gender-bias/.

33. "Mentor Tip Sheet," Andie & Al, accessed January 4, 2022, https://andie andal.com/wp-content/uploads/2021/08/Mentor-Tip-Sheet.7.21.pdf.

34. David Kearney, "Mentors, Mentees, & The Rules of Engagement," *Linke-dIn*, November 9, 2020, https://www.linkedin.com/pulse/mentors-mentees -rules-engagement-david-kearney/.

35. Susan Madsen, "Understanding Women's Negative Interactions With Each Other in the Workplace," *Forbes*, January 25, 2022, https://www.forbes.com /sites/forbescoachescouncil/2022/01/25/understanding-womens-negative -interactions-with-each-other-in-the-workplace/?sh=2ae08af92be4.

36. Susan R. Madsen and Maureen S. Andrade, "Unconscious Gender Bias: Implications for Women's Leadership Development," *Journal of Leadership Studies* 12, no. 1 (2018): 65.

37. "10 Best Ways to Make New Manager Training More Effective," *Forbes*, November 5, 2021, https://www.forbes.com/sites/forbeshumanresources council/2021/11/05/10-best-ways-to-make-new-manager-training-more -effective/?sh=2de6e23a2931 *See also, Deepa Purushothaman, Lisen Strom-berg, and Lisa Kaplowitz, "5 Harmful Ways Women Feel They Must Adapt in Corporate America," Harvard Business Review, October 31, 2022.*

38. Herminia Ibarra, *Working Identity: Unconventional Strategies for Rein-venting Your Career* (Boston: Harvard Business Publishing, 2004).

Chapter 12

1. Jessica Nordell, *The End of Bias: A Beginning: The Science and Practice of Overcoming Unconscious Bias* (New York: Metropolitan Books, 2021).

2. Michael Hammer, "Deep Change: How Operational Innovation Can Transform Your Company," *Harvard Business Review,* April 2004, https://hbr.org/2004/04/deep-change-how-operational-innovation-can-transform-your-company.

3. Michael Bucy et al., "Losing from Day One: Why Even Successful Transformations Fall Short," McKinsey & Company, December 7, 2021, https://www.mckinsey.com/capabilities/people-and-organizational-performance/our-insights/successful-transformations .

4. Scott Keller and Colin Price, *Beyond Performance: How Great Organizations Build Ultimate Competitive Advantage* (New York: Wiley, 2011).

5. Lili Duan, Emily Sheeren, and Leigh M. Weiss, "Tapping the Power of Hidden Influencers," *McKinsey Quarterly,* March 1, 2014, https://www.mckinsey.com/capabilities/people-and-organizational-performance/our-insights/tapping-the-power-of-hidden-influencers.

6. Bill Taylor, "Persuading Your Team to Embrace Change," *Harvard Business Review,* April 12, 2022, https://hbr.org/2022/04/persuading-your-team-to-embrace-change.

7. Mary Sharp Emerson, "7 Reasons Why Change Management Strategies Fail and How to Avoid Them," Professional Development, Harvard Division of Continuing Education, Nov 18, 2022, https://professional.dce.harvard.edu/blog/7-reasons-why-change-management-strategies-fail-and-how-to-avoid-them/.

8. Gorbatai, Boroş, and Ullman, "Why Middle Managers Struggle."

9. Duan, Sheeran, and Weiss, "Tapping the Power."

10. M. Lansu, and I. Bleijenbergh, and Y. Benschop, "Just Talking? Middle Managers Negotiating Problem Ownership in Gender Equality Interventions," *Scandinavian Journal of Management* 36, no. 2 (2020): 101110.

11. Bourke and Dillon, "The Diversity and Inclusion Revolution."

12. Erika Andersen, "Change Is Hard. Here's How to Make It Less Painful," *Harvard Business Review,* April 7, 2022, https://hbr.org/2022/04/change-is-hard-heres-how-to-make-it-less-painful.

13. J.R. Maxwell and Kirk Rieckhoff, "America 2021: Making Change Happen, Against the Odds," McKinsey & Company, February 19, 2021, https://www.mckinsey.com/industries/public-and-social-sector/our-insights/america-2021-making-change-happen-against-the-odds.

14. Scott Edinger, "Motivating People Starts with Building Emotional Connections," *Harvard Business Review,* July 21, 2022, https://hbr.org/2022/07/motivating-people-starts-with-building-emotional-connections.

15. Andrew White, Michael Smets, and Adam Canwell, "Organizational Transformation Is an Emotional Journey," *Harvard Business Review,* July 18, 2022, https://hbr.org/2022/07/organizational-transformation-is-an-emotional-journey.

16. David Rock, "The Fastest Way to Change a Culture," *Forbes,* May 24, 2019, https://www.forbes.com/sites/davidrock/2019/05/24/fastest-way-to-change-culture/?sh=2c92dc683d50.

17. John P. Kotter, "Leading Change: Why Transformation Efforts Fail," *Harvard Business Review,* May-June 1995, https://hbr.org/1995/05/leading-change-why-transformation-efforts-fail-2.

18. Emily Balcetis, *Clearer, Closer, Better: How Successful People See the World* (New York: Ballantine Books, 2020).

19. Jennifer Mueller, *Creative Change: Why We Resist It...How We Can Embrace It* (Boston: Houghton Mifflin Harcourt, 2017).

20. Rosabeth Moss Kanter, "Ten Reasons People Resist Change," *Harvard Business Review,* September 25, 2012, https://hbr.org/2012/09/ten-reasons-people-resist-chang.

21. Taylor, "Persuading Your Team."

22. Kanter, "Ten Reasons."

23. Katica Roy, David G. Smith, and W. Brad Johnson, "Gender Equity Is Not Zero Sum," *Harvard Business Review,* December 31, 2020, https://hbr.org/2020/12/gender-equity-is-not-zero-sum.

24. Members of High-Status Groups are Threatened by Pro-Diversity Organizational Messages," *Journal of Experimental Social Psychology* 62, (2016): 58-67.

25. Lisa S. Kaplowitz et al., "How Men Benefit From Close Relationships With Women At Work," *Forbes,* March 18, 2021, https://www.forbes.com/sites/ellevate/2021/03/18/how-men-benefit-from-close-relationships-with-women-at-work/?sh=104d80ac1264.

26. Christine Ro, "Why Do We Still Distrust Women Leaders?" BBC, January 19, 2021, https://www.bbc.com/worklife/article/20210108-why-do-we-still-distrust-women-leaders/.

27. Anna Patty, "Women Are Just As Ambitious As Men, Unless Companies Hold Them Back," *The Sydney Morning Herald,* April 5, 2017, https://www.smh.com.au/business/workplace/women-are-just-as-ambitious-as-men-unless-companies-hold-them-back-20170405-gvedtx.html.

28. Laura J. Kray et al., "The Effects of Implicit Gender Role Theories on Gender System Justification: Fixed Beliefs Strengthen Masculinity to Preserve

the Status Quo," *Journal of Personality and Social Psychology* 112, no.1 (2017): 98.

29. Negin Sattari, Sarah DiMuccio, and Ludo Gabriele, "When Managers Are Open, Men Feel Heard and Interrupt Sexism," *Catalyst,* December 3, 2021, https://www.catalyst.org/reports/managers-openness-sexism/.

30. Michael Kaufman, "The AIM Framework: Addressing and Involving Men and Boys to Promote Gender Equality and End Gender Discrimination and Violence," *UNICEF,* March 31, 2003, https://www.michaelkaufman .com/wp-content/uploads/2009/01/kaufman-the-aim-framework.pdf.

31. Kaufman, "The AIM Framework."

32. Kaufman, "The AIM Framework."

ACKNOWLEDGMENTS

We could not have written this book without the comments, criticisms, suggestions, nudges, laughter, and support of a great many people. In fact, we're proud of the diverse community we turned to for help and the people who agreed to roll up their sleeves and give us a hand. Many of our reviewers and commentators were old friends, but we have made some new friends in writing this book.

In alphabetical order and without suggesting the nature and extent of the help they provided us, here they are: Jody Adler, Katie A. Ahern, Irma Alvarado, Abby Baker, Dee Baker, Kate Bensen, Jennifer A. Berman, Barbara J. Best, Kay Bowers, Michael Chisholm, Sarah Collins, Charlie and Rochelle Curtis, Candace P. Davis, Adi Dina, Elizabeth Dougherty, Lynne Flater, Christopher Haigh, Margaret Hanson, Cynthia Harris, Les Harris, Bethany W. Harris, Jackie Haynes, Erika Heilman, Barbara Kavanagh, Frances H. Krasnow, Ursula Laskowski, Wendy A. Manning, Roseanne Rega, Sarah Shoblaske, Pam Simon, Alicia Simons, Anna Stagner, Jonathan Star, Ellen Rozelle Turner, Angela Vasandani, Anthony Warren, Sara White, and Jennifer Zordani.

We'd also like to thank everyone at our publisher, Nicholas Brealey. We have had the pleasure of publishing this, our third book, with them. We could not have done it without the strong support of Iain Campbell in London and Michelle Surianello in Boston. Once again it has been a pleasure to work with their teams to get this book published.

And once again we would like to end with a huge thanks to the hundreds of women (and men) who have shared their stories, experiences, and situations with us. As we promised, we have not included any names or other identifying characteristics.

REFERENCES

Abouzahr, Katie, Matt Krentz, Claire Tracey, and Miki Tsusaka. "Dispelling the Myths of the Gender 'Ambition Gap.'" *Boston Consulting Group.* April 5, 2017. https://www.bcg.com/publications/2017/people-organization-leadership -change-dispelling-the-myths-of-the-gender-ambition-gap/

Acker, Joan. "Hierarchies, Jobs, Bodies: A Theory of Gendered Organizations." *Gender & Society* 4, no. 2 (1990): 139-158.

Ahlman, Austin. "Build Back Better Dies...Again." *The American Prospect,* April 28, 2022. https://prospect.org/politics/build-back-better-dies-again/.

Al-Khateeb, Zac. "What is the Rooney Rule? Explaining NFL Mandate to Interview Minority Candidates, its Effectiveness and Criticism." *The Sporting News,* March 28, 2022. https://www.sportingnews.com/us/nfl/news /what-is-rooney-rule-nfl-minority-candidates-effectiveness-criticisms/1k4 m7oilxr8nv1xjs9f9bw2k7d.

Alemany, Luisa, Mariarosa Scarlata, and Andrew Zacharakis. "How the Gender Balance of Investment Teams Shapes the Risks They Take." *Harvard Business Review.* December 24, 2020, https://hbr.org/2020/12/how-the -gender-balance-of-investment-teams-shapes-the-risks-they-take#:~:text =Gender-,How%20the%20Gender%20Balance%20of%20Invest ment%20Teams%20Shapes%20the%20Risks,issues%20are%20on%20the %20table.&text=Women%20are%20more%20risk%20averse,received%20 wisdom%20seem%20to%20suggest

Amabile, Teresa M. and Steven J. Kramer. "The Power of Small Wins." *Harvard Business Review.* May 2011, https://hbr.org/2011/05/the-power-of-small-wins.

Amble, Brian. "Collaboration and Gender." *Management Issues,* June 1, 2012. https://www.management-issues.com/news/6495/collaboration-and-gender/.

American Institute of Architects. "Diversity in the Profession of Architecture: Key Findings 2015." Accessed December 18, 2021. https://www.architec-turalrecord.com/ext/resources/news/2016/03-Mar/AIA-Diversity-Survey/ AIA-Diversity-Architecture-Survey-02.pdf.

Ammerman, Colleen and Boris Groysberg. "How to Close the Gender Gap," *Harvard Business Review,* May 2021. https://hbr.org/2021/05/how-to-close-the-gender-gap.

Andersen, Erika. "Change is Hard. Here's How to Make It Less Painful." *Harvard Business Review*, April 7, 2022. https://hbr.org/2022/04/change-is-hard-heres-how-to-make-it-less-painful.

Andi, Simge, Meera Selva, and Rasmus Kleis Nielsen. "Women and Leadership in the News Media 2020: Evidence from Ten Markets," *Reuters Institute online*, March 8, 2020. https://reutersinstitute.politics.ox.ac.uk/women-and-leadership-news-media-2020-evidence-ten-markets.

Andie & Al. "Mentor Tip Sheet." Accessed January 4, 2022. https://andieandal.com/wp-content/uploads/2021/08/Mentor-Tip-Sheet.7.21.pdf.

Anti-Defamation League. "When Women Are the Enemy: The Intersection of Misogyny and White Supremacy." July 20, 2018. https://www.adl.org/resources/reports/when-women-are-the-enemy-the-intersection-of-misogyny-and-white-supremacy

Arnand, Rohini and Mary-Frances Winters. "A Retrospective View of Corporate Diversity Training from 1964 to the Present." *Academy of Management Learning & Education* 7, no. 3 (2008): 356-372.

Asmelash, Leah. "Women Are Told More Lies Than Men in Workplace Reviews, New Research Suggests. And That Can Prevent Gender Equality." *CNN,* May 25, 2020. https://www.cnn.com/2020/05/25/us/women-workplace-gender-bias-study-trnd/index.html.

Aten, Jason. "Xerox's Former CEO Made a Controversial Statement About Work-Life Balance. Why She's Not Wrong." *Inc.,* March 17, 2022. htttps://www.inc.com/jason-aten/xeroxs-former-ceo-made-a-controversial-statement-about-work-life-balance-why-shes-not-wrong.html#:~:text=In%20an%20interview%20with%20CNBC,to%20all%20your%20kids'%20games.

Atewologun, Doyin, Tinu Cornish, and Fatima Tresh, "Unconscious Bias Training: An Assessment of the Evidence for Effectiveness," *Equality and Human Rights Commission Research Report 113*, March 2018, https://www.equalityhumanrights.com/en/publication-download/unconscious-bias-training-assessment-evidence-effectiveness.

Audette, Andre P. "Gender Equality Supports Happiness and Well-Being." *The Gender Policy Report,* September 13, 2019, https://genderpolicyreport.umn.edu/gender-equality-supports-happiness/.

Ayewologun, Doyin Tinu Cornish, and Fatima Tresh, "Unconscious Bias Training: An Assessment of the Evidence for Effectiveness," Equality and Human Rights Commission Research Report 113, March 2018, https://www.equality

humanrights.com/en/publication-download/unconscious-bias-training
-assessment-evidence-effectiveness.

Badal, Sangeeta Bharadwaj. "The Business Benefits of Gender Diversity." Gallup. January 20, 2014, https://www.gallup.com/workplace/236543/business
-benefits-gender-diversity.aspx.

Bailinson, Peter, William Dechard, Diana Ellsworth, and Maital Guttman. "Understanding Organizational Barriers to a More Inclusive Workplace." *McKinsey & Company*, June 23, 2020. https://www.mckinsey.com /business-functions/people-and-organizational-performance/our-insights /understanding-organizational-barriers-to-a-more-inclusive-workplace.

Balcetis, Emily. *Clearer, Closer, Better: How Successful People See the World.* New York: Ballantine Books, 2020.

Banaji, Mahzarin R., Max H. Bazerman, and Dolly Chugh. "How (Un)Ethical Are You?" *Harvard Business Review*, December 2003. https://hbr .org/2003/12/how-unethical-are-you

Banaji, Mahzarin. "Mind Bugs: The Science of Ordinary Bias." *Harvard University Center for Ethics*, September 22, 2010. https://ethics.harvard.edu /mahzarin-banaji-mind-bugs-science-ordinary-bias

Barker, Kim and Ellen Gabler. "Charlie Rose Made Crude Sexual Advances, Multiple Women Say." *New York Times*, November 20, 2017. https://www .nytimes.com/2017/11/20/us/charlie-rose-women.html.

Bax, Bianca, Andrew Schwedel, Fai Assakul, and Nicole Bitler. "Working Women and the War for Talent," Bain & Company, 2022, https://www .bain.com/insights/working-women-and-the-war-for-talent/.

BBC News. "Young Goldman Sachs Bankers Ask for 80-hour Week Cap," March 19, 2021, https://www.bbc.com/news/business-56452494.

Beheshti, Naz. "How 'Greedy' Jobs and Inflexible Schedules Impact the Gender Pay Gap." *Forbes*, December 5, 2019. https://www.forbes.com/sites /nazbeheshti/2019/12/05/how-greedy-jobs-and-inflexible-schedules -impact-the-gender-pay-gap/?sh=5c50d79c6707.

Beiner, Camila. "Childcare Is Getting More Support from Some Private Companies." *NPR*, January 4, 2022. https://www.npr.org/2022/01/04/1064124004 /child-care-is-getting-more-support-from-some-private-companies.

Belkin, Lisa. "The Opt-Out Revolution." *New York Times*. October 26, 2003, https://www.nytimes.com/2003/10/26/magazine/the-opt-out-revolution .html. See also, https://www.pewresearch.org/fact-tank/2018/11/29/more -than-one-in-ten-u-s-parents-are-also-caring-for-an-adult/.

Bennett, Benjamin, Isil Erel, Léa H. Stern, and Zexi Wang. "Paid Leave Pays Off: The Effects of Paid Family Leave on Firm Performance." *National*

Bureau of Economic Research, December 2020. https://www.nber.org
/papers/w27788.

Beyoud, Lydia and Andrew Ramonas. "Shareholders Up Demands for Workforce Diversity Data Seen by Few." *Daily Labor Report,* June 7, 2021. https://
news.bloomberglaw.com/esg/shareholders-up-demands-for-workplace
-diversity-data-seen-by-few.

Bezrukova, Katerina, Chester S. Spell, Jamie L. Perry, and Karen A. Jehn. "A
Meta-Analytical Integration of over 40 Years of Research on Diversity
Training Evaluation." *Psychological Bulletin* 142, no. 11 (2016): 1227-1274.

Big Bet Initiate. "Unitive: Addressing Bias Through Blind Recruitment." Accessed
December 4, 2021. http://bigbetinitiative.com/unitive-addressing-bias
-through-blind-recruitment/.

Booker, Brakkton. "NFL Announces New Rules to Tackle Lack of Diversity in its Coaching, Executive Ranks." *NPR,* May 19, 2020. https://www
.npr.org/2020/05/19/858702029/nfl-announces-new-rules-to-tackle
-lack-of-diversity-in-its-coaching-executive-ra.

Bourke, Juliet and Bernadette Dillon. "The Diversity and Inclusion Revolution: Eight Powerful Truths." *Deloitte Review* 22, January 22, 2018. https://
www2.deloitte.com/content/dam/insights/us/articles/4209_Diversity-and
-inclusion-revolution/DI_Diversity-and-inclusion-revolution.pdf.

Brassel, Sheila, Tara Van Bommel, and Katharina Robotham. "Three Inclusive Team Norms That Drive Success," *Catalyst.* Accessed January 1, 2022.
https://www.catalyst.org/reports/inclusive-team-norms-success.

Brescoll, Victoria L. "Lead with Their Hearts? How Gender Stereotypes of Emotion Lead to Biased Evaluations of Female Leaders." *The Leadership Quarterly* 27 (2016): 415-428.

Bresman, Henrik and Amy C. Edmondson. "Research: To Excel, Diverse Teams
Need Psychological Safety." *Harvard Business Review,* March 17, 2022.
https://hbr.org/2022/03/research-to-excel-diverse-teams-need-psychological
-safety.

Bruce, Maryann. "Mentoring Matters: The Importance of Female Mentorship." *Forbes,* October 26, 2021. https://www.forbes.com/sites/committee
of200/2021/10/26/mentoring-matters-the-importance--of-female
-mentorship/?sh=1c4449c0ccaa.

Buchholz, Katharina. "How Has the Number of Female CEOs in Fortune 500
Companies Changed Over the Last 20 Years?" March 10, 2022. https://
www.weforum.org/agenda/2022/03/ceos-fortune-500-companies-female/.

Burlington Industries v. Ellerth, 524 U.S. 742 (1998); *Faragher v. City of Boca
Raton, 524 U.S. 775* (1998).

Burrell, Darrell Norman, Shanel Lu, Preston Vernard Leicester Lindsay, Sharon L. Burton, Roderick French, Aikyna Finch, Quatavia McLester, and Delores Springs. "Sexual Harassment Training Focusing Solely on Protecting Organizations from Lawsuits Won't Change a Toxic Culture for Women to an Inclusive One." *International Journal of Public Sociology and Sociotherapy* 1, no. 1 (2021): 12-25.

Byham, Tacy. "Women CEOs' Highest Representation on the Fortune 500 List Still Isn't Enough." *Forbes*, August 3, 2020. https://www.forbes.com/sites /forbescoachescouncil/2020/08/03/women-ceos-highest-representation-on -the-fortune-500-list-still-isnt-enough/?sh=5c6b8a835aa8.

Byham, Tracy. "Where Are the Women in the C-Suite?" *Forbes*, March 1, 2021. https://www.forbes.com/sites/forbescoachescouncil/2021/03/01/where -are-the-women-in-the-c-suite/?sh=4b115a684ece.

Cahn, Naomi. "Women's Status and Pay in the C-Suite: New Study." *Forbes*, February 19, 2021. https://www.forbes.com/sites/naomicahn/2021/02/19 /womens-status-and-pay-in-the-c-suite--new-study/?sh=3d2757f63762.

California Secretary of State. Women on Boards (SB 826). Sacramento, California Secretary of State 2018. https://www.sos.ca.gov/business-programs /women-boards.

Cappelli, Peter and Anna Tavis. "The Performance Management Revolution." *Harvard Business Review*, October 2016. https://hbr.org/2016/10/the -performance-management-revolution.

Cappelli, Peter. "In a Hybrid Office, Remote Workers Will Be Left Behind." *Wall Street Journal*, August 13, 2021. https://www.wsj.com/articles/hybrid -workplace-promotions-11628796072.

Carucci, Ron. "To Retain New Hires, Spend More Time Onboarding Them." *Harvard Business Review*, December 3, 2018. https://hbr.org/2018/12/to -retain-new-hires-spend-more-time-onboarding-them.

Cassella, Megan. "The Pandemic Drove Women Out of the Workforce. Will They Come Back?" *Politico*, July 22, 2021, https://www.politico.com/news/2021 /07/22/coronavirus-pandemic-women-workforce-500329.

Catalyst. "Pyramid: Women in S&P 500 Companies." February 9, 2022. https:// www.catalyst.org/research/women-in-sp-500-companies/.

Catalyst. "Why Diversity and Inclusion Matter." June 24, 2020, https://www .catalyst.org/research/why-diversity-and-inclusion-matter/.

Catalyst. "Research: Women in Management (Quick Take)." March 1, 2022. https://www.catalyst.org/research/women-in-management/.

Cecchi-Dimeglio, Paola. "How Gender Bias Corrupts Performance Reviews, and What to Do About It." *Harvard Business Review*, April 12, 2017. https://

hbr.org/2017/04/how-gender-bias-corrupts-performance-reviews-and
-what-to-do-about-it.

Center for Women and Business at Bentley University. "Men as Allies: Engaging Men
to Advance Women in the Workplace." Spring 2017, https://www.ceoaction
.com/media/1434/bentley-cwb-men-as-allies-research-report-spring
-2017.pdf.

Cesario, Angela. "Andie Kramer and Al Harris: Empowering Women and
Engaging Men to Deal with Gender Bias." *Above the Law*, May 8, 2017.
https://abovethelaw.com/lawline-cle/2017/05/08/andie-kramer-and-al
-harris-empowering-women-and-engaging-men-to-deal-with-gender-bias/.

Cespedes, Frank V. "How to Conduct a Great Performance Review." *Harvard
Business Review*, July 8, 2022. https://hbr.org/2022/07/how-to-conduct
-a-great-performance-review.

Chang, Edward H., Katherine L. Milkman, Dena M. Gromet, Robert W. Rebele,
Cade Massey, Angela L. Duckworth, and Adam M. Grant. "The Mixed
Effect of Online Diversity Training." *Proceedings of the National Academy
of Sciences* 116, no. 16 (2019): 7778-7783.

Chilazi, Siri, Iris Bohnet, and Oliver Hauser. "Achieving Gender Balance at All Levels
of Your Company." *Harvard Business Review*, November 30, 2021. https://
hbr.org/2021/11/achieving-gender-balance-at-all-levels-of-your-company

Chui, Michael and Anna Bernasek. "Forward Thinking on Economic Recov-
ery and Gender Equality with Laura Tyson." *Mckinsey Global Institute's
Forward Thinking*. Podcast audio. July 28, 2021. https://www.mckinsey
.com/featured-insights/gender-equality/forward-thinking-on-economic
-recovery-and-gender-equality-with-laura-tyson.

Cohen, Carol Fishman. "A New Way to Explore the Pause in Your Career." *Harvard Business Review*, March 23, 2022. https://hbr.org/2022/03/a-new-way
-to-explain-the-pause-in-your-career.

Cohen, Carol Fishman. "Return-to-Work Programs Come of Age." *Harvard
Business Review*, October 2021. https://hbr.org/2021/09/return-to-work
-programs-come-of-age.

Collier, Anne E. "Men in the Mix: How to Engage Men on Issues Related to
Gender in the Legal Profession." American Bar Association, 2021. https://
www.americanbar.org/content/dam/aba/administrative/women/men-in
-mix-report_feb2.pdf.

Collins, Lois M. "Who's Helping Around the House? It's a He Said, She
Said Situation." *Deseret News*, October 12, 2021. https://www.deseret
.com/2021/10/12/22698901/do-men-or-women-help-more-around-the
-house-american-family-survey-childcare-cleaning-chores?fr=operanews.

Cook, Jackie. "What Will it Take to Close the Gender Pay Gap for Good?" *Morningstar,* February 22, 2021. https://www.morningstar.com/articles /1025601/what-will-it-take-to-close-the-gender-pay-gap-for-good.

Coqual. "What Majority Men Really Think About Diversity and Inclusion (And How to Engage Them in It)." August 2020. https://coqual.org/wp-content /uploads/2020/09/CoqualMajorityMenBelongingKeyFindings090720.pdf.

Correll, Shelley J. and Caroline Simard. "Research: Vague Feedback Is Holding Women Back." *Harvard Business Review,* April 29, 2016. https://hbr .org/2016/04/research-vague-feedback-is-holding-women-back.

Correll, Shelley J., Katherine R. Weisshaar, Alison T. Wynn, and JoAnne Delfino Wehner. "Inside the Black Box of Organizational Life: The Gendered Language of Performance Assessment." *American-Sociological Review* 85, no. 6 (2020): 1022-1050.

Covert, Bryce. "The Secret to Getting More Women on Corporate Boards: The $100,000 Threat." *Politico,* February 25, 2022. https://www.politico .com/news/magazine/2022/02/25/california-companies-women-boards -quotas-00010745.

Cowen, Tyler. "Of Course Stereotypes Are Holding Women Back." *Pittsburgh Post-Gazette.* November 25, 2021. https://www.post-gazette.com/opinion /Op-Ed/2021/11/26/Tyler-Cowen-Of-course-stereotypes-are-holding -women-back/stories/202111260009.

Crenshaw, Kimberlé. *On Intersectionality: Essential* Writings. New York: The New Press, 2017.

Culbert, Samuel A. *Get Rid of the Performance Review! How Companies Can Stop Intimidating, Start Managing—and Focus on What Really Matters.* Dublin: Business Plus, 2010.

Culleton, Billy. "State Lawmakers Continue Push to Increase Diversity in Corporate Boardrooms." *Multistate.* March 17, 2021, https://www.multi state.us/insider/2021/3/17/state-lawmakers-continue-push-to-increase -diversity-in-corporate-boardrooms.

Davis, Jeffery. "The Bias Against Difference and How it Gets in the Way of Creativity and Collaboration." *Psychology Today.* June 25, 2020, https:// www.psychologytoday.com/us/blog/tracking-wonder/202006/the -bias-against-difference.

Day, David V. Stephen J. Zaccaro, and Stanely M. Halpin, eds. *Leader Development for Transforming Organization: Growing Leaders for Tomorrow.* Mahway: Lawrence Erlbaum Associates, 2004.

DeBara, Deanna. "Gender Diversity: Benefits, Challenges & Strategies." *Hourly,* September 26, 2022. https://www.hourly.io/post/gender-diversity.

Delizonna, Laura. "High-Performing Teams Need Psychological Safety. Here's How to Create It." *Harvard Business Review*, August 24, 2017. https://hbr .org/2017/08/high-performing-teams-need-psychological-safety-heres -how-to-create-it.

Denend, Lyn, Paul Yock, and Dan Azagury. "Research: Small Wins Can Make a Big Impact on Gender Equality." *Harvard Business Review*, November 6, 2020. https://hbr.org/2020/11/research-small-wins-can-make-a-big-impact-on -gender-equality#:~:text=Change%20management-,Research%3A%20 Small%20Wins%20Can%20Make%20a%20Big%20Impact%20on %20Gender,look%20at%20their%20own%20organization.&text =Health%20technology%20is%20a%20growing,tools%2C%20and%20 health%20care%20IT./

Denend, Lyn, Stacey McCutcheon, Mike Regan, Maria Sainz, Paul Yock, and Dan Azagury. "Analysis of Gender Perceptions in Health Technology: A Call to Action." *Analysis of Biomedical Engineering* 48, no. 5 (2020): 1573-1586.

Dew, Nicole. "These 17 Companies Help Employees with Child Care." *The Penny Hoarder,* August 15, 2022. https://www.thepennyhoarder.com/make-money /career/companies-with-child-care/.

Dias, Felipe A., Joseph Chance, and Arianna Buchanan. "The Motherhood Penalty and the Fatherhood Premium in Employment During Covid-19: Evidence from the United States." *Research in Social Stratification and Mobility* 69 (2020): 1-4.

Dill, Kathryn and Angela Yang. "Companies Are Cutting Back on Maternity and Paternity Leave: Many Employers Dial Down How Much Paid Time Off They Give New Moms and Dads." *Wall Street Journal*, August 22, 2022. https://www.wsj.com/articles/the-surprising-benefit-some-companies -are-taking-awayparental-leave-11661125605.

Dixon-Fyle, Sundiatu, Kevin Dolan, Vivian Hunt, and Sara Prince, "Diversity Wins: How Inclusion Matters." *McKinsey & Company*, May 19, 2020. https://www.mckinsey.com/featured-insights/diversity-and-inclusion /diversity-wins-how-inclusion-matters.

Dobbin, Frank and Alexandra Kalev. "How Companies Should Set—and report DEI Goals." *Harvard Business Review*, September 29, 2022. https://hbr .org/2022/09/how-companies-should-set-and-report-dei-goals.

Dobbin, Frank and Alexandra Kalev. "Training Programs and Reporting Systems Won't End Sexual Harassment. Promoting More Women Will." *Harvard Business Review*, November 15, 2017. https://hbr.org/2017/11 /training-programs-and-reporting-systems-wont-end-sexual-harassment -promoting-more-women-will.

Dobbin, Frank and Alexandra Kalev. "Why Diversity Programs Fail." *Harvard Business Review*, July-August 2014. https://hbr.org/2016/07/why-diversity -programs-fail.

Dobbin, Frank and Alexandra Kalev. "Why Doesn't Diversity Training Work? The Challenge for Industry and Academia." *Anthropology Now* 10, no. 2 (2018) 48-55.

Dobbin, Frank and Alexandra Kalev. "Why Sexual Harassment Programs Backfire." *Harvard Business Review*, May-June 2020. https://hbr.org/2020 /05/why-sexual-harassment-programs-backfire.

Dover, Tessa L., Brenda Major, and Cheryl R. Kaiser. "Members of High-Status Groups Are Threatened by Pro-diversity." *Journal of Experimental Social Psychology* 62, (2016): 58-67.

Dow, Nicole. "These 17 Companies Help Employees with Child Care." *The Penny Hoarder*, August 15, 2022. https://www.thepennyhoarder.com/make -money /career/companies-with-child-care/.

Du Mez, Kristen Kobes. *Jesus and John Wayne: How White Evangelicals Corrupted a Faith and Fracture a Nation.* New York: Liveright Publishing Corporation, 2020.

Duan, Lili, Emily Sheeran, and Leigh M. Weiss. "Tapping the Power of Hidden Influencers." *McKinsey & Company*, March 1, 2014. https://www.mckinsey .com/capabilities/people-and-organizational-performance/our-insights /tapping-the-power-of-hidden-influencers.

Eagly, Alice H. and Steven J. Karau. "Role Congruity, Theory of Prejudice Toward Female Leaders." *Psychological Review* 109, no. 3 (2002): 573-598.

Edinger, Scott. "Motivating People Starts with Building Emotional Connec-tions." *Harvard Business Review*, July 21, 2022. https://hbr.org/2022/07/ motivating-people-starts-with-building-emotional-connections.

Edmondson, Amy. "Psychological Safety and Learning Behavior in Work Teams." *Administrative Science Quarterly* 44, no. 2 (1999): 350-383.

El-Bawab, Nadine. "Employers Offer Stipends for Babysitting and Tutoring to Sweeten Childcare Benefits and Win Over Workers." *CNBC*, July 9, 2021. https://www.cnbc.com/2021/07/09/employers-sweeten-child-care-benefits -to-win-over-workers-.html#:~:text=The%20Path%20Forward -,Employers%20offer%20stipends%20for%20babysitting%20and%20 tutoring%20to%20sweeten%20child,benefits%20and%20win%20 over%20workers&text=As%20working%20parents%20juggled %20their,coronavirus%20pandemic%2C%20companies%20took%20notice.

Ellison, Sarah. "Inside the Final Days of Roger Ailes's Reign at Fox News." *Vanity Fair,* September 22, 2016. https://www.vanityfair.com/news/2016/09/roger-ailes -fox-news-final-days.

Elsesser, Kim. *Sex and the Office: Women, Men and the Sex Partition That's Dividing the Workplace.* Lanham: Rowman & Littlefield, 2014.

Elsesser, Kim. "Goldman Sachs Won't Take Companies Public if They Have All-Male Corporate Boards." *Forbes*, January 23, 2020. https://www.forbes .com/sites/kimelsesser/2020/01/23/goldman-sachs-wont-take-companies -public-if-they-have-all-male-corporate-boards/?sh=2ee3e13a9475.

Ely, Robert J. "The Effects of Organizational Demographics and Social Identity on Relationship Among Professional Women." *Administrative Quarterly* 39, no. 2, (1994): 203-238.

Ely, Robin J. and Irene Padavic. "What's Really Holding Women Back?" *Harvard Business Review.* March-April 2020, https://hbr.org/2020/03/whats -really-holding-women-back

Ely, Robin J., Erica Gabrielle Foldy, and Maureen A. Scully, eds. *Reader in Gender, Work and Organization.* Hoboken: Wiley-Blackwell, 2003.

Ely, Robin J., Pamela Stone, and Colleen Ammerman. "Rethink What You Know about High-Achieving Women." *Harvard Business Review*, December 2014. https://hbr.org/2014/12/rethink-what-you-know-about-high-achieving-women.

Emerson, Joelle. "Don't Give Up on Unconscious Bias Training – Make It Better." *Harvard Business Review*, April 28, 2017. https://hbr.org/2017/04/dont-give-up -on-unconscious-bias-training-make-it-better.

Emerson, Mary Sharp. "7 Reasons Why Change Management Strategies Fail and How to Avoid Them," Professional Development, Harvard Division of Continuing Education, Nov 18, 2022, https://professional.dce.harvard.edu/blog /7-reasons-why-change-management-strategies-fail-and-how-to-avoid- them/.

Facebook. "Managing Unconscious Bias." Accessed January 3, 2022. https:// managingbias.fb.com/.

Fan, Jennifer S. "Innovating Inclusion: The Impact of Women on Private Company Boards." *Law Review* 46, no. 2 (2019): 354-413.

Fawcett, Charles C. Securities Exchange Act Release No. 56770, 91 S.E.C. Docket 2594. November 8, 2007.

Feintzeig, Rachel. "More Companies Say Targets Are the Key to Diversity." *Wall Street Journal,* September 30, 2015. https://www.wsj.com/articles/more -companies-say-targets-are-the-key-to-diversity-1443600464.

Feldblum, Chai R and Victoria A. Lipnic. "EEOC Special Task Force on the Study of Harassment in the Workplace." Equal Employment Opportunity Commission, June 6, 2016. https://www.eeoc.gov/select-task-force -study-harassment-workplace.

Fels, Anna. "Do Women Lack Ambition?" *Harvard Business Review*. April 2004, https://hbr.org/2004/04/do-women-lack-ambition.

Ferrante, Mary Beth. "Before Breaking the Glass Ceiling, Women Must Climb the Maternal Wall." *Forbes,* October 31, 2018. https://www.forbes.com/sites/marybethferrante/2018/10/31/before-breaking-the-glass-ceiling-women-must-climb-the-maternal-wall/?sh=740c5679c519.

Joan C. Williams and Kate Massinger, "Need a Good Parental Leave Policy? Here It Is," *Harvard Business Review*, November 23, 2015. https://hbr.org/2015/11/need-a-good-parental-leave-policy-here-it-is.

Ferreira, Emily and Rich Fuerstenberg. "The Pressure Is on to Modernize Time Off Benefits: 6 Survey Findings." *Mercer Health News*, January 16, 2019. https://www.mercer.us/our-thinking/healthcare/the-pressure-is-on-to-modernize-time-off-benefits-6-survey-findings.html.

Fischer, Agneta H. "Sex Differences in Emotionality: Fact or Stereotype?" *Feminism & Psychology* 3, no. 3 (1993): 303-318.

Fitzsimons, Grainne, Aaron Kay, and Jae Yun Kim. "'Lean In' Messages and the Illusion of Control." *Harvard Business Review*, July 30, 2018. https://hbr.org/2018/07/lean-in-messages-and-the-illusion-of-control#:~:text=Researchers%20found%20a%20downside%20to%20messages%20of%20empowerment.&text=In%20a%20world%20in%20which,favor%20men%20at%20women's%20expense%3F.

Flanagan, Caitlin. "The Problem with HR." *The Atlantic*, July 2019. https://www.theatlantic.com/magazine/archive/2019/07/hr-workplace-harrassment-metoo/590644/

Flood, Michael and Richard Hoswon, eds. *Engaging Men in Building Gender Equality*. Newcastle: Cambridge Scholars Publishing, 2016.

Forbes. "10 Best Ways to Make New Manager Training More Effective." November 5, 2021. https://www.forbes.com/sites/forbeshumanresourcescouncil/2021/11/05/10-best-ways-to-make-new-manager-training-more-effective/?sh=513008d62931.

Ford, Richard Thompson. "Perverse Effects of Antidiscrimination Law." *New York Times*, June 30, 2015. https://www.nytimes.com/roomfordebate/2014/03/24/if-gays-can-marry-and-be-fired-for-doing-so/perverse-effects-of-antidiscrimination-law.

Forscher, Patrick S., Calvin K. Lai, Jordan R. Axt, Charles R. Ebersole, Michelle Herman, Patricia G. Devine, and Brian A. Nosek. "A Meta-Analysis of Procedure to Change Implicit Measures." *Journal of Personality and Social Psychology* 117, no. 3, 522-559.

Foschi, Martha. "Double Standards for Competence: Theory and Research." *Annual Review of Psychology* 26, no. 1 (2000): 21-42

Fox, Wendy J. "Women Aren't Opting Out of the Workforce They Are Being Forced Out." *Ms. Magazine,* October 22, 2020. https://msmagazine.com /2020/10/22/jobs-women-work-workforce-opt-out-forced-out-wage -gap-gender/.

Friedman, Ron. "High-Performing Teams Don't Leave Relationships to Chance." *Harvard Business Review,* September 14, 2022. https://hbr.org/2022/09/high -performing-teams-dont-leave-relationships-to-chance.

Fry, Richard. "Some Gender Disparities Widened in the U.S. Workforce During the Pandemic." Pew Research Center, January 14, 2022. https:// www.pewresearch.org/fact-tank/2022/01/14/some-gender-disparities -widened-in-the-u-s-workforce-during-the-pandemic/.

Fuhrmans, Vanessa. "Where Are All the Women CEOs?" *Wall Street Journal,* February 6, 2020. https://www.wsj.com/articles/why-so-few-ceos-are-women -you-can-have-a-seat-at-the-table-and-not-be-a-player-11581003276.

Fuller, Pamela and Mark Murphy. *Leaders Guide to Unconscious Bias How to Reframe Bias, Cultivate Connection, and Create High-Performing Teams.* New York: Simon & Schuster, 2020.

Gabler, Ellen, Jim Rutenberg, Michael M. Grynbaum, and Rachel Abrams. "NBC Fires Matt Laure, the Face of 'Today.'" *New York Times,* November 9, 2017. https://www.nytimes.com/2017/11/29/business/media/nbc-matt-lauer .html.

GapJumpers. "Performance Over Privilege & Pedigree." Accessed November 13, 2021, https://www.gapjumpers.me/.

Gaudiano, Paolo. "Women's Equality in the Workplace Requires Greater Inclusion." *Forbes,* March 8, 2022. https://www.forbes.com/sites/paologaudiano/2022 /03/08/womens-equality-in-the-workplace-requires-greater-inclusion/?sh =5c7fb2582eb4.

Gavett, Gretchen. "The Problem With 'Greedy Work.'" *Harvard Business Review,* September 28, 2021.https://hbr.org/2021/09/the-problem-with-greedy -work.

Gerdemn, Dina. "How Gender Stereotypes Kill a Woman's Self-Confidence." *Harvard Business School.* February 25, 2019. https://hbswk.hbs.edu/item/how -gender-stereotypes-less-than-br-greater-than-kill-a-woman-s-less-than -br-greater-than-self-confidence.

Gill, Rosalind and Shani Organ. "Confidence Culture and the Remaking of Feminism." *New Formation* 91, no. 91 (2017): 16-36.

Gillin, Heather. "How Career Interruptions Affect Women." *Texas A&M Today,* March 9, 2020. https://today.tamu.edu/2020/03/09/how-career-interruptions

-affect-women/#:~:text=Wage%20penalties,level%20all%20influence%20
wage%20penalties..

Gino, Francesca. "Why It's So Hard to Speak Up Against a Toxic Culture." *Harvard Business Review*, May 21, 2018. https://hrb.org/2018/05/why-its-so-hard
-to-speak-up-against-a-toxic-culture

Glazebrook, Kate. "What Is Blind Hiring? A Guide to Blind Recruitment."
Be Applied, November 27, 2018. https://www.beapplied.com/post/what
-is-blind-hiring.

Global News Wire. "Diversity and Inclusion (D&I) World Market Report:
Diverse Companies Earn 2.5 Times Higher Cash Flow Per Employee and
Inclusive Teams Are More Productive by Over 35%." August 9, 2022.
https://www.globenewswire.com/news-release/2022/08/09/2494604/0/en
/Diversity-and-Inclusion-D-I-Global-Market-Report-2022-Diverse-Com
panies-Earn-2-5-Times-Higher-Cash-Flow-Per-Employee-and-Inclusive
-Teams-Are-More-Productive-by-Over-35.html.

Gloor, Jamie L., Gudrun Sander, and Alyson Meister. "What to Do About Employees Who Consciously Exclude Women." *Harvard Business Review*, November 8, 2021. https://hbr.org/2021/11/what-to-do-about-employees-who
-consciously-exclude-women.

Goldberg, Steven. *The Inevitability of Patriarchy*. New York: William Morrow
and Company, 1973.

Goldin, Claudia. *Career and Family: Women's Century-Long Journey Toward
Equity*. Princeton: Princeton University Press, 2021.

Goldman Sachs. "Executive Officers." Accessed April 2, 2022, https://www
.goldmansachs.com/about-us/people-and-leadership/leadership/executive
-officers//.

Google. "Action #1 Hiring." Accessed April 3, 2022. https://about.google
/belonging/diversity-annual-report/2022/hiring.

Google. "Guide: Raise Awareness About Unconscious Bias." Accessed April 7,
2022. https://rework.withgoogle.com/print/guides/5079604133888000/.

Gorbatai, Andreéa, Smaranda Boroşs, and Katherine Ullman. "Why Middle Managers Struggle to Implement DEI Strategies." *Harvard Business
Review*, October 13, 2022. https://hbr.org/2022/10/why-middle-managers
-struggle-to -implement-dei-strategies.

Graf, Nikki, Anna Brown, and Eileen Patten. "The US Gender Pay Gap Is Narrowing but Persistent." *World Economic Forum*, April 12, 2018. https://
www.weforum.org/agenda/2018/04/the-narrowing-but-persistent-gender
-gap-in-pay.

Grant, Adam. "Why So Many Men Don't Stand Up for Their Female Colleagues." *The Atlantic*, April 29, 2014. https://www.theatlantic.com/business/archive /2014/04/why-men-dont-stand-up-for-women-to-lead/361231/.

Gratton, Lynda. "How to Do Hybrid Right." *Harvard Business Review*, May-June 2021. https://hbr.org/2021/05/how-to-do-hybrid-right.

Green, Jeff. "Corporate America Loves the Rooney Rule but Does It Work?" *Financial Post*, March 21, 2022. https://financialpost.com/pmn/business -pmn/corporate-america-loves-the-rooney-rule-but-does-it-work.

Green, Tiffany L. and Nao Hagiwara. "The Problem with Implicit Bias Training." *Scientific American*, August 28, 2020. https://www.scientificamerican .com/article/the-problem-with-implicit-bias-training/.

Haider, Monica. "Kathy Hochul Is Now One of Nine Female Governors, But Narrowing Gender Gap Requires Less Scrutiny." *Forbes*, August 27, 2021. https://www.forbes.com/sites/monicahaider/2021/08/27/kathy-hochul-is -now-one-of-nine-female-governors-but-narrowing-gender-gap-requires -less-scrutiny/?sh=5bc6f49265e5.

Hakim, Catherine. "Women, Careers, and Work-Life Preferences." *British Journal of Guidance & Counseling* 34, no. 3 (2006): 279-294.

Hammer, Michael. "Deep Change: How Operational Innovation Can Transform Your Company." *Harvard Business Review*, April 2004. https://hbr.org/2004/04/ deep-change-how-operational-innovation-can-transform-your-company.

Han-He, Camilla. "Why It's Time to Rewrite the Narrative on Career Breaks." LinkedIn, March 1, 2022. https://www.linkedin.com/pulse/why-its-time -rewrite-narrative-career-breaks-camilla-han-he/?src=aff-ref&trk=aff-ir _progid%3D8005_partid%3D10078_sid%3D_adid%3D449670&clickid =TVr3WR2vwxyNTfTW9LwVOwjEUkDRckWlwWd8Ts0&mcid=685196 2469594763264&irgwc=1.

Hancock, Bryan, Elizabeth Hioe, and Bill Schaninger. "The Fairness Factor in Performance Management." McKinsey & Company, April 5, 2018. https://www .mckinsey.com/business-functions/people-and-organizational-performance /our-insights/the-fairness-factor-in-performance-management].

Hartley, Robert Paul, Ajay Chaudry, Melissa Boteach, Estelle Mitchell, and Kathryn Menefee. "A Lifetime Worth of Benefits; The Effect of Affordable, High-Quality Childcare on Family Income, the Gender Earnings Gap, and Women's Retirement Security." Center on Poverty & Social Policy and National Women's Law Center, March 2021. https://www.povertycenter .columbia.edu/publication/2021/childcare/women-lifetime-earnings.

He, Joyce and Sarah Kaplan. "The Debate About Quotas." *Gender and the Economy*. October 26, 2017, https://www.gendereconomy.org/the-debate-about-quotas//.

Hewlett, Sylvia Ann and Carolyn Buck Luce. "Off-Ramps and On-Ramps Keeping Talented Women on the Road to Success." *Harvard Business Review*, March 2004. https://hbr.org/2005/03/off-ramps-and-on-ramps-keeping -talented-women-on-the-road-to-success.

Hewlett, Sylvia Ann, Melinda Marshall, and Laura Sherbin. "How Diversity Can Drive Innovation." *Harvard Business Review*. December 2013, https:// hbr.org/2013/12/how-diversity-can-drive-innovation.

Hewlett, Sylvia Ann. "Executive Women and the Myth of Having It All." *Harvard Business Review*, April 2002. https://hbr.org/2002/04/executive-women -and-the-myth-of-having-it-all.

Hideg, Ivona, Anja Krstic, Raymond Trau, and Tanya Zarina. "Do Longer Maternity Leaves Hurt Women's Careers?" *Harvard Business Review*, September 14, 2018. https://hbr.org/2018/09/do-longer-maternity-leaves-hurt -womens-careers.

Hiscox, Michael J., Tara Oliver, Michael Ridgway, Lilia Arcos-Holzinger, Alastair Warren, and Andrea Willis. "Going Blind to See More Clearly: Unconscious in Australian Public Service (APS) Shortlisting Process." *Behavioral Economics Team of the Australian Government*, November 14, 2016. https://behaviouraleconomics.pmc.gov.au/projects/going-blind- see-more-clearly-unconscious-bias-australian-public-service-aps-short listing.

Holmes, Aaron. "AI Could Be the Key to Ending Discrimination in Hiring, but Experts Warn It Can Be Just as Biased as Humans." *Business Insider*, October 8, 2019. https://www.businessinsider.com/ai-hiring-tools-biased-as-humans -experts-warn-2019-10.

Horowitz, Juliana Menasce and Ruth Igielnik. "A Century After Women Gained the Right to Vote, Majority of Americans See Work to Do on Gender Equality." Pew Research Center, July 7, 2020. https://www.pewresearch .org/social-trends/2020/07/07/a-century-after-women-gained-the-right-to -vote-majority-of-americans-see-work-to-do-on-gender-equality/.

Horwitz, Sujin K., and Irwin B. Horwitz. "The Effects of Team Diversity on Team Outcomes: A Meta-Analytic Review of Team Demography." *Journal of Management* 33, no. 6 (2007): 987-1015.

Houser, Kimberly and Jamillah Bowman Williams. "Board Gender Diversity A Path to Achieving Substantive Equality in the U. S." *William and Mary Review* 63, (2021): 497.

Huang-Menders, Celeste. "The Fight to Protect Contraception Rights After Dobbs." *Women's Media Center*. August 4, 2022, https://womensmediacenter .com/fbomb/the-fight-to-protect-contraceptive-rights-after-dobbs.

Hyde, Janet Shilbey. "The Gender Similarities Hypothesis." *American Psychological Association* 60, no. 6 (2005): 581-592.

Ibarra, Herminia, Nancy M. Carter, and Christine Silva. "Why Men Still Get More Promotions Than Women." *Harvard Business Review*, September 2010. https://hbr.org/2010/09/why-men-still-get-more-promotions-than-women.

Ibarra, Herminia, Robin J. Ely, and Deborah M. Kolb. "Women Rising: The Unseen Barriers." *Harvard Business Review.* September 2013, https://hbr.org/2013/09/women-rising-the-unseen-barriers.

Ibarra, Herminia. *Working Identity: Unconventional Strategies for Reinventing Your Career.* Boston: Harvard Business Press, 2004.

Jacquemont, David, Dana Maor, and Angelika Reich. "Losing From Day One: Why Even Successful Transformations Fall Short." *McKinsey & Company*, December 7, 2021. https://www.mckinsey.com/capabilities/people-and-organizational-performance/our-insights/successful-transformations.

Jagannathan, Meera. "Want to Support Your Female Colleague – Particularly in a Male-Dominated Field? Do This One Thing." *Market Watch*, August 11, 2021. https://www.marketwatch.com/story/want-to-support-your-female-colleagues-particularly-in-a-male-dominated-field-do-this-one-thing-11628697541.

Jaser, Zahira, Dimitra Petrakaki, Rachel Starr, and Ernesto Oyarbide-Magaña. "Where Automated Job Interviews Fall Short." *Harvard Business Review*, January 27, 2022. https://hbr.org/2022/01/where-automated-job -interviews-fall-short.

Jessen-Howard, Steven, Rasheed Malik, and MK Falgout. "Costly and Unavailable: America Lacks Sufficient Child Care Supply for Infants and Toddlers." Center for American Progress, August 4, 2020. https://www.americanprogress.org/article/costly-unavailable-america-lacks-sufficient-child-care-supply-infants-toddlers/.

Johansson, Anna. "Why Workplace Diversity Diminishes Groupthink and How Millennials Are Helping." *Forbes,* July 20, 2017. https://www.forbes.com/sites/annajohansson/2017/07/20/how-workplace-diversity-diminishes-groupthink-and-how-millennials-are-helping/?sh=33c1e3ba4b74.

Johnson, Stefanie K., David R. Hekman, and Elsa T. Chan. "If There Is Only One Woman in Your Candidate Pool, There's Statistically No Chance She'll be Hired." *Harvard Business Review*, April 26, 2016. https://hbr.org/2016/04/if-theres-only-one-woman-in-your-candidate-pool-theres-statistically-no-chance-shell-be-hired.

Johnson, Stephanie K., Ksenia Keplinger, Jessica F. Kirk, and Liza Barnes. "Has Sexual Harassment at Work Decreased Since #MeToo?" *Harvard Business Review*, July 18, 2019. https://hbr.org/2019/07/has-sexual-harassment-at-work-decreased-since-metoo.

Johnson, W. Brad and David G. Smith. "How Men Can Confront Other Men About Sexist Behavior." *Harvard Business Review*, October 16, 2020. https://hbr .org/2020/10/how-men-can-confront-other-men-about-sexist-behavior.

Kahneman, Daniel. *Thinking, Fast and Slow.* New York: Macmillan, 2011.

Kalev, Alexandra and Frank Dobbin. *Getting to Diversity: What Works and What Doesn't.* Boston: Harvard University Press, 2022.

Kalev, Alexandra and Frank Dobbin. "The Surprising Benefits of Work/Life Support." *Harvard Business Review*, September – October 2022. https://hbr .org/2022/09/the-surprising-benefits-of-work-life-support#:~:text =The%20lessons%20these%20examples%20offer,also%20boosts%20 diversity%20among%20managers.

Kanter, Rosabeth Moss. "Ten Reasons People Resist Change." *Harvard Business Review*, September 25, 2012. https://hbr.org/2012/09/ten-reasons-people -resist-chang.

Kanter, Rosabeth Moss. "The Interplay of Structure and Behavior: How System Dynamics Can Explain or Change Outcomes by Gender or Social Category." Harvard Business School. Accessed January 3, 2022, https://www .hbs.edu/faculty/Shared%20Documents/conferences/2013-w50-research -symposium/kanter.pdf.

Kaplan, Steven N. and Morten Sorensen. "Are CEOs Different? Characteristics of Top Managers." No. w23832, National Bureau of Economic Research, September 2017. https://www.nber.org/papers/w23832.

Kaplowitz, Lisa S., Kristina Durante, W. Brad Johnson, and David G. Smith. "How Men Benefit from Close Relationships with Woman at Work." *Forbes*, March 18, 2021. https://www.forbes.com/sites/ellevate/2021/03/18/ how-men-benefit-from-close-relationships-with-women-at-work/?sh =3a770cec1264.

Kaufman, Michael. "Addressing and Involving Men and Boys to Promote Gender Equality and End Gender Discrimination and Violence." UNICEF, March 31, 2003. https://www.michaelkaufman.com/wp-content/uploads /2009/01/kaufman-the-aim-framework.pdf.

Kearney, David. "Mentors, Mentees, & The Rules of Engagement." LinkedIn, November 9, 2020. https://www.linkedin.com/pulse/mentors-mentees-rules -engagement-david-kearney/.

Kelan, Elisabeth. "Why Aren't We Making More Progress Towards Gen- der Equality?" *Harvard Business Review*, December 21, 2020. https://hbr .org/2020/12 /why-arent-we-making-more-progress-towards-gender-equity/.

Keller, Scott and Colin Price. *Beyond Performance: How Great Organization Build Ultimate Competitive Advantages.* New York: Wiley, 2011.

KFF. "Paid Leave in the U.S." December 17, 2021. https://www.kff.org/womens
    -health-policy/fact-sheet/paid-leave-in-u-s/.

King, Michelle. "We Need to Stop Fixing Women and Start Fixing Workplace."
    Evoke, October 10, 2019. https://www.evoke.org/articles/october-2019/big
    -ideas/we-need-to-stop-fixing-women-start-fixing-workplaces.

Kingo, Audrey Goodson. "Is a Stay-at-Home Spouse the Secret to Executive Suc-
    cess?" *Chief*, June 29, 2021. https://chief.com/articles/stay-at-home-spouse.

Kirk, Gwyn and Margo Okazawa-Rey. *Women's Lives: Multicultural Perspec-
    tives*. Boston: McGraw-Hill, 2004.

Klotz, Ann Marie. "'The Journey to the Top.' Women's Paths to University Pres-
    idency," PhD diss. DePaul University, 2014.

Kluch, Sofia and Megan Brenan. "U.S. Women Feel Less Respected Than Euro-
    pean, Canadian Peers." Gallup, March 8, 2019. https://news.gallup.com
    /poll/247205/women-feel-less-respected-european-canadian-peers.aspx.

Kolev, Julian, Yuly Fuentes-Medel, and Fiona Murray. "Is Blinded Review
    Enough? How Gendered Outcomes Arise Even Under Anonymous Evalua-
    tion." National Bureau of Economic Research, Working Paper 25759, April
    2019. https://www.nber.org/papers/w25759

Kolmar, Chris. "Average Paid Maternity Leave in the U.S. [2022]: U.S. Mater-
    nity Leave Statistics." *Zippia*, January 5, 2022. https://www.zippia.com
    /advice/average-paid-maternity-leave/.

Kotter, John P. "Leading Change: Why Transformation Efforts Fail." *Harvard
    Business Review*, May-June 1995. https://hbr.org/1995/05/leading-change
    -why-transformation-efforts-fail-2.

Kowitt, Beth. "Are Women on a Collision Course with the Covid Ceiling?"
    Fortune, October 4, 2021. https://fortune.com/longform/covid-women-in
    -leadership-corporate-maerica-pandemic-effects/.

Kramer, Andrea S. and Alton B. Harris. "How Do Your Workers Feel About
    Harassment? Ask Them." *Harvard Business Review*, January 29, 2018. https://
    hbr.org/2018/01/how-do-your-workers-feel-about-harassment-ask-them.

Kramer, Andrea S. and Alton B. Harris. *Breaking Through Bias*. 2nd ed. Boston:
    Nicholas Brealey Publishing, 2016.

Kray, Laura J., Laura Howland, Alexandra G. Russell, and Lauren M. Jackman.
    "The Effects of Implicit Gender Role Theories on Gender System Justifica-
    tion: Fixed Beliefs Strengthen Masculinity to Preserve the Status Quo."
    Journal of Personality and Social Psychology 112, no.1 (2017): 98-115.

Krentz, Matt, Justin Dean, Jennifer Garcia-Alonso, Miki Tsusaka, and Elliot
    Vaughn. "Fixing the Flawed Approach to Diversity." *Boston Consulting Group*,

January 17, 2019. https://www.bcg.com/publications/2019/fixing-the-flawed
-approach-to-diversity.

Krizan, Zlatan and Angie Hunt. "Gender Roles: Men and Women Are Not So
Different After All." *Iowa State University News*, January 29, 2015. https://
www.news.iastate.edu/news/2015/01/29/genderdifferences.

Krouse, Sarah. "BlackRock: Companies Should Have At least Two Female
Directors." *Wall Street Journal*, February 2, 2018. https://www.wsj.com
/articles/blackrock-companies-should-have-at-least-two-female
-directors-1517598407/.

Kulik, Carol T., Molly B. Pepper, Loriann Roberson, and Sharon K. Parker. "The
Rich Get Richer: Predicting Participation in Voluntary Diversity Training." *Journal of Organization Behavior* 28, no. 6, 753-769.

Kwok, Navio, and Winny Shen. "Leadership Training Shouldn't be for Top
Performers." *Harvard Business Review*, January 20, 2022. https://hbr
.org/2022/01/leadership-training-shouldnt-just-be-for-top-performers
#:~:text=The%20case%20for%20a%20broader%20approach%20to%20
employee%20development.&text=Senior%20leaders%20often%20
receive%20most,they%20have%20the%20most%20experience.

Lai, Calvin K., Maddalena Marini, Steven A. Lehr, Carlo Cerruti, Jiyun-Eliza-
beth L. Shin, Jennifer A. Joy-Gaba, Arnold K. Ho, Bethany A. Teachman,
Sean P. Wojcik, Sena Koleva, Rebecca S. Frazier, Larisa Heiphetz, Eva Chen,
Rhiannon Turner, Jonathan Haidt, Selin Kesibir, Carlee Beth Hawkins,
Hillary Schaefer, Sandro Rubichi, Giuseppe Sartori, Christopher M. Dial,
N. Sriram, Mazarin R. Banaji, and Brian A. Nosek. "Reducing Implicit
Racial Preferences: A Comparative Investigation of 17 Interventions." *Jour-
nal of Experimental Psychology: General* 143, no. 4 (2014): 1765-1785.

Lansu, M., I. Bleijenbergh, and Y. Benschop. "Just Talking? Middle Managers
Negotiating Ownership in Gender Equality Interventions." *Scandinavian
Journal of Management* 36, no. 2 (2020): 1-9.

Lauzen, Martha M. "The Celluloid Ceiling: Behind-the-Scenes Employment
of Women on the Top US Films of 2020." Center for the Study of Women
in Television & Film. 2021, https://womenintvfilm.sdsu.edu/wp-content
/uploads/2022/01/2021-Celluloid-Ceiling-Report.pdf.

Lenney, Ellen. "Women's Self-Confidence in Achievement Settings." *Psychological Bulletin* 84, no. 1 (1977): 1-13.

Leonard, Bill. "Don't Exclude White Males from Diversity and Inclusion Programs." Society for Human Resource Management, February 12, 2013. https://
www.shrm.org/resourcesandtools/hr-topics/behavioral-competencies

/global-and-cultural-effectiveness/pages/whitemales-diversity-inclusion
.aspx.

Lewiss, Resa E., W. Brad Johnson, David G. Smith, and Robin Naples, "Stop
Protecting 'Good Guys.'" *Harvard Business Review*, August 1, 2022.https://
hbr.org/2022/08/stop-protecting-good-guys.

Lilienfeld, Scott O. and Hal Arkowitz. "Why 'Just Say No' Doesn't Work." *Scientific American,* January 1, 2014. https://www.scientificamerican.com
/article/why-just-say-no-doesnt-work/.

Lim, Dawn. "BlackRock Must Hit ESG Targets or Pay More to Borrow Money."
Wall Street Journal. April 7, 2021, https://www.wsj.com/articles/blackrock
-must-hit-esg-targets-or-pay-more-to-borrow-money-11617769833
#:~:text=The%20firm%20struck%20a%20financing,Latino%20
employees%20in%20its%20workforce./.

Lindsey, Alex, Eden King, Ashley Membere, and Ho Kwan Cheung. "Two Types of
Diversity Training that Really Work." *Harvard Business Review,* July 28, 2017.
https://hbr.org/2017/07/two-types-of-diversity-training-that-really-work.

LinkedIn. "A New Way to Represent Career Breaks on LinkedIn." March 1, 2022.
https://news.linkedin.com/2022/march/new-way-to-represent-career
-breaks-on-linkedin.

Lippmann, Walter. *Public Opinion.* Piscataway: Transaction Publishers, 1946.

Livingston, Gretchen and Deja Thomas. "Among 41 Countries, only U.S. Lacks
Paid Parental Leave." Pew Research, December 16, 2019. https://www.pewre
search.org/fact-tank/2019/12/16/u-s-lacks-mandated-paid-parental-leave/.

Lorenzo, Rocío, Nicole Voigt, Karin Schetelig, Annika Zawadzki, Isabelle
Welpe, and Prisca Brosi. "The Mix That Matters: Innovation Through
Diversity." Boston Consulting Group. April 26, 2017, https://www.bcg
.com/publications/2017/people-organization-leadership-talent
-innovation-through-diversity-mix-that-matters

Lublin, Joann S. and Sarah Krouse. "State Street to Start Voting Against Companies That Don't Have Women Directors." *Wall Street Journal*, March 7, 2017.
https://www.wsj.com/articles/state-street-says-it-will-start-voting-against
-companies-that-dont-have-women-directors-1488862863.

Luisa Paúl, María. "14-year-old's Arthritis Meds Denied After Arizona Abortion Ban, Doctor Says." *The Washington Post*, October 5, 2022. https://
www.washingtonpost.com/nation/2022/10/05/abortion-arizona-arthritis
-prescription-refill/.

Mackenzie, Lori Nishiura, JoAnne Wehner, and Shelley J. Correll. "Why Most
Performance Reviews Are Biased, and How to Fix Them." *Harvard Business*

Review, January 11, 2019.https://hbr.org/2019/01/why-most-performance
-evaluations-are-biased-and-how-to-fix-them.

Mackenzie, Megan. *Beyond the Band of Brothers: The US Military and the Myth
that Women Can't Fight.* Cambridge: Cambridge University Press, 2015.

Madsen, Susan. "Understanding Women's Negative Interactions With Each
Other in the Workplace." *Forbes,* January 25, 2022. https://www.forbes.com
/sites/forbescoachescouncil/2022/01/25/understanding-womens-negative
-interactions-with-each-other-in-the-workplace/?sh=64cdbe0d2be4.

Madsen, Susan and Maureen Andrade. "Unconscious Gender Bias: implications for Women's Leadership Development." *Journal of Leadership Studies*
12, no. 1 (2018): 62-67.

Magee, Kate. "This is Adland '17: Part One: Gender." *Campaign Live,* January 19, 2017.
https://www.campaignlive.co.uk/article/adland-17-part-one-gender/1421095

Mallik, Mita. "Maternity Leave Isn't Enough to Retain New Moms." *Harvard Business Review,* November 30, 2020, https://hbr.org/2020/11/maternity-leave
-isnt-enough-to-retain-new-moms.

Mandel, Hadas. "The Individual and Structural Aspects of Gender Inequality
at Work." Oxford Human Rights Hub, May 2, 2017. https://ohrh.law.ox.ac
.uk/the-individual-and-structural-aspects-of-gender-inequality-at-work/.

Marshall, Mallika. "Toxic Workplaces Can Take a Toll on Your Mental and
Physical Health, Surgeon General Says." CBS Boston, October 24, 2022.
https://www.cbsnews.com/boston/news/toxic-workplaces-mental-physical
-health-surgeon-general-report-vivek-murthy/.

Martin, Courtney E. "Arianna Huffington: The Visionary." *Glamour,* October 31,
2011. https://www.glamour.com/story/arianna-huffington#:~:text=%22If
%20my%20daughters%2C%20and%20women,simply%20sticking%20
your%20neck%20out.%22.

Masterson, Victoria. "Here's What Women's Entrepreneurship Looks Like
Around the World." World Economic Forum, July 20, 2022. https://
www.weforum.org/agenda/2022/07/women-entrepreneurs-gusto
-gender/#:~:text=Women%20started%2049%25%20of%20new,to%20
business%20ownership%2C%20say%20experts.

Mason, Betsy. "Making People Aware of Their Implicit Biases Doesn't Usually
Change Minds. But Here Is What Does Work." *PBS,* June 10, 2020. https://www
.pbs.org /newshour/nation/making-people-aware-of-their-implicit-biases
-doesnt -usually-change-minds-but-heres-what-does-work.

Martinovich, Milenko. "Many Americans Still Underestimate the Risks of Smoking, Stanford Scholars Say." *Stanford News Service,* August 22, 2017. https://

news.stanford.edu/press-releases/2017/08/22/americans-misinformed
-smoking/.

Maxwell, J.R. and Kirk Rieckhoff. "America 2021: Making Change Happen, Against the Odds." McKinsey & Company, February 19, 2021. https://www .mckinsey.com/industries/public-and-social-sector/our-insights/america -2021-making-change-happen-against-the-odds.

McGregor, Jena. "How Most Leadership Training Programs Fail Women." *The Washington Post,* October 23, 2017. https://www.washingtonpost .com/news/on-leadership/wp/2017/10/23/how-most-leadership-training -programs-fail-women//

McKinsey & Company. "Intersection: Delivering on Diversity, Gender Equality, and Inclusion." Last modified 2020, https://www.mckinsey.com/~/media /McKinsey/Email/Intersection/2020/12/2020-12-02.html?cid=other-eml -dni-mip-mck&hlkid=70fd350403c64c0e8d518beb3d801299&hctky=1136 0948&hdpid=e0a58a6c-14cb-43fa-959c-cbafe7b1ee24.

Meta. "Executives," Media Gallery. Accessed April 2, 2022, https://about.face book.com/media-gallery/executives/.

"Women in the Workplace 2022," LeanIn.Org and McKinsey & Company, October 18, 2022, https://www.mckinsey.com/featured-insights/diversity -and-inclusion/women-in-the-workplace.

Microsoft. "Microsoft Inclusion Journey." Accessed January 1, 2022. https:// www.microsoft.com/en-us/inclusion-journey/learn.

Miller, Claire Cain. "How Other Nations Pay for Child Care. The U.S. Is an Outlier." *New York Times,* October 6, 2021. https://www.nytimes.com/2021/10 /06/upshot/child-care-biden.html.

Miller, Claire Cain. "Is Blind Hiring the Best Hiring?" *New York Times Magazine*, February 25, 2016. https://www.nytimes.com/2016/02/28/magazine /is-blind-hiring-the-best-hiring.html.

Milligan, Ellen and Todd Gillespie. "Diversity at Elite Law Firms is so Bad Clients Are Docking Fees." *Bloomberg Law*, October 5, 2021. https://news .bloomberglaw.com/business-and-practice/diversity-at-elite-law-firms-is -so-bad-clients-are-docking-fees.

Modestino, Alicia Sasser, Jamie J. Ladge, Addie Swartz, and Alisa Lincoln. "Childcare Is a Business Issue." *Harvard Business Review*, April 29, 2021. https://hbr.org/2021/04/childcare-is-a-business-issue.

Moniz, Michelle, Ryan Howard, and Michael Englesbe. "How U.S. Employers Can Support Women's Health" *Harvard Business Review*, June2, 2022. https://hbr.org/2022/06/how-u-s-employers-can-support-womens-health.

Moran, Gwen. "What Will It Take for Employers to Offer On-Site Day Care." *Fast Company,* February 16, 2016. https://www.fastcompany.com/3056440 /what-will-it-take-for-employers-to-offer-on-site-day-care.

Moss-Racusin, Corinne A., John F. Dovidio, Victoria L. Brescoll, Mark J. Graham, and Jo Handelsman. "Science Faculty's Subtle Gender Biases Favor Male Students." *Proceedings of the National Academy of Sciences* 109, no. 41 (2012): 16474-16479.

Mueller, Jennifer, Sarah Harvey, and Alec Levenson. "How to Steer Clear of Group Think." *Harvard Business Review,* March 7, 2022, https://hbr .org/2022/03/how-to-steer-clear-of-groupthink.

Mueller, Jennifer. *Creative Change: Why We Resist It . . . How We Can Embrace It.* Boston: Houghton Mifflin Harcourt, 2017.

NAPL. "Representation of Women and Minority Equity Partners Among Partners: Little Changed in Recent Years." April 2019, https://www.nalp.org/0419research.

Nathoo, Zulekha. "Why Diverse Hires Can't Always Escape Tokenism." *BBC,* September 6, 2021. https://www.bbc.com/worklife/article/20210902-why -diverse-hires-cant-always-escape-tokenism/.

National Bureau of Labor Statistics. "What Data Does the BLS Publish on Family Leave?" September 23, 2021. https://www.bls.gov/ncs/ebs/factsheet/ family-leave-benefits-fact-sheet.htm.

Newton-Small, Jay. "Critical Mass: What Happens When Women Start to Rule the World." Harvard Kennedy School. Accessed January 3, 2022. https:// iop.harvard.edu/get-involved/study-groups/critical-mass-what-happens -when-women-start-rule-world-led-jay-newton.

Nordell, Jessica. *The End of Bias: A Beginning: The Science and Practice of Overcoming Unconscious Bias.* New York: Metropolitan Books, 2021.

O'Connor, David. "Increasing Law Firm Diversity." in Diversity and Inclusion Committee Newsletter, Winter 2020. https://www.americanbar.org/groups /tort_trial_insurance_practice/publications/committee-newsletters /increasing_law_firm_diversity/.

Ohlheiser, Abby. "How James Damore Went from Google Employee to Right-Wing Internet Hero." *The Washington Post,* August 12, 2017. https:// www.washingtonpost.com/news/the-intersect/wp/2017/08/12/how-james -damore-went-from-google-employee-to-right-wing-internet-hero/.

Oliver, Lori A. and Jessica M. Norris, "Corporate Governance Emerging Best Practices Series: Gender-Diverse Boards." *The National Law Review,* August 18, 2020. https://www.natlawreview.com/article/corporate-governance -emerging-best-practices-series-gender-diverse-boards.

Ortutay, Barbara. "Women Say They Do Most Chores, Childcare; AP NORC Poll." *AP News*, December 14, 2021. https://apnews.com/article/coronavirus-pandemic-business-lifestyle-health-us-news-21e5e959e9f53c0f3060cabf8c521ff1.

Paluck, Elizabeth Levy, and Donald P. Green. "Prejudice Reduction: What Works? A Review and Assessment of Research and Practice." *Annual Review of Psychology* 60, (2009): 339-367.

Parker, Kim and Cary Funk. "Gender Discrimination Comes in Many Forms for Today's Working Women." Pew Research, December 14, 2017. https://www.pewresearch.org/fact-tank/2017/12/14/gender-discrimination-comes-in-many-forms-for-todays-working-women/.

Patty, Anna. "Women Are Just as Ambitious as Men, Unless Companies Hold Them Back." *The Sydney Morning Herald*, April 5, 2015. https://www.smh.com.au/business/workplace/women-are-just-as-ambitious-as-men-unless-companies-hold-them-back-20170405-gvedtx.html.

Paturel, Amy. "Where Are All the Women Deans?" *Association of American Medical Colleges News*, June 11, 2019. https://www.aamc.org/news-insights/where-are-all-women-deans.

Paul, Kelly. "The Benefits of Taking Time to Tackle Unconscious Bias." *Energy and Technology*, August 17, 2020. https://eandt.theiet.org/content/articles/2020/08/the-benefits-of-taking-time-to-tackle-unconscious-bias/.

Pease, Bob. *Undoing Privilege: Unearned Advantage in a Divided World*. London: Zed Books, 2010.

Peppercorn, Susan. "How to Tell If a Prospective Employer values Psychological Safety." *Harvard Business Review*, September 1, 2022. https://hbr.org/2022/09/how-to-tell-if-a-prospective-employer-values-psychological-safety.

Pew Research. "For Both Moms and Dads, More Time Spent on Childcare." June 15, 2017. https://www.pewresearch.org/ft_17-06-14_fathers_1965_2015/.

Phillips, Katherine W. "How Diversity Makes Us Smarter." *Greater Good Magazine*, September 18, 2017. https://greatergood.berkeley.edu/article/item/how_diversity_makes_us_smarter.

Pincus, Fred L. and Howard J. Ehrlich eds. *Race and Ethnic Conflict*. New York: Routledge, 1999.

Prime, Jeanine and Corinne A. Moss-Racusin. "Engaging Men in Gender Initiatives: What Change Agents Need to Know." Catalyst, May 4, 2009. https://www.catalyst.org/research/engaging-men-in-gender-initiatives-what-change-agents-need-to-know/.

Promundo-US. "So, You Want to be a Male Ally for Gender Equality? (And You Should): Results of a National Survey, and a Few Things You

Should Know." 2019. https://www.equimundo.org/resources/male-ally ship/.

Purushothaman, Deepa, Lisen Stromberg, and Lisa Kaplowitz. "5 Harmful Ways Women Feel They Must Adapt in Corporate America," *Harvard Business Review*, October 31, 2022. https://hbr.org/2022/10/5-harmful-ways -women-feel-they-must-adapt-in-corporate-america.

Quinn, Holly. "Are Your Job Descriptions as Inclusive as You Think They Are?" *Technically*, April 29, 2022. https://technical.ly/company-culture /how-to-write-inclusive-job-descriptions/.

Quinn, Melissa. "Sotomayor Says Supreme Court Adjusted Argument Format Partly Over Interruptions of Female Justices." CBS News online, October 14, 2021. https://www.cbsnews.com/news/supreme-court-justice-sonia-sotomayor-oral -arguments-female-justices-interruptions/

Ratner, Rebecca K. and Dale T. Miller. "The Norm of Self-Interest and Its Effects on Social Action." *Journal of Personality and Social Psychology* 81, no. 1 (2001): 5-16.

Regents of the University of California v. Allan Bakke. 438 U.S. 265 98 S. Ct. 2733 57 L.Ed.2d 750.

Regents of the University of California, Petitioner, v. Allan Bakke. 438 U.S. 265 98 S. Ct. 2733 57 L.Ed.2d 750.

Reynolds, Alison and David Lewis. "Teams Solve Problems Faster When They're More Cognitively Diverse." *Harvard Business Review*, March 30, 2017. https://hbr.org/2017/03/teams-solve-problems-faster-when-theyre-more- cognitively-diverse.

Ridgeway, Cecilia. *Framed by Gender: How Gender Inequality Persists in the Modern World*. New York: Oxford University Press, 2011.

Rivera-Torres, Pilar, Rafael Angel Araque-Padilla, and María José Montero-Simó. "Job Stress Across Gender: The Importance of Emotional and Intellectual Demands and Social Support in Women." *International Journal of Environmental Research and Public Health* 10, no. 1 (2013): 375-389.

Ro, Christine. "Why Do We Still Distrust Women Leaders?" *BBC*, January 19, 2021. https://www.bbc.com/worklife/article/20210108-why-do-we-still-distrust -women-leaders/

Rock, David and Heidi Grant. "Why Diverse Teams Are Smarter." *Harvard Business Review*. November 4, 2016, https://hbr.org/2016/11/why-diverse-teams -are-smarter.

Rock, David, and Paulette Gerkovich. "Why Diverse Teams Outperform Homogenous Teams." Neuroleadership Institute, June 10, 2021. https://neuro leadership.com/your-brain-at-work/why-diverse-teams-outperform -homogeneous-teams/.

Rock, David. "The Fastest Way to Change a Culture." *Forbes*, May 23, 2019. https://www.forbes.com/sites/davidrock/2019/05/24/fastest-way-to-change-culture/?sh=14ee92b43d50.

Rosalsky, Greg. "The Case for Revolutionizing Childcare." *NPR*, May 17, 2022. https://www.npr.org/sections/money/2022/05/17/1098524454/the-case-for-revolutionizing-child-care-in-america.

Ross, Laura. "Similarity Bias in Hiring and How to Avoid It." *Vervoe*, May 2, 2022. https://vervoe.com/similarity-bias-in-hiring/.

Rossander, Michael, Denise Salin, Lina Viita, and Stefan Blomberg. "Gender Matters: Workplace Bullying, Gender, and Mental Health." *Frontiers in Psychology* 11, (2020): 1-13.

Roy, Katica, David G. Smith, and W. Brad Johnson. "Gender Equity Is Not Zero Sum," *Harvard Business Review*, December 31, 2020. https://hbr.org/2020/12/gender-equity-is-not-zero-sum#:~:text=To%20move%20toward%20a%20fairer,need%20to%20dismantle%20the%20fallacy.&text=It's%20easy%20to%20see%20why,men%20identified%20as%20the%20problem%3F.

Sandberg, Sheryl. *Lean In: Women, Work, and the Will to Lead*. New York: Knopf, 2013.

Sattari, Negin, Sarah DiMuccio, and Ludo Gabriele. "When Managers Are Open Men Feel Heard and Interrupt Sexism." Catalyst, December 3, 2021. https://www.catalyst.org/media-release/manager-openness-men-interrupting-sexism/.

Schulte, Brigid and Stavroula Pabst. "How Companies Can Support Single Parents." *Harvard Business Review*, June 28, 2021. https://hbr.org/2021/06/how-companies-can-support-single-parents.

Schulte, Brigid. "Survey: Majority of Men Want Flexible Work." *The Washington Post*, October 21, 2014. https://www.washingtonpost.com/news/local/wp/2014/10/21/survey-majority-of-men-want-flexible-work/.

Sergeant, Desmond Charles and Evangelos Himonides. "Orchestrated Sex: The Representation of Male and Female Musicians in World-Class Symphony Orchestras." *Frontiers in Psychology,* August 16, 2019. https://www.frontiersin.org/articles/10.3389/fpsyg.2019.01760/full.

Shalal, Andrea. "Aging Population to Hit U.S. Economy Like a 'Ton of Bricks' -U.S. Commerce Secretary." *Reuters*, July 12, 2021. https://www.reuters.com/world/us/aging-population-hit-us-economy-like-ton-bricks-us-commerce-secretary-2021-07-12/.

Sheinin, Dave, Michael Lee, Emily Giambalvo, Artur Galocha and Clara Ence Morse. "How the NFL Blocks Black Coaches." *The Washington Post*, Sep-

tember 21, 2022. https://www.washingtonpost.com/sports/interactive/2022
/nfl-black-head-coaches/.

Sherf, Elad N., Subrahmaniam Tangirala, and Katy Connealy Weber. "It's Not My
Place! Psychological Standing and Men's Voice and Participation in Gender
Parity Initiatives." *Organizational Science* 28, no. 2 (2017): 193-210.

Sherman, Gabriel. "The Revenge of Roger's Angels." *New York Times*, September 5, 2016. http://nymag.com/intelligencer/2016/09/how-fox-news-women
-took-down-roger-ailes.html.

Shook, Ellyn. "How to Set—and Meet—Your Company's Diversity Goals." *Harvard Business Review*, June 25, 2021. https://hbr.org/2021/06/how-to-set-and
-meet-your-companys-diversity-goals.

Singal, Jesse. "Awareness Is Overrated." *The Cut*, July 17, 2014. https://www.the
cut.com/2014/07/awareness-is-overrated.html/.

Singer, Jenny. "How Many Men at CBS Had Heard That Eliza Dushku Was Sexually Threatened on Tape?" *Forward*, December 19, 2018. https://forward
.com/schmooze/416342/cbs-sexual-harassment-scandal-implicates-top
-execs-showrunner-actors-and.

Slater, Ben. "Recruiting, Fast and Slow: Lessons from Human Psychology." *Beamery*,
March 8, 2017. https://beamery.com/resources/blogs/recruiting-fast-and
-slow-lessons-from-human-psychology.

Smith, Allen. "SHRM Research: More Employers Are Offering Paid Leave."
SHRM, September 15, 2020. https://www.shrm.org/resourcesandtools/legal
-and-compliance/employment-law/pages/more-paid-leave-offered
.aspx#:~:text=The%20letter%20presents%20research%20from,paid%20
extended%20family%20care%20leave.

Smith, David G., Judith E. Rosenstein, and Margaret C. Nikolov. "How Performance
Evaluations Hurt Gender Equality." *Behavioral Scientist*, June 26, 2018. https://
behavioralscientist.org/how-performance-evaluations-hurt-gender-equality/.

Smith, Kelly Anne. "Biden's Build Back Better Plan Is Dead. Now What?" *Forbes*,
March 2, 2022. https://www.forbes.com/advisor/personal-finance/build
-back-better-plan-dead/.

Sommers, Christina Hoff. "Blind Spots in the 'Blind Audition' Study." *Wall
Street Journal*, October 20, 2019. https://www.wsj.com/articles/blind-spots-in
-the-blind-audition-study-11571599303.

Spar, Debora L. "Good Fellows: Men's Role & Reason in the Fight for Gender
Equality." *Daedalus* 149, no.1, (2020): 222-235.

Stamarski, Caitlin S. and Leanne S. Son Hing. "Gender Inequalities in the
Workplace: The Effects of Organizational Structures, Processes, Practices,
and Decisions Makers' Sexism." *Frontiers in Psychology* 6 (2015): 1-20.

Steel, Emily. "Fox Establishes Workplace Culture Panel After Harassment Scandal." *New York Times*, November 20, 2017. https://www.nytimes.com /2017/11/20/business/media/fox-news-sexual-harassment.html.

Steel, Emily. "How Bill O'Reilly Silenced His Accusers." *New York Times*, April 4, 2018. https://www.nytimes.com/2018/04/04/business/media/how-bill-oreilly -silenced-his-accusers.html.

Steinpreis, Rhea E., Katie A. Anders, and Dawn Ritzke. "The Impact of Gender on the Review of the Curricula Vitae of Job Applicants and Tenure Candidates: A National Empirical Study." *Sex Roles* 41, no. 7 (1999): 509-528.

Stewart, Edward C. *Culture in the Communication Age.* London: Routledge, 2002.

Sumagaysay, Levy. "Not a 'Woke Mission': NASQAQ, SEC Say Push for Diversity on Corporate Boards is What Investors Want." *MarketWatch*, August 29, 2022. https://www.marketwatch.com/story/not-a-woke-mission-nasdaq-sec -push-for-diversity-on-corporate-boards-is-what-investors-want-11661821759.

Sun, Rachel. "UI Employees Say Memo on Abortion, Contraception Creating Chill Effect in Classroom." *NWPB*, October 3, 2022. https://www.nwpb .org/2022/10/03/ui-employees-say-memo-on-abortion-contraception -creating-chilling-effect-in-classroom/.

Taylor, Bill. "Persuading Your Team to Embrace Change." *Harvard Business Review*, April 12, 2022.https://hbr.org/2022/04/persuading-your-team-to-embrace -change.

Teare, Gené and Ann Shepherd. "2020 Study of Gender Diversity in Private Company Boardrooms." *CRUNCHBASE NEWS*, March 1, 2021. https://news .crunchbase.com/news/2020-diversity-study-on-private-company-boards/.

The National Alliance for Caregiving. "Caregiving in the US 2020." https://www .caregiving.org/research/caregiving-in-the-us/caregiving-in-the-us-2020/.

The White House. "Fact Sheet: The American Families Plan." Last modified April 28, 2021. https://www.whitehouse.gov/briefing-room/statements-releases /2021/04/28/fact-sheet-the-american-families-plan/.

Timmins, Beth. "Little Change in Gender Pay Over Past 25 Years, Study Finds." *BBC*, December 6, 2021. https://www.bbc.com/news/business-59542790.

Tinsley, Catherine H. and Robin J. Ely. "What Most People Get Wrong About Men and Women." *Harvard Business Review*. May-June 2018, https://hbr .org/2018/05/what-most-people-get-wrong-about-men-and-women.

Turban, Stephen, Dan Wu, and Letian (LT) Zhang. "When Gender Diversity Makes Firms More Productive." *Harvard Business Review*. February 11, 2019, https://hbr.org/2019/02/research-when-gender-diversity-makes-firms -more-productive.

Tyson, Jim, "Most Companies Increase Spending on Diversity Training: Survey." *CFO Dive*, May 13, 2021. https://www.cfodive.com/news/most-companies -increase-spending-diversity-training-survey/600149/.

U.S. Equal Employment Opportunity Commission. "EEO-1 Component 1 Data Collection." Accessed March 3, 2022. https://www.eeocdata.org/EEO1 /home/index.

University of California. "University of California Performance Management for Senior Administrators." Accessed March 2022. https://regents.university ofcalifornia.edu/policies/smgperfform.pdf.

Variety. "Report Card on Female Representation in Hollywood Shows Few Women at the Top." December 13, 2017, https://variety.com/2017/biz/news /women-in-leadership-roles-hollywood-1202638260/.

Von Drehle, David. "Of course, the SBC Hasn't Fixed Its Sexual Abuse Problem. Look at Its Theology." *The Washington Post*. June 11, 2021, https://www .washingtonpost.com/opinions/2021/06/11/sbc-has-bad-sexist-theology -course-bad-culture-follows/.

Walsh, Nuala. "How to Encourage Employees to Speak Up When They See Wrong Doing." *Harvard Business Review*, February 4, 2021. https://hbr.org/2021 /02/how-to-encourage-employees-to-speak-up-when-they-see-wrong doing.

Warner, Judith, Nora Ellmann, and Diana Boesch. "The Women's Leadership Gap: Women's Leadership by the Numbers." Center for American Progress, November 20, 2018. https://www.americanprogress.org/issues/women /reports/2017/05/21 /432758/womens-leadership-gap/.

Weber, Lauren. "How to Expand Diversity in the Workplace." *Wall Street Journal*. January 9, 2021, https://www.wsj.com/articles/how-to-expand-diversity-in -the-workplace-11610204183.

Weingarten, Elizabeth, and Liz Kofman-Burns. "Is Your Leadership Develop-ment Program Undermining Your DEI Goals?," *Harvard Business Review*, October 6, 2022, https://hbr.org/2022/10/is-your-leadership-development -program-undermining-your-dei-goals.

Wheeler, Melissa and Victor Sojo. "One Unconscious Bias Is Keeping Women Out of Senior Roles." *Business Insider*, March 8, 2017. https://www.business insider.com/women-in-senior-roles-workplace-equality-2017-3.

White, Andrew, Michael Smets, and Adam Canwell. "Organizational Transfor-mation Is an Emotional Journey." *Harvard Business Review*, July 18, 2022. https://hbr.org/2022/07/organizational-transformation-is-an-emotional -journey.

William, Jamillah Bowman and Jonathan M. Cox. "The New Principle-Practice Gap: The Disconnect Between Diversity Beliefs and Actions in the Workplace." *Sociology of Race and Ethnicity* 8, no. 2 (2022): 301-314.

Williams v. Saxbe, 413 F. Supp. 654 (D.D.C. 1976).

Williams, Joan C., Rachel M. Korn, and Asma Ghani. "To Build a DEI Program That Works, You Need Metrics." *Harvard Business Review*, October 12, 2022. https://hbr.org/2022/10/to-build-a-dei-program-that-works-you-need-metrics.

Wilson, Margo and Martin Daly. "Competitiveness, Risk Taking, and Violence: The Young Male Syndrome." *Ethology and Sociobiology* 6, issue 1 (1985): 59-73

Wittenberg-Cox, Avivah. "Gender Initiatives Are Culture Change Initiatives." *Harvard Business Review*, October 14, 2015. https://hbr.org/2015/10/gender-initiatives-are-culture-change-initiatives.

World Economic Forum. "How Has the Number of Female CEOs in Fortune 500 Companies Changed Over the Last 20 Years?" March 10, 2022. https://www.weforum.org/agenda/2022/03/ceos-fortune-500-companies-female/.

Yellen, Janet L. "The History of Women's Work and Wages and How It Has Created Success for Us All." *The Brookings Institution*, May 2020. https://www.brookings.edu/essay/the-history-of-womens-work-and-wages-and-how-it-has-created-success-for-us-all/.

Zahid, Amel. "Onsite Childcare—How to Get Started? Lessons from the Pioneers." LinkedIn, March 14, 2018. https://www.linkedin.com/pulse/onsite-childcare-how-get-started-lessons-from-pioneers-amel-zahid/.

Zheng, Lily. "How to Show White Men That Diversity and Inclusion Efforts Need Them." *Harvard Business Review*, October 28, 2019. https://hbr.org/2019/10/how-to-show-white-men-that-diversity-and-inclusion-efforts-need-them.

INDEX

ABOUT THE AUTHORS

Andrea Kramer and Alton Harris are co-authors of two award-winning books: *Breaking Through Bias (Second Edition): Communication Techniques for Women to Succeed at Work* (Nicholas Brealey, 2020) and *It's Not You, It's the Workplace: Women's Conflict at Work and the Bias That Built It* (Nicholas Brealey, 2019). Andie and Al are also the authors of hundreds of articles on diversity, overcoming gender stereotypes, and building inclusive workplaces that have been featured in numerous national media outlets. They are contributing writers to *Harvard Business Review*'s *"On Women and Leadership"* (2019), and Andie is a contributing writer on gender issues in the workplace for Forbes.com.

Together and separately, Andie and Al speak and lead workshops across the country to help women, men, and organizations eliminate gender inequality and build more inclusive and productive workplaces. In *Beyond Bias*, they present for the first time in fully-developed form, PATH: a comprehensive, multifaceted initiative to eliminate gender inequality in all of its manifestations in every type of workplace. PATH offers a practical, effective, and realistic way for companies to begin to finally make significant progress in ridding their workplaces of gender inequality by making them more fair, inclusive, and satisfying for everyone. PATH is not another call for individuals to become more aware of their biases and make diligent efforts to stop their influence on their behaviors. Quite the contrary, PATH is a concrete, step-by-step program by which organizations can make the changes in their personnel management practices that will finally lead to the end of hurtful, pernicious, and persistent workplace gender inequality.

Andie is the founding member of ASKramer Law LLC. She is a

former partner in an international law firm, where she established its Gender Diversity Committee and served on both the firm's Management Committee and Compensation Committee. She was named one of the 50 Most Influential Women Lawyers in America by the *National Law Journal* for her "demonstrated power to change the legal landscape, shape public affairs, launch industries, and do big things." She cofounded the Women's Leadership and Mentoring Alliance (WLMA), which has been highly successful in providing mentorship opportunities for aspiring women across the country.

Al was a founding partner of a Chicago law firm that merged into a large national law firm. In the firm that he founded, Al served for many years as the managing partner and then as a member of its Executive and Compensation Committees. In these roles, he had extensive experience mentoring and advising women in many career fields. Al's extensive research, astute observations, and pragmatic voice have made him a nationally recognized advocate for women's career advancement, getting men into the conversation for advancing gender equality, and building truly inclusive workplaces.

Andie and Al are married, have a daughter who is a medical doctor, and live in Chicago with their rescue dogs and rescue cats.

Ready to start working toward gender equality?

So are we.

Visit our website at AndieAndAl.com for the latest on our speaking engagements and other books

To learn more about implementing the PATH Program in your organization, go to PathBeyondBias.com

Or send us a note at
Info@AndieAndAl.com

Andrea S. Kramer and Alton B. Harris are also authors of:

It's Not You, It's the Workplace   Breaking Through Bias
9781473697270   9781529317299

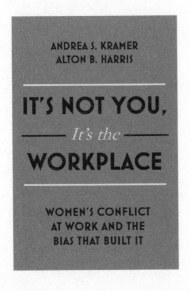

Read on for an excerpt from

Breaking Through Bias

Communication Techniques for Women to
Succeed at Work

Second Edition

ANDREA S. KRAMER
ALTON B. HARRIS

INTRODUCTION TO
SECOND EDITION

There is a wide disparity in women's and men's career achievements. This book is about how you as a woman with—or about to begin—a career can avoid falling victim to this disparity. It is about how you—right now, just the way you are—can advance as far and as fast as your talent, hard work, and commitment will take you. Achieving such success depends on your understanding of the nature, causes, and operation of gender stereotypes; how they foster biases; and how these biases operate to hold women back. It also depends on your willingness to use the communication techniques that will allow you to avoid or overcome these biases. Before jumping directly into these matters, let's look closely at the extent of the persistent and vexing disparities between women's and men's representation in senior leadership.

Disparities in Women's and Men's Career Achievements

In corporate America, women make up 48 percent of entry-level career employees but only 38 percent of first-tier managers, 34 percent of senior managers, 30 percent of vice presidents, 26 percent of senior vice presidents, and 21 percent of executives in the C-suite.[1] In Fortune 500 companies, women make up only 9.5 percent of the top earners,[2] constitute only 12.5 percent of CFOs,[3] only 6.6 percent of CEOs,[4] and only 22.5 percent of board members.[5] Outside of corporate America, women fare no better. They make up 47 percent of law firm associates but only 20 percent of equity partners.[6] Women are over 50 percent of medical students[7] but only 25 percent of full professors, 18 percent of department chairs, and 16 percent of deans at medical schools.[8] Women are just 27 percent of tenure track professors at four-year colleges and universities,[9] despite making up 54 percent of full-time students.[10] With respect to political office, women make up only 24 percent of the members of the US House of Representatives, 23 percent of US senators, 28 percent of state legislators, 18 percent of state governors, and 23 percent of the mayors of the 100 largest American cities.[11] Of the 250 top-grossing Hollywood films of 2017, women made up just 18 percent of the directors, executive producers, producers, writers, cinematographers, and editors.[12]

Many more similar statistics are available, but the point should be clear enough: women are not moving into senior leadership positions in business, the professions, academia, government, and entertainment in numbers anywhere near comparable to men. And discouragingly, women have made virtually no progress in changing this situation since the 1990s. As this graph from the US Census Bureau dramatically

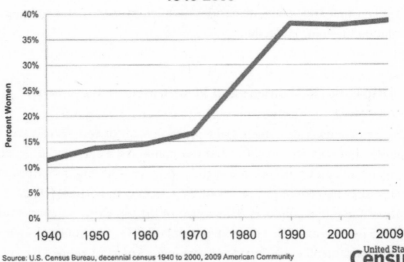

Percentage of Managers Who Are Women: 1940-2009

Source: U.S. Census Bureau, decennial census 1940 to 2000, 2009 American Community

illustrates, between 1970 and 1990 women made steady and rapid progress, increasing their representation among corporate managers from about 16 percent to more than 35 percent. Since then, however, women's progress has been nonexistent.[13]

The US Census Bureau graph stops at 2009, but the Bureau of Labor Statistics reports that things had not significantly improved by 2016,[14] and the 2019 LeanIn and McKinsey study on women in the workplace makes clear that there has been no progress since then.[15] Indeed, as LeanIn and McKinsey concluded in their 2018 report, "Progress isn't just slow. It's stalled."[16]

Perhaps equally troubling as women's lack of increased representation in senior leadership ranks is the fact that when women do gain access to those ranks, they are largely concentrated in "feminized" positions such as human resources. And regardless of the type of management position they hold, women are paid less than men in similar positions.[17]

Why the Achievement Disparity?

The difference in women's and men's career achievements is often explained by claiming that women prefer to spend time with their children rather than pursuing career success; they don't ask (or don't want) to move up to senior leadership positions; and they lack the ambition, confidence, and core competencies needed to successfully compete against men. These claims, however, are all patently false.

A growing body of research makes clear that women are just as talented, ambitious, and committed to career advancement as men. For example, a 2017 study by the Boston Consulting Group found "on average, women entered the workforce with the same—or higher—levels of ambition as men, in terms of their desire to hold leadership positions or be promoted.... [I]t is also unequivocal: having children does not affect women's desire to lead. The ambition levels of women with children and women without children track each other almost exactly over time."[18] Moreover, recent psychological research finds that "one's sex has little or no bearing on personality, cognition and leadership."[19] Indeed, as a review of hundreds of studies on cognitive performance (such as math ability), personality and social behaviors (such as leadership), and psychological well-being (such as self-esteem) found, there are more similarities than differences between men and women.[20]

Writing in the *Harvard Business Review*, Catherine Tinsley and Robin Ely conclude that "on average, the sexes are far more similar in their inclinations, attitudes, and skills than popular opinion would have us believe. [There are] sex differences in various settings, including the workplace—but those differences are not rooted in fixed gender traits. Rather, they stem from organizational structures, company practices, and patterns of interaction that position men and women differently, creating systematically different experiences for them."[21] This is confirmed by a 2011 report by Catalyst which found that even when women do everything they are told to do to get ahead, they still fail to advance as far and as fast as men.[22] In other words, women with high ambition, terrific abilities, can-do attitudes, and appropriate behavioral characteristics are systematically disadvantaged in relation to men in their pursuit of career advancement.

So what is the problem? Why are women at such a disadvantage in comparison to men when it comes to career achievement? A recent American Bar Association (ABA) report on why experienced women lawyers leave the legal profession provides a key insight. This ABA report concludes, "It is clear that women lawyers on average do not advance along the same trajectory as men," for they "have far less access to the building blocks for success than men."[23] Indeed, the ABA found that "women report being four to eight times more likely to be overlooked for advancement, denied a salary increase or bonus, treated as a token representative for diversity, lack access to business development opportunities, perceived as less committed to their career, and lack access to sponsors." Thus, women's *experience* in the pursuit of career success in large law firms is very different from that of their male counterparts. Our research makes clear that this sharply differentiated workplace experience of women and men is also found in virtually all other professions, business settings, academia, and politics.[24]

Gender Bias

The question is: what accounts for women's and men's very different workplace experiences and their divergent representation in senior leadership? The answer to that question is the focus of this book: pervasive, persistent gender stereotypes and the biases that flow from them. We first discuss what these stereotypes and biases are, why they are most pronounced in workplaces led and dominated by men with decidedly masculine cultures, and how these stereotypes and biases operate to create obstacles to women's career advancement. Most importantly, we then go on to spell out in detail the concrete, practical, effective steps women can take to avoid or overcome these discriminatory obstacles. In other words, this book is about the myriad ways in which gender stereotypes and their ensuing biases hold women back and how women can break through these biases to achieve career success *and* satisfaction.

Implicit Gender Bias

A person holds an implicit gender bias when she or he unconsciously— that is, without any conscious awareness—assumes, expects, or anticipates that men will be better than women at critical workplace tasks, that women are better at and have a greater responsibility for childcare than men, that women and men are best suited for different societal roles, and that men should play leadership roles and women should play supporting roles. Implicit gender bias has numerous variants: motherhood bias (mothers pursuing careers are hurting their small children), self-limiting bias (women's assumption that certain careers, positions, and tasks are not appropriate for women), agentic bias (discomfort with women who do not conform to traditional feminine behavior norms), negative bias (communal women are not cut out for leadership roles), and affinity bias (a preference for associating with and supporting people who are like you).

Implicit gender bias and its variants affect people's actions, decisions, and judgments. They influence how people relate to women and men, decide what assignments and projects to give them, evaluate their performance, and provide them with feedback. Although implicit gender bias and its variants adversely affect women's career advancement, these concepts do not involve bad intentions or malevolent motivations. Implicit biases result not from consciously held beliefs, but from deep-seated, long-established stereotypes we have acquired simply by growing up in this society and being exposed to contemporary media, entertainment, politics, and education.

Explicit Gender Bias

In writing the first edition of this book, we focused almost exclusively on implicit gender bias. We assumed that explicit gender bias—the open, intentional, aggressive, and hostile expression of sexist and misogynistic views[25]—was so socially unacceptable that it did not pose a serious threat to women's careers. While that assumption may have been justified in late 2015 when we submitted our manuscript, Donald Trump's presidential campaign and election have made it apparent that that assumption is no longer justified. Beginning with Trump's campaign, the media has been flooded with crude, angry, and mean-spirited criticisms of women. Indeed, explicit gender bias has now become so prevalent that we are convinced it poses a real and very severe threat to women's career advancement. Our change of heart is nicely captured by Cheryl Strayed when she writes:

> I've never been under the illusion that sexism had vanished, [but] before Trump was elected there was a history-lesson element to the stories I told of my first consciousness about what it meant to be female in America, a quality that had made the sexism I

experienced as a girl seem antiquated and nearly extinct. The message was: *This is the way it used to be! Isn't that amazing?* In witnessing the presidential campaign and Trump's eventual election, I've concluded that I had it wrong. This isn't how it used to be. It is the way it is . . . . This election wasn't simply a political contest. It was a referendum on how much America still hates [strong, ambitious] women.[26]

Explicit gender bias exists on a continuum of discriminatory gender-specific behaviors that includes implicit gender bias, incivility to and microaggressions against women, inappropriate sexual comments, unwelcomed touching, actionable sexual harassment, and criminal sexual assault. As we wrote in the *Harvard Business Review*, because these discriminatory behaviors are all related and interconnected, they need to be "addressed collectively, because sexual harassment [and other forms of explicit gender bias are] far more likely in organizations that experience offenses on the 'less severe' end of the spectrum than in those that don't."[27] As a consequence, this book's continuing focus on implicit gender bias remains highly relevant. Misogynistic criticism of women striving to achieve true gender equality is tolerated only when there is a pervasive, unconscious assumption that women are somehow less capable, less qualified, and less entitled to play leadership roles than men. Therefore, to effectively attack such explicit gender bias, implicit gender bias must also be attacked. And that, of course, is precisely the objective of this book.